Joanne.

With my best wishes.

Uncle Hugh.

January, 1996.

The Sword of Damocles

Vice Admiral Sir Hugh Mackenzie, KCB, DSO+, DSC.

The Sword of Damocles

some memories of
Vice Admiral Sir Hugh Mackenzie,
KCB, DSO+, DSC

First published in the United Kingdom in 1995 by The Royal Navy
Submarine Museum

ISBN 0 9526696 0 9

Produced by Alan Sutton Publishing Ltd, Stroud, Glos.
Printed in Great Britain by WBC Ltd, Bridgend.

CONTENTS

To

MAUREEN

Who has shared my love for the Royal Navy, who has stood by me over these many years, and without whose active encouragement this book would never have been completed. In love and gratitude.

Preface

I have never kept any personal diaries or detailed written records of any periods of my life; therefore, apart from my official Midshipman's Journal covering the years 1930 to 1933 and which I still possess, the story in this book is based almost entirely on memory, which, alas, is now fading more rapidly than I would wish. For the War years, 1939 to 1945, I have, however, made full use of the Public Records Office at Kew and all the information it holds on Submarine operations, including individual submarine Patrol Reports, which has helped to substantiate, or on occasion correct, my recollections. For those chapters covering the Polaris Programme, fortunately I have been able to refresh my memory from various papers I have had access to and from my 'desk diaries' giving my engagements throughout the five and a half years with which I was concerned.

The world, this country, the Royal Navy, are all very different from what they were when I first became fully conscious of all that they represented, each in their own unique way. I hope that this account of some seventy-five years of change may add to people's awareness of those changes, but will also demonstrate that certain principles, particularly a sense of service and acceptance of duty and responsibility, remain an essential part of an evolving world, and can play their part without detriment to a full and happy life.

There is an omission from the story I have told which I now correct: there is virtually no mention of the significance of religion in my life. Perhaps this is because from my very earliest years a firm belief in God and Christian principles was instilled in me and became so ingrained in me that He and they were, so to speak, automatically there, overseeing what I did, whatever the circumstances and whatever my failings; it would not be right for anyone to suppose, because it is not specifically mentioned, that my faith and belief in a Christian manner of thinking has not been basic to the way I have tried to conduct my life.

Many, many people have played a part in my life and have thus contributed to this story; to them, too numerous to list, I record my thanks and gratitude. To the Public Record Office, the R.N. Submarine Museum, the Imperial War Museum and the Naval Historical Branch of the Ministry of Defence I tender my warmest thanks. But, particularly, there are two people I must mention: John Wingate, who, after cornering me late at night at a Submarine Officers' Reunion, finally persuaded me to put pen to paper and record my submarine experiences; and Patrick Sullivan-Tailyour who subsequently took on the burden of translating all my efforts into something that would find favour with a publisher; to them both I am especially and forever grateful.

H.S.M.
Sylvan Lodge, Puttenham
March 1995

Chapter One

'The Lucky Thirteen'

With origins lost in the dim myths of the past, superstitions were an ever present element in the life of a sailor in the first half of this century. None were taken too seriously, but amongst them was the dictum that it was unlucky to set sail on a Friday, and doubly so if the Friday happened to be the 13th day of the month. Consequently, it was no surprise to me that amongst the crew of HMS *Thrasher* there were a few grim and gloomy forebodings, and perhaps a general sense of uneasy apprehension, when she was unexpectedly ordered to sail for war patrol on Friday, 13th February 1942. World War II was at its gloomiest and in the Mediterranean the 8th, 10th and 1st Submarine Flotillas of the Royal Navy, based respectively at Gibraltar, Malta and Alexandria in Egypt, were the only British naval forces actively engaged in offensive operations against the Axis powers of Germany and Italy, whose air forces virtually controlled all that moved on the surface of that inland sea.

That month, HMS *Thrasher*, a T-class submarine, was lying alongside her Depot Ship HMS *Medway* in Alexandria harbour, having returned from her seventh Mediterranean war patrol towards the end of January; *her* seventh but *my* third, as I had only been in command since October of the previous year. We were due to sail on our next patrol on Sunday, 15th February and all preparations were geared to that.

About mid-day on Friday the 13th, I was sent for by the Captain of the First Submarine Flotilla, Captain S.M. Raw, and told that we were to sail that evening so as to be on patrol off Suda Bay on the North coast of Crete by early morning on Monday, 16th February, intelligence reports having indicated there was an important enemy ship to be intercepted. Sammy Raw apologised for cutting short our rest period in harbour and sailing us on the 13th, but war being war there was no option.

Accordingly, the final preparations for patrol were hurriedly completed that afternoon and at 16.30 HMS *Thrasher* left harbour and set course for the Kaso Strait at the east end of Crete: once at sea, I informed the crew of our destination and the reason for the sudden departure from Alexandria. The routine dive to obtain a 'trim' quickly re-established normality and *Thrasher* proceeded on her way. She followed the normal passage procedure of making as much ground as possible on the surface at night, then dived by day at the economical speed of 2–3 knots in order to conserve battery power.

The Kaso Strait was negotiated without incident on Sunday, 15th February and that night *Thrasher* turned to the westward along the north coast of Crete. In the early hours of Monday the 16th, in poor, misty visibility, three darkened ships were sighted heading for the port of Candia; a torpedo attack on the surface was attempted but an effective firing position could not be obtained before the ships gained the shelter of the known mined zone. An hour after first sighting, the attack was abandoned and *Thrasher* proceeded at full speed so as to be able to dive at dawn off Suda Bay.

With the rising sun, came a gloriously fine Mediterranean day. Maximum visibility, cloudless blue sky, with not a breath of wind to ruffle the glassy surface of the sea, and as a background, to the south the snow-clad mountains of Crete were shining brilliantly in the sun. It was tempting to keep the periscope raised for longer than prudence dictated in order to gaze on this strikingly beautiful view. But the realities of the situation prevailed, a dived patrol keeping careful periscope watch for the expected enemy ship had to be maintained, notwithstanding the very adverse conditions: conditions anathema to any submarine commanding officer, with the water so crystal clear that the whole hull, 30 feet below the surface, would be conspicuously visible to any patrolling aircraft; and the sea so mirror-like that raising the periscope or firing torpedoes would create a disturbance like an erupting dolphin.

There was considerable activity off Suda Bay throughout the forenoon; small coastal craft, unescorted, creeping in and out, and patrol vessels hanging around on apparent anti-submarine searches, but fortunately no aircraft. So *Thrasher* could remain at periscope depth, to maintain a vigilant search for the target we hoped would appear.

Just before noon, a possible target materialised: a merchant vessel to the north-east, heading for Suda Bay. Was it what we were waiting for? The answer soon became clear: with five escorts, one ahead, one on each bow and one on each quarter, and with two aircraft circling overhead, the enemy obviously thought she was an important ship. Three of the escorts were heard to be transmitting on Asdics, this being the first reported use of such equipment in the Mediterranean theatre of submarine operations; hitherto enemy A/S forces had relied on hydrophones for detecting submerged submarines. *Thrasher* manoeuvred into a favourable position to fire torpedoes.

In the early stages, the attack was carried out with the submarine mainly at a depth of 80 feet, coming to periscope depth every 3 minutes for a snap look; but as the attack developed the interval between looks had to be shorter and we could afford time to go only to 50 feet. All went well until the crucial moment when the sights were coming 'on' for firing a salvo of four torpedoes from broad on the beam of the target; one of the escorts was heading directly for us, too close for comfort or safety, and *Thrasher* was forced deep to avoid being run down. "Missed DA" (Director Angle); the doomed cry of the submarine captain who fails to get his shot off when the sights come on! But there was still hope . . . turning on to a much broader and less favourable track (when torpedoes would be fired from a position on the quarter of the ship, which would therefore be presenting less of a target) *Thrasher* returned to periscope depth as soon as the escort had been heard to pass overhead. A quick look was reassuring and almost immediately the first of a salvo of four torpedoes was on its way, with the remaining three following at intervals of ten seconds.

Within moments of the discharge of the first torpedo, a dull, muffled explosion shook the submarine severely, to be followed by the rat-tat-tat of machine gun bullets hitting the water around the 'attack' periscope which had been raised to aim the subsequent torpedoes of the salvo. It seemed obvious that one of the escorting aircraft had sighted and attacked us; not unexpected in the prevailing conditions! With the four torpedoes on their way, *Thrasher* immediately went to a depth of 270 feet and set course to retire from the scene of action; five minutes later the three Asdic equipped escorts were to be heard actively hunting in close proximity, but not before two loud, distant explosions, ten seconds apart, seemed to indicate that half the salvo of torpedoes had found its mark.

For a quarter of an hour *Thrasher* then endured constant attacks by the hunting escorts who dropped a total of 33 depth-charges, including concentrated patterns of 10 and 7, the last being too close for comfort, bringing down the cork dusting from overhead, smashing lights and, more seriously, breaking the control room deep depth gauge. Otherwise there was no significant damage and the A/S vessels then appeared to lose contact while *Thrasher* continued to steal quietly away. On returning to periscope depth an hour and a half later, three escorts and aircraft could be seen hunting in the area of the last depth-charge attack; a mast and tall pillar of yellowish-grey smoke marked the position of the original target.

Soon after surfacing that night, orders were received to proceed to patrol in the Gulf of Taranto and *Thrasher* set course accordingly. The sea was still glassy calm; but after midnight and out in the open Mediterranean clear of the western end of Crete, *Thrasher* began to roll slowly in the slight swell. There was nothing in this to disturb the even tenor of the middle watch, but I, asleep in my cabin next to the control room, was suddenly awoken by a rhythmic banging immediately overhead. Something loose was rolling about outside the pressure hull in the casing under the gun, an unwelcome noise, and dangerous when one's very existence could depend on absolute silence. I ordered the Officer of the Watch to send someone down from the bridge to investigate.

In no time at all, I was told that there seemed to be a bomb (about three feet long overall) lying on the casing beneath the muzzle of the gun. There was also a hole in the side of the casing, abreast the breech of the gun, so another bomb might be lying on top of the pressure hull, causing the noise that had awoken me. By then, I was on the bridge and went down onto the casing to look at things myself.

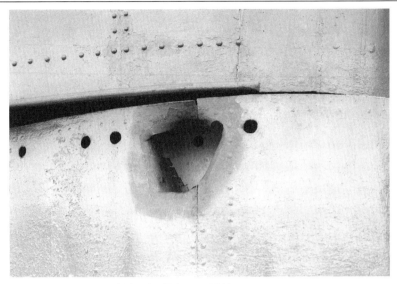

Bomb hole under gun of *Thrasher*, February 1942.

Sure enough, there was a bomb, about 100 lbs. in weight, lying peacefully on the casing. Further aft, there indeed was a hole in the gun-casing obviously made by an object of about the same size; further investigation confirmed that a second bomb lay inside the gun casing. Remembering the moment of firing torpedoes on the previous day, I concluded the escorting aircraft had dropped more than one bomb (the muffled explosion heard at the time). Two had hit us but failed to go off.

'What to do?' This was an emergency of which neither I nor anyone else on board had had any experience. I hoped that, having been subjected to a good dose of sea water at a pressure of some 130 lbs. per square inch when *Thrasher* had been at a depth of 270 feet, neither bomb was likely to be in a very dangerous state. But they must be got rid of as quickly as possible.

The First Lieutenant and Second Coxswain, being those responsible for all matters to do with the casing, were summoned to the bridge. The first bomb could be disposed of easily. By carrying or dragging it right forward and putting it in a sack, with the submarine going full speed astern, it could be lowered over the bows and let go. The second was much more difficult, it could only be reached by a long crawl through the casing. It would have to be dragged out along the same route before being taken up to the bows. There it could, like the first bomb, be dropped overboard.

Lieutenant Roberts and Petty Officer Gould volunteered readily to take on the job. So, with the Torpedo Officer, Sub-Lieutenant Fitzgerald, standing guard on the casing to act as communication link, they set about this dangerous task.

Meanwhile, *Thrasher* lay stopped, rolling uneasily in the long swell. It was a dark night but visibility was good. Tension on the bridge was high. The lookouts re-doubled their vigilance. Should the enemy discover us again (and they had been hunting us not long since), the submarine would have to dive. The chances of those on the casing getting back in time to be safely down the conning tower hatch were slim. But if they were crawling inside the casing retrieving the second bomb, their chances were zero.

Time dragged. There were many anxious moments, but within two hours of first discovering these unwelcome 'passengers', both bombs had been safely ditched. The second had proved particularly difficult with Roberts and Gould lying on their stomachs whilst manhandling the bomb through the casing, and the bomb itself emitting an alarming 'twanging' sound whenever it was moved.

Notwithstanding the trauma and difficulties, Roberts took full measurements of the bombs and noted their particular markings which, when subsequently analysed, revealed that they had been made in a factory in Czechoslovakia. I have wondered ever since whether I, and all in *Thrasher*, owe our lives to some unknown dissident worker in that factory who sabotaged the mechanism of the bombs? Or was it an error by the pilot who dropped his load from too low an altitude for all the bombs to 'arm' before they hit the water? We shall never know.

With the 'casing party' safely back on the bridge, tension eased for all of us who had been aware of these dramatic events taking place in the middle of the night. The majority of the ship's company, those off watch, had not been disturbed. I hoped that they had slept peacefully through it all. *Thrasher* resumed her way towards the Gulf of Taranto. The incident was behind us. We had carried out an apparently successful attack. We had survived the subsequent 'bollocking', and the fortunes of war had been on our side.

The rest of the patrol was without incident, except for days, and nights, of incessant gales and foul weather. Heavy units of the Italian fleet, which were expected to be met leaving or returning to Taranto never came within our orbit. *Thrasher* finally returned to base, to HMS *Medway* in Alexandria on the 8th March.

I did not make much of the 'bombs incident' in the official typed Patrol Report which, as customary, I handed in on arrival alongside *Medway*. Beyond a brief factual account in the main narrative, the appropriate section for Personnel included the following: "I should like to bring to your notice Lieutenant P. S.W. Roberts, Royal Navy, and Petty Officer T.W. Gould ON C/JX 147945 for their excellent conduct when acting as 'bomb disposal party' on 17th February."

This comparatively brief treatment did not satisfy higher authority, as I was soon to discover, being abruptly wakened at about 4 pm on the afternoon of our return to harbour. I was ordered to report immediately to Captain (S). Sammy Raw then told me that at the express direction of the C-in-C, Admiral Sir Andrew Cunningham, to whom Captain Raw had reported, I was to render full recommendations for an award or decoration for Roberts and for Gould. I complied accordingly, and wrote up the incident more fully. No mention was made of what the award should be, this being left entirely to the Honours and Awards Committee in London, but with the full-hearted backing of 'A.B.C.', (as the C-in-C was known throughout the Fleet), it was likely to be significantly more than a 'Mention in Despatches'. In forwarding *Thrasher*'s Patrol Report to the Admiralty he remarked, ". . . the coolness and courage displayed by Lieutenant Roberts and Petty Officer Gould in disposing of the bombs was of the highest order."

Several months passed, and with them several exciting patrols. The events of February 16th/17th were almost forgotten when we were shaken, I think that is the right word, by the news that Roberts and Gould had each been awarded the Victoria Cross. A great personal honour to themselves and, as they and I felt, also to their fellow submariners, which I am sure was the reason behind A.B.C.'s decision to make a special mark of the affair.

Thrasher completed thirteen war patrols in the Mediterranean before returning safely home to the United Kingdom just before Christmas 1942. It seemed not unnatural, then, that the media christened her 'The Lucky Thirteen'.

Chapter Two

Childhood

But, of course, these exciting events lay in the future, so let me start at the beginning.

About a year after the end of World War One a small, red-haired boy in his nursery was asked what he was going to do when he grew up. Without hesitation the answer was, "Be a sailor." The next question, "How do you spell sailor?" I got it wrong, replying, "s-a-i-l-e-r". I can see to this day our nursemaid, Eva McCrum, daughter of the Asylum's electrician, a red-hot left wing Clydesider, quietly putting me right. From then on, if all went well, my destiny seemed settled. Nobody queried it or tried to persuade me otherwise, and if ever my future was discussed it was simply that I was "going to join the Navy".

I was born on 3rd July 1913 in the house, 'Ruigh-Ard' to give it its Gaelic name, the residence of the Medical Superintendent of the Inverness District Asylum. Our home was beautifully situated on a hillside three miles to the north-west of Inverness, with a wonderful view out to the east over the Moray Firth and to the south, across the Great Glen. My father occupied this post for some twenty-five years and the circumstances surrounding it provided, in our eyes anyway, the most wonderful upbringing for his children. As we grew up, my two elder brothers, myself, and our younger sister, were given unlimited scope for adventure and experience in the then completely unspoilt country. We enjoyed every opportunity for all kinds of outdoor activities with the Highlands on our doorstep. The beauty and attraction of their hills, glens, rivers and lochs has never dimmed.

The daily life of this large lunatic asylum – as it was then called – with some 800 to 1,000 inmates at any one time, inevitably had its impact, but no special measures were taken to shelter us growing children from it. Were they 'lunatics' as they were commonly referred to in the parlance of the day? No, they were not, just unfortunate mentally disturbed people. These men and women were under treatment in the Asylum so that they could be cured and then returned to the villages, crofts, glens and straths of the northern Highlands and of the Hebrides from whence they had come. But some, of course, were incurable and were permanent residents. A number worked in the large garden around our house and once beyond infancy we were in daily contact with them. They helped us to look after our tame rabbits, gave us swings, supervised early tree-climbing and answered our questions. We soon learnt to talk only to those who could answer, and not to address those more troubled in mind.

I have no idea why I so positively decided my future at such an early age, but I have never regretted it. I was not following in the footsteps of any relation, close or distant, and we had no direct contact with the sea other than my mother coming from a well-known Aberdeen shipbuilding family. Perhaps it was triggered by the recently ended Great War, with all its triumphs and tragedies as seen through the scarcely comprehending eyes of a small child, or by the occasional distant sight from the top windows of our home of dark hulls on the horizon as ships of the Grand Fleet went about their business, to or from their base in the Cromarty Firth. The net result was that when the Atlantic Fleet paid the post-war annual Autumn visit to Invergordon, a small excited boy was always amongst those going on board whatever awe inspiring battleship was 'Open to Visitors'. HMS *Warspite*, still proudly bearing her honourable scars from the battle of Jutland, was the first of His Majesty's Ships in which I set foot. And though it came about in the course of time that my views on battleships as a whole were not all that complimentary, I always retained a 'soft spot' for that great and noble ship. And, in time, nothing gladdened my heart more than that the third nuclear submarine in the Royal Navy should bear the same name.

The shrubberies, lawns, banks and gravel paths of the extensive garden around our home gave ample scope through the first few years of life for every sort of fun and games. As we grew, activities were expanded over the Asylum's private estate; its roads, woods, farmlands, reservoirs and ponds. And behind the house and beyond the Asylum estate was Dunain Hill rising to nearly 1,000 feet, oak and pine woods at its base, where primroses flowered in the spring; heather, bracken, rocks and crags on its steeply rising slopes, and a small cap of fir trees at its very top. From there in fine weather could be seen the dim outline of Ben Nevis at the far distant end of the Great Glen, where it towered above Fort William.

It was an idyllic playground for growing children, the scene of many happy family picnics in summer; a neighbouring gamekeeper raised no objection to our presence on his domain, provided we took care to give him no grounds for complaint. Alas, no longer; Dunain is now under a dark blanket of the ubiquitous spruce tree blotting out all its distinctive features. Where, I wonder, have the sheld-duck gone, whose nests we found under the hill's great boulders, a site they must have used from time immemorial but fraught with immense difficulties in getting their ducklings down to the sea, three miles distant. Where, too, are the kestrels nesting in a particular crag year by year? Do they still survive?

The pond across the road from the house was a source of endless enjoyment, fishing and boating in the summer, skating in the winter. The skilled craftsmen in the Asylum's workshops, one of whom was an expert boatbuilder from the fishing village of Avoch in the neighbouring Black Isle, had built the most perfect sixteen ft. rowing boat, her timbers all from a

Brothers and sisters of self (the author) top, Alec, left, Charles, right, Margaret, centre.

great home-grown larch tree. I could find to this day the exact spot where it was felled. After long and careful parental instructions we were allowed to handle her on our own; she was called 'Margaret', after my young sister. There was soon added a smaller eight ft. dinghy. The seed was sown for my lasting love of being afloat, in any form.

The pond held a stock of brown trout, soon to be well educated in the various forms of artificial fly or other lure with which we tried to catch them. They spawned in the stream which fed the pond, and became individually so well-known to us that honour was satisfied if they just deigned to rise to the fly presented to them, no pressing need to kill and eat them. Potting rats with an air gun around the smelly duck pond, and in the adjacent hen run; stalking the rabbits which had ventured outside the plantations of young trees; and, later pursuing such game as poachers allowed to survive on the Asylum's farmlands, were our introductions to shooting. This was exciting to a youngster but all kept, on the whole, to within accepted rules and practices.

A close-knit family, we had a happy upbringing; our parents were kind and tolerant, though strict when necessary. We were well housed and well fed, during the war (1914–18) and its aftermath there were no drastic shortages and the Asylum's farm and gardens provided a back-up, but variety was lacking. Our staple nursery diet seemed to be tripe and porridge.

Father, Dr Mackenzie, and self.

Mother, self and grandmother.

How we rejoiced when our father returned from an invitation to stalk, fish, or shoot and a haunch of venison, a salmon or game would appear in the larder. It was long before the day of refrigerators and freezers; what could not be immediately consumed within the family was distributed amongst neighbours and friends. So we grew up imbued from an early age with a love and knowledge of the Highlands, wildlife, nature and all things outdoors, but also given a unique opportunity to absorb an understanding of the personal fortunes and misfortunes of our fellow human beings; for all of which I have been forever grateful.

Formal education was not neglected. Summer and winter alike, come rain or snow, every weekday a Governess bicycled out from Inverness to teach us the three 'R's', and much else; so that when in due course my brothers and I went on to boarding school we were not lacking in the essentials. Time never hung on our hands and when not engaged in formal lessons, or outdoor pursuits, books were avidly devoured. Our tastes were omnivorous, from Sir Walter Scott's Waverley Novels and Dickens to P.G. Wodehouse, John Buchan, Jack London, Henty, plus anything concerning wild life or sport in the Highlands. But Edgar Wallace and his detective stories were not welcome, they were thought to contain too much of crime and violence. Radio was still in its infancy, barely beyond 'cat's whisker' crystal sets, and was beyond our means until years later. Television did not exist so we did not miss it! Despite the latter's many genuine benefits in the fields of education, arts, entertainment and sport, and in the alleviation of loneliness, especially for the aged, I cannot help wondering whether a child can resist the examples of crime, violence and sex so constantly portrayed nowadays? Or will its behaviour reflect these examples? In our day, we were fortunate not to be so beset.

My parents were not rich, but reasonably well-off. Their status could be outwardly marked in those days by possession of the pre-war 'model T' Ford, to be succeeded soon after the war by a more comfortable version. Our chauffeur, ex-coachman, had converted easily from horses to horsepower and was an expert at getting his charges to their destinations and safely home again. Ice and snow, with heavy drifting in winter, presented the worst hazards, but the rough metalled roads and inevitable punctures made any journey an exciting adventure. Children's parties, to which I was usually a very reluctant starter, much preferring some more favoured 'ploy' at home, were a common entertainment. In the winter months they gave rise to many long journeys in darkness over snow-bound roads, us children well wrapped in thick rugs and with hot water bottles at our feet. They were fun in the end, but putting on our 'party clothes' was anathema!

Inverness itself was rarely visited, except for regular attendance at Ness Bank Church on Sunday mornings, all arrayed in our 'Sunday best'. The pews were hard, the sermons long, but the weekly discipline did us no harm; and at the right times of the year the sight of salmon jumping in the River Ness alongside the Church was ample recompense. If we ventured into town on other occasions, it was straight to the fishing tackle shops and taxidermists to hear the latest news from the salmon rivers and deer forests of the North.

At nine years of age, I was sent to preparatory school, to Cargilfield at Barnton on the outskirts of Edinburgh. My elder brother was then Head

Boy, to be followed similarly by my other brother a year later, which shielded me from utter loneliness and other hazards to be faced by a new boy. Fortunately, I found few difficulties in acclimatising to this new way of life, even to the cold of the dormitories. Most marked was the lack of electric lighting, only a few buildings boasted this, the remainder being lit by dim and spluttering gas mantles. Lessons were either boring, interesting or impossibly difficult, depending, as everywhere, on the individual master. While simple arithmetic was tolerable, algebra rapidly reduced me to tears, which laid the foundation to a lifelong aversion to anything to do with 'Higher Maths', a dislike only to be overcome when later professional needs were paramount.

Many of the boys were fatherless – casualties of the Great War. The whole school was redolent of the War, exemplified by the completion in 1923 of a beautiful memorial chapel and the attached Library. There, whenever time was free, I studied 'The Times History of the Great War', until I knew by heart the major events within its many volumes. Half the masters had fought on the Western Front, some still suffering from wounds. Those masters who had not seen active service were elderly, but also were the more patient with their pupils. The senior classics master, H.C. Benbow, took endless trouble with the mysteries of Latin and, for those sufficiently advanced, Greek. He was a loveable figure dressed in an old tweed suit, his ancient pipe constantly being re-filled with a pungent but sweet smelling herbal mixture of his own concoction. From him I learnt the art of tying the smallest and daintiest of trout flies, the same as he cast on his trout fishing holidays in Cumbria. It was a pursuit that gave me much enjoyment, until my eyes eventually found the strain too much. The very first salmon I caught was taken with a fly I had 'cooked up' and tied myself.

It was accepted from the start that the school should prepare me for taking the exams to get me into the Royal Naval College, Dartmouth; and as I progressed from form to form, lessons and teaching were adjusted accordingly. Latin I continued to learn, but no Greek. I wish it had been otherwise, for I have always regretted a lack of knowledge of the Classics. My contemporaries, many destined for the Public Schools of Fettes or Loretto in Scotland, or Winchester, Rugby or Sedbergh in England had the advantage. Small for my age and lightly built, I made no mark on the playing fields; rugger and hockey in the winter months, cricket in the summer. Competition was intense with other prep schools around Edinburgh, and, if not actively participating in the Wednesday and Saturday afternoon matches, we provided a shrill-voiced chorus to urge on our heroes of the first XV, XI, or whatever. If I had a penchant for anything, it was long-distance running. Any musical talents were conspicuously absent, on being tried for the choir I was contemptuously dismissed out-of-hand as a 'growler'. Obviously tone deaf, I was of no further interest. Despite this, listening to good music has always given me great pleasure.

Two years passed and then, halfway through the Autumn term of 1924, I suffered a major mishap and, for the second time in my short life, I nearly died. The first had been at the age of about two when under anaesthetic (chloroform in those days) on the kitchen table at home in Ruigh-Ard for a simple operation to remove a small gland from my neck, my heart appeared to fail. I have no recollection of this, other than a lasting dislike of the smell of chloroform, but was told by my mother many years later that there were a few very critical moments before things were returned to normal.

Now, on this second occasion at school, my appendix erupted. On the evening of a third day in bed (by which time the pain in my abdomen was excruciating), the school doctor at last laid his finger on the exact tender spot, diagnosed the trouble, had me wrapped in a blanket and took me forthwith in his car to an Edinburgh nursing home, 35 Drumsheugh Gardens, where I was operated on at midnight by a leading Edinburgh surgeon, Sir David Wilkie; but not, unfortunately, in time to prevent the abscess bursting.

For about a week I lay with two tubes protruding from my stomach, oozing a thick and most foul smelling green liquid. A very unpleasant few days were only alleviated by the kind and solicitous attention of the surgeon, doctors and nurses; of the latter, the first I was to see on recovering consciousness was the self-same Sister who had tended me on the kitchen table at Ruigh-Ard in Inverness some eight years before. I recognised her with a spasm of joy and relief, but, to keep everything in perspective, was promptly violently sick!

Recovery and convalescence was slow and protracted and it was many months before I was allowed to resume normal activities. This afforded me scope for much reading. Any books about the Royal Navy and its role in the Great War were greedily devoured. 'Taffrail' was my favourite author, and before I left the nursing home I knew by heart the tactics and movements of every British unit in the Battle of Jutland and the fate of every individual ship. But not only Jutland; Heligoland Bight, Coronel, Falklands, Dogger Bank, Gallipoli – I knew them all.

On return to school, work was progressively directed more and more towards the exams I would have to pass to achieve my ambition. A new Headmaster took over, young compared to his predecessor; an ex-judge from the Indian Civil Service we were told, refreshing in his outlook and forthright in making clear what was permissible and what was not in the way of conduct and behaviour. He went on to be for many years the highly regarded and much respected Headmaster of Sherborne, Canon A.R. Wallace. I felt his heavy hand on only one occasion and learnt never again to repeat the misdemeanour responsible, but it was what he said rather than what he did that had the more lasting impact.

And so to the Autumn of 1926, when for the first time I left my native Scotland and in the company of George Murray (another boy from Cargilfield also hoping to join the Navy) travelled by train to London under close parental escort. Short though the visit was to be, only a day or two, there was excitement enough for a 13 year-old. It was my first look at England, the changing countryside as the train sped south from Waverley to Kings Cross, the mining villages and industrial towns of the North to the far horizons and flatness of East Anglia, and finally, the bustle, noise, and hurly-burly of the capital city, with its careering red buses so different from the clanking trams of its sister north of the Border. The object of the visit was to appear before the Interview Board set up by the Admiralty and to undergo a Medical examination; to assess whether one was, respectively, intelligent enough ('good officer material' in modern phraseology) and medically fit for the Royal Navy.

Quaking in my shoes, I entered a large, barely furnished room in some grey, uninviting Government building in Tothill Street, Westminster, and was told promptly to 'sit down' before a long table on the other side of which sat five middle-aged gentlemen, none of whom had much of a welcoming smile. It was a paralysing experience, enough to make any youngster tongue-tied – but I suppose it succeeded in separating the sheep from the goats.

The atmosphere soon softened and the questioning was unexpectedly friendly. The barrage contained none of the things I had been briefed to expect ("What was the number of the taxi that brought you here?" and other matters of elementary observation) but concentrated on home life and my expectations for the future. After an ordeal of fifteen minutes, I was released, feeling I had acquitted myself reasonably well. Then followed the medical part, my naked body being thumped and banged and examined in detail, nothing aroused more interest or suspicion than the large and ugly scar from my appendicitis operation. Fortunately, when I quoted the name of the surgeon who had performed it, all doubts subsided, and as far as I could tell, everything had gone well.

Back at Cargilfield anxious weeks followed, awaiting the results. Consternation and dismay greeted them on arrival; though both George Murray and I had satisfactorily passed the Interview, our hopes of going on to the final hurdle of the written Entrance Exams were totally dashed by our both being failed for 'eyesight' in our Medical tests. My father, convinced there was nothing wrong with my eyes, immediately lodged an appeal and meantime arranged for me to see a leading eye specialist in Edinburgh. George's widowed mother followed suit. His reports being favourable, another visit to London ensued, to the old Queen Anne's Mansions building for a further quick test on our eyes by the Medical Director General's Department; we both passed, to great relief all round.

Some thirty years later, going through my father's papers, I came across the Edinburgh specialist's report. Dr. Paterson wrote, "despite very slight astigmatism in one eye this boy's eyesight is wholly up to the standards required by the Navy; in his early forties he will probably require to wear glasses." Prophetic words, for at the age of 42 I had just acquired my first pair of spectacles! I have no conception as to why both George and I failed the original eye test. Neither of us had any trouble in the routine eye tests that followed during the next 3½ years at Dartmouth, but I have always suspected that poor lighting, by gas, in our early days at Cargilfield may have had something to do with it.

A month later, accompanied by our parents, George and I were again on our way to London. In the train in the next-but-one compartment, was another small boy, in the blazer of Merchiston Castle preparatory school, Edinburgh. We viewed each other suspiciously – Merchiston was always a rival to Cargilfield. Later, in the same term at Dartmouth and joining submarines together, Robbie Alexander was to become a lifelong friend, but sadly dying a few days before his eightieth birthday, as these words are being penned. For all of two days, a motley crowd of about 150 small boys assembled each morning in a large hotel near Bedford Square, each sitting at separate desks under close invigilation and doing their best to cope with the varied papers set by The Lords Commissioners of the Admiralty for the granting of Naval Cadetships.

The papers taxed me fully, and there was no time to get to know the other candidates, any spare moment was immediately snatched by the representative of Messrs. Gieves Ltd., the naval outfitters. Like a vulture hanging in the sky on the look-out for prey, he seized on every potential cadet to measure him up for his future uniform and take orders for every necessary item of clothing and accessories from boots to hair brushes. A naval officer at the start of his career was thus inevitably in the clutches of Gieves.

I enjoyed the luxury of staying with my parents in the Langham Hotel, just opposite the B.B.C. at the top of Regent Street; and the fun of an evening car drive down Regent Street at over 45 m.p.h. in an open Rover, latest model, belonging to kind cousins who had come to show us the sights of London. There were no speed limits, no traffic lights, no pedestrian crossings in those days, and the streets were virtually empty.

Within three weeks, and before the end of the autumn term, 1926, came the exam results. All was well, both George Murray and I had passed. We were thrilled, the school was pleased.

Beyond the sadness of saying 'Goodbye' to friends, masters and boys alike, I had no regrets at leaving Cargilfield, all thoughts being on the Christmas holidays immediately ahead and the new life on the horizon. But as the years went by I came to realise just how much I owed to the thorough grounding, in both work and play, that I had received in my four years there.

Chapter Three

The 'Anson' Term

On a cold, grey January morning in 1927, fifty-one naval cadets assembled at Paddington station in London to catch the midday train to Kingswear in Devon, on the other side of the river Dart from the Royal Naval College, Dartmouth, where nearly all of us were to lodge for nearly four years, until July, 1930. All in brand new uniforms, unfamiliar and unsure of ourselves, we were greeted by our term officer, Lieutenant D.P. Evans. 'Dippy' was his nickname, and we were mustered and marshalled by our Term Cadet Captain D.P. Dreyer (now Admiral Sir Desmond Dreyer), assisted by our Cadet Captain, R.C. Hammond-Chambers-Borgnis, until a sense of order prevailed. We became the 'Anson' Term, and were to remain together throughout our passage through the College, the first five terms in the Junior College, the sixth in an intermediate stage, and the remainder in the Senior College. The top of the tree was reached in our eleventh term, by which time we were only forty-eight strong.

As new boys we were twenty-four hours ahead of the rest of the College, which gave us much needed time to settle in and assimilate the rules and conventions governing daily life and routine. These were not only those that might be termed 'official', but, vital to future equanimity of body and spirit, the unofficial customs known as 'guff', a practice common in almost any school whereby the seniors imposed their will on the juniors. Chief Petty Officer Massey, a bearded figure and by far the oldest human being with whom we had daily contact, a pensioner retired after 22 years service in the Navy, was our instructor and guide in all such matters. He rapidly became our friend and 'Father Confessor' for the years ahead. Once the twenty-four hours' grace expired, we were forever on the run; everything had to be done 'at the double', from classroom to classroom, when passing the 'gun-rooms' of terms senior to our own – as time progressed, we deliberately walked past the gun-rooms of junior terms!

Throughout waking hours there was little time when we were not under pressure, we were very ready for bed and sleep at the end of each day. On the playing fields, with which the College was superbly equipped, it was the same, 'Dippy' Evans ensuring we were never still. "Chop, chop!" was his battle cry as he urged us to ever greater efforts. And if the wet weather of the West Country caused the 'Grounds Unfit' notice to go up because of rain-sodden fields, we were sent off running along the Devon roads, the minimum stint being to 'Black Cottage' and

Self on joining Dartmouth, 1927.

back, a small, dark cottage about 1½ miles away on the coast road to Slapton and beyond.

We were lucky having such a man as 'Dippy' Evans as our Term Officer; true to form as a Cambridge rugger Blue, he was a great enthusiast for all team games and I must have been a disappointment to him, not that he ever showed any such feeling. Physically one of the smallest in the term, I did not shine at any organised game. He kept us up to the mark in everything. His standards were high, he expected us to match them in every respect and we had to be 'on the ball' at all times. But he was always kind and approachable, a figure much liked and admired and certainly not one to be feared. He was then unmarried, his whole heart and mind were devoted to bringing us up as 'Officers and Gentlemen' and to fit us for future service to our country as Naval Officers.

It was reassuring to see him years later, soon after World War II, when he was Commodore of the Barracks in Portsmouth. He was unchanged, except that, now being relatively recently married, the example he had always set as how to give, and to get the best out of life was even fuller than before. We did not see much of the other term officers, of whom there were seven, but enough to recognise that each had his own traits of character, quickly apparent as they, in turn, as Duty Officer passed through the dormitories on nightly 'rounds', the final act to every day. Term Cadet Captains and Cadet Captains (the 'prefects' directly responsible to the term officer for our conduct and behaviour) changed each term and our happiness, or the reverse, were much dependent on them; on the whole we were lucky, but there were some we regarded as a 'pain in the neck'. I think those latter suffered more than we did; never going so far as to be openly mutinous, the term's 50-strong 'dumb insolence' could win the day. No doubt we all learnt from such experience.

The Captain of the College, which came within the parish of the Commander-in-Chief, Plymouth, was responsible directly to the Board of Admiralty for the overall well-being of the College and its inhabitants as a Naval Establishment. For the first two years, until January 1929, we were under Captain (later Admiral) M.E. Dunbar-Nasmith, VC, a very distinguished submariner from the Great War, who had been decorated with the VC for his exploits in the Dardanelles and Sea of Marmora. He was succeeded for the remainder of our time by Captain S.J. Meyrick, just as much 'God' to us as his predecessor, but quickly given the nickname of 'Fog-horn' from the manner in which his booming voice carried across the parade ground. Under the Captain, the total Naval Staff of the College numbered twenty-eight, including the eight Term Officers. An Engineer Commander had charge of the Engineering Workshops and Machine Shops and he supervised with three Lieutenants (E) our instruction and training in the then 'state-of-the-art' Marine Engineering. In order to teach us sailing and the handling of small boats, a fleet of two-oared and four-oared rowing boats, service whalers and cutters, the latter with either dipping lug or Montague rigs, were kept afloat on the River Dart. We were encouraged to make maximum use of these in the summer months, as an alternative to organised games. For other lessons in seamanship, there were large and well-equipped instructional rooms within the heart of the main college building, manned by an indomitable quartet of ex-Chief Petty Officers; boatswains through-and-through, with fingers like marline spikes, they had an unplumbable depth of knowledge, the like of which I doubt exists today.

By far the major part of our time was rightly taken up by education in Mathematics, History and English, Science, Geography, and Modern Languages. Under the Headmaster (initially C.E. Ashford, CB, MVO, LLD, MA, latterly E.W.E. Kempson, MC, MA) there were five Heads of Department. There was one for each of the above subjects, supported by thirty Masters; three serving Instructor Branch officers taught Navigation and a solitary serving Lieutenant Commander, a qualified 'Torpedo Officer' taught Electrics. Many masters had been there for years, others being comparatively fresh from University and more flexible in their approach. But one and all were utterly dedicated to the task of instilling in us, some bright, some dense, as much learning and knowledge of their respective subjects as they could possibly encompass within the restricted time available. Beyond this, each had his own particular interest; art, music,

Admiral of the Fleet Earl Jellicoe at Dartmouth in the Admiral's Cricket Match, 1928.

natural history, medieval weapons, ornithology, and so on, all of which they were happy to share with any cadet who showed an interest.

Being at this time about eighty thousand strong overall, the Royal Navy was served by an Officer structure needing an entry of 150 cadets annually. We were individually very small cogs fitting into an enormous wheel revolving regularly to provide its officers. To help us understand how we fitted into this gigantic machine, every term each cadet was issued with what was known as 'The Blue Book'. This listed the members of the Board of Admiralty, the C-in-C Plymouth and the Officers, Masters and Cadets at the College, in full. I still have my complete lot, and they make interesting reading; they also demonstrate how the 'Term' system, which segregated each entry into its own age group and maintained this 'age discrimination' for 3½ years, helped engender profound loyalties to particular causes. If we could not get to personally know fellow cadets of different ages, at least we could learn to be aware of them by name and follow any changes in the hierarchy. The Blue Books gave us an overall view, not entirely superficial, of our progress through the College relative to others.

I enjoyed life at Dartmouth, from the very first day right through to the end, creature comforts were better than at my prep. school and to my juvenile mind the food was especially so. Roast chicken on Sundays, irreverently referred to as 'Seagull' by the stewards who dished it out, was a luxury unheard of at Cargilfield. Jehu, ex-Marine, fastest with the trolleys and at serving out the grub – hence his name – stands out in memory; "Bread is the staff of life" and "He also serves who only stands and waits" were two of his favourite quotations.

I won no prizes, never became a Cadet Captain, never got my 'Colours' for any form of games or sport; in all, a thoroughly undistinguished cadet, a 'late developer' if ever there was one. I remained one of the smallest cadets in the term and did not begin to grow until after I had left the College. The discipline and constant rushing to and fro presented no problems, and bullying, as far as I could see and from my own experience, was non-existent. And sex, as now portrayed as permeating, or even dictating, so much of life today, was neither a worry nor concern. It never then crossed my mind, or life – but then, as I have said, I was a late developer!

After two years there was a change of Term Officer, Lieutenant A.M. Kimmins (Tony Kimmins to all who knew him) replacing 'Dippy' Evans. He was a talented pilot in what was soon to be revitalised as the Fleet Air Arm and in our eyes an officer distinguished as having flown the only aeroplane to be launched by catapult from a submarine, the M2. He was also the author of that successful play *While Parents Sleep*. His wife was the daughter of Admiral Sir Michael Hodges, soon to be C-in-C Plymouth. Tony Kimmins was totally different from his predecessor, just as kind and as approachable but more relaxed. He allowed us more freedom to do as we wished outside class-room hours; organised games were no longer 'de rigueur' for everybody, nor did we have to conform to a stipulated task every afternoon.

Together with John Young, a fellow cadet from Helensburgh on the Clyde, with an equal interest in birds and ornithology as myself, I took full advantage. We scoured the surrounding countryside to note its bird life, anything within ten miles radius we considered within reach, accepting having to run most of the way, and there was little we did not find. We certainly kept fit and found much of interest, ravens at Start Point, buzzards along the cliffs and in almost every wood; sparrow hawks close by the College . . . we got beautiful photographs of the latter at their nest. But one summer's day we nearly met our end.

Returning from Slapton Lea along the shore below the cliffs, the incoming tide suddenly cut off further progress, so unwilling to retrace our steps – a long way, and time was getting short – we decided to climb the 200ft. cliff above us. This was against all the College rules, which strictly forbade any cadet venturing on the cliffs, because one had been killed a year earlier.

I led upwards, making steady progress with John following until within about eight feet from the top. There was no clear way on. The thought of descending was horrific, as some of our footholds had been dislodged. Then I spied a possible way to the top, six feet to my right, making use of a precarious foothold half way across but as I stretched out and put my weight on it, it crumbled and cascaded in a shower of earth 200 feet down to the beach below. By the mercy of God, or whoever looks after stupid cadets, some long bramble tendrils were hanging down the cliff to my right from overhead. As my foothold gave I made a desperate grab for them with both hands and thus swung across the cliff face to the point I had been aiming for; from there I had no difficulty in reaching the cliff top. But what of John?

He was marooned. The thorny life-line that had saved me was beyond his reach and he was quite unable to move up or down. After a quick consultation, we agreed I should seek help, a rope, or anything to help him get up the remaining eight feet, even if this meant our misdemeanour being revealed. I rushed off to look for the nearest farm. Across the first field I noticed a ten- to twelve-foot sapling growing out of the hedge. It did not seem to be secure and after some heaving and tugging I was able to pull it clear. Hastening back to the cliff top, I anchored myself and pushed the length of young tree down to John. It was just long enough. In a trice he was beside me on the grass. We hurried, thankfully, back to the College, determined to say nothing of our escapade, but from then on we had greater respect for the cliffs, and for the College rules.

As the summer term of 1930 drew towards its end there was noticeable quietness in the Anson Term, everyone was 'swotting' hard for the final passing-out exams (see Appendix I). It was rammed into us again and again that these were crucial, our fate depending on how well we did. Certainly the exams were a test of how much of all the knowledge crammed into us we

'Anson' Term, Dartmouth 1930. Self third from right bottom row.

had retained. Also, admittedly, this was not the wider, broad-brush, more liberal knowledge that another system of education might have given us. But – and it is a large 'BUT' – everything that we were taught throughout our time at Dartmouth had one sole design; to prepare Naval Cadets as fully as practicable for a life of service to King and Country in the Royal Navy. If we, or our parents, had wanted something else, we should not have volunteered – as plain as that!

I have heard many criticisms of the system over the years and some may have a measure of validity, for example, the immediate relevance of filing away for hours on end at a 6-inch block of brass was not apparent, but given that it taught us the basics of working with metal perhaps it was worth it. Or should the time have been better spent? I am not an 'educationalist' and cannot judge. Looking back, on balance I believe Dartmouth has very largely produced the right answer to meet the needs of the Royal Navy; two World Wars, The Falklands and, more recently, The Gulf go to prove it.

When I joined the Anson Term in January 1927, I was about half-way up, or down, in educational order of merit; academically I had progressed steadily upwards throughout the 3½ years and I was not disappointed that I had remained undistinguished, with no prizes, no awards. Life had been fun and I had learnt much. Thus equipped I was ready to begin the next voyage; to explore, to venture, to learn, to enjoy. I had no particular ambition to rise high in the Navy; to do my best and, as fate willed, to meet the next step as it came remained the sum of my aspirations.

In 1930, due to cuts in the Navy, there was no Cadet Training Cruiser to ease the change from life ashore to life afloat. With Dartmouth behind us, and after a spell of leave, we would go directly to the Gunrooms of the Fleets, Atlantic or Mediterranean, or of the more far-flung Squadrons; China, East Indies, South Africa, America and West Indies. We were given no choice; our fate all depended, we imagined, on Their Lordships' whim. It meant that, from having been 'top dogs' at Dartmouth, we came down with a crash to being the very lowest of the low, the accustomed status of midshipmen – but now even they had a stratum of inferior beings below them, sea-going cadets as we would be called.

We could look forward to wider horizons than the mouth of the river Dart and, of some significance to our unworldly eyes, our pay went up from two shillings a week at Dartmouth (provided, in fact, by our parents, not the Navy or Government) to the princely sum of five shillings a day (twenty-five pence in present day currency); but here again the Admiralty took its cut for, until we were finally promoted to Midshipman, our parents contributed four-fifths of this. The Treasury was as close-fisted then as it is now! Those whose parents could afford to give their sons an allowance were naturally better off; those not in the same boat made do with their pay. I cannot recall anyone grumbling. We were all treated alike and 'discrimination' was a word not yet invented.

But all this was still in the future. The end of our time at Dartmouth had been marked by an Anson term dinner at the Criterion restaurant in Piccadilly, London. For many of us this was our first experience of the discomfort of formal evening dress – a tradition which was to be with us for many years ahead, and which, like many other apparently irksome twists and turns in life, we learnt on reflection to accept with equanimity. After this dinner we dispersed all over the country on summer leave, which for me was to last until the end of September, the longest leave to come my way for many, many years. We were not to meet again in like circumstances until January 1977, the Golden Jubilee of our joining Dartmouth, by which time war, the passing years and wide dispersal had depleted our numbers from forty nine to fourteen. World War Two accounted for eighteen of those missing, including the brightest and best. Both term officers, 'Dippy' Evans and Tony Kimmins, were unfortunately also dead. Admiral Sir Desmond Dreyer, our first Term Cadet Captain, was our Guest of Honour and surprised us all by his depth of knowledge of how his early charges had fared.

I made the most of my leave; two glorious months at home in the Highlands with the whole family together at Ruigh-Ard for what, in the event, was to be the last time. My elder brother Charles was on leave from Sandhurst, with the later career in the Cameron Highlanders and the Parachute Regiment; my other brother Alec, home from Magdalene College, Cambridge, and my sister Margaret from her school, Heatherly, in Inverness. Happy times, culminating in the two days of the Northern Meeting in September, Inverness's great annual social occasion.

Young men were in much demand to make up evenly balanced parties for the two nights' dancing, and the Atlantic Fleet provided a ready source, its annual visit to Invergordon being timed to coincide. I was sorry for those officers thus induced to try their hands – or rather, feet – at a reel or Scottish country dance whilst clad in full naval Ball Dress – no uniform could have been less suitable. I was lucky to be wearing a kilt. The Northern Meeting Rooms with the specially hung and sprung floor, moving to the rhythm of two hundred pairs of feet above it, on which we danced each night through to the early hours, are sadly no more. In the midst of such carefree times, nemesis of course arrived, in the shape of my official appointment 'By Command of Their Lordships', ordering me to join HMS *Ramillies* of the 1st Battle Squadron in the Mediterranean Fleet as a Naval Cadet. I had instructions to take passage in the P&O liner *Rawalpindi*, sailing from Tilbury on a date in early October. Some eight to ten others of my term, also bound for the Mediterranean Fleet, duly joined with me on the given date. We explored this great ship and congratulated ourselves on having such luxurious first-class accommodation, albeit on the lowest cabin deck. Our destination was Marseilles, where we were to join HMS *Revenge*, the flagship of the 1st Battle Squadron, for onward passage to our respective ships, dispersed around the coasts of Greece and Yugoslavia on the Med. Fleet's second Summer Cruise.

The prospects of about a week on board this pride of the P&O fleet were enthralling, only slightly dampened when we realised a fellow passenger was Vice-Admiral Sir William Wordsworth Fisher – 'the Great Agrippa' as he was known – going out to command the 1st Battle Squadron, and becoming Second-in-Command of the Mediterranean Fleet. He was accompanied by his wife and lovely daughter Rosamond who captured our youthful hearts immediately but was much too efficiently guarded by the Flag Lieutenant from the likes of us. No one could mistake the Admiral, a man of great and commanding stature, with a voice to match, carrying for miles. It was rumoured he once directed by voice alone his ships entering Grand Harbour in Malta, whilst standing on the battlements below the Castile. 'W.W.' kept, after our initial introduction to him, a kindly and fatherly eye on us, and in deference to his presence we minded our Ps and Qs throughout the voyage.

After a brief call at Gibraltar we were soon at Marseilles. The group of wide-eyed cadets joining *Revenge* were very small beer compared to all the firing of gun salutes, parading of guards and bands, fanfares of bugles and musical honours which accompanied the new admiral hoisting his flag on board. To say that we were totally *de trop* would be no exaggeration. There was no room in the gunroom for us, other than for a first or second 'shift' at meal times; neither did there appear to be any job for us, except on the Saturday morning when in accordance with normal practice we were all put to work cleaning the Gunroom brasswork. The senior midshipman in charge of this unskilled workforce knew only one word in the English language, 'bloody'; no matter how hard we sweated, polished and burnished, his verdict on our efforts never rose above this.

Eventually time would run out and we would be dismissed, and so back to the bare cabin, totally empty of furniture, not even a chair or table, in the officers' cabin flat. There we wiled away the days it took to steam from Marseilles to a remote bay on the west coast of Greece, calling at Malta en route. In Dragamesti Bay *Revenge* joined up with the rest of the 1st Battle Squadron. We hoped there were exciting times ahead, but this first voyage was not the happiest introduction to life afloat.

Chapter Four

The Mediterranean Fleet, 1930–33

On Friday, 17th October 1930, I and four other cadets from the Anson Term thankfully left our temporary home and joined *Ramillies*. We were given twenty-four hours to 'sling our hammocks', those supremely practical and comfortable beds (once one had got into them) in which we were to sleep until finally reaching the rank of Acting Sub Lieutenant. The next two days were a revelation, for we were in the throes of an Admiral's Inspection. 'W.W.' had wasted no time in ensuring he was known to his squadron.

So began two years and ten months in the Mediterranean Fleet – at that time one of the most powerful fleets in the world; one squadron of five 15" gun battleships, one aircraft carrier, eight cruisers in two squadrons, thirty six destroyers in four flotillas, a flotilla of five submarines, plus repair and depot ships and auxiliary craft to provide logistic support, maintenance and hospital service. Until 1st May, 1931, I served as a 'sea-going cadet', thereafter as a Midshipman. I spent a fortnight in the aircraft carrier, *Glorious*, to gain air experience; and three months in the summer of 1932 in the destroyers, *Worcester* and *Achates*, of the Third Destroyer Flotilla, to gain 'small ship' experience. For the remainder of my (midshipman) Snotty's time the gun rooms of the battleships of the First Battle Squadron were to be home to me and my four Anson term-mates who had joined *Ramillies*. We remained in *Ramillies* until transferring to destroyers in May 1932, while a month later *Ramillies* returned to the U.K. to re-commission. At the end of our destroyer time, in August, we found ourselves together again in another battleship, *Resolution*, remaining in her until she, in turn, left the Mediterranean station to re-commission at home in the following year. Once again, in early April, 1933, we were transferred to yet another battleship, *Queen Elizabeth*. None of us were thrilled by this latest edict of the appointing authorities in the Admiralty. We envied so many of our contemporaries given the chance of leave at home, when their ships left the station to re-commission. The treatment meted out to us strengthened my evolving prejudice against 'big ship' life and so had a lasting effect on my future.

Resolution, then under the command of Captain Max K. Horton, later in World War II to be Flag Officer Submarines and C-in-C Western Approaches, had the most efficient Captain I ever served under, demanding the very highest standards from officers and men alike. He was promoted

HMS *Ramillies* in floating dock, Malta 1931.

HMS *Ramillies* firing main and secondary armament and high angle guns 1931.

HMS *Ramillies*, full power trial 1931.

Rear Admiral in October 1932, and was relieved by Captain C.E. Turle, who may not have had quite the same qualities as Max Horton, but was the best big ship ship-handler I have ever known. On 31st October 1932, *Resolution* took over from *Queen Elizabeth* as Fleet Flagship, the latter returning to the UK to re-commission; simultaneously, Admiral Sir William Fisher relieved Admiral Sir Ernle Chatfield at Commander-in-Chief, and so, once again, we were directly under the eyes of 'W.W.'

Gun-room life varied from ship to ship throughout the fleet. Much depended on the 'snotties' nurse, usually one of the ship's Lieutenant Commanders selected by the Captain to be responsible for midshipmen's training, welfare and discipline. In day-to-day existence, the Sub-Lieutenant who presided over the gun-room mess featured more significantly, it was he who had the power to make life tolerable or intolerable.

No-one could describe the gun-room itself as luxurious. It was a sparsely furnished and plainly painted steel box, with no lining other than corticene on the deck underfoot, with a hatch through to the gun-room pantry where the Maltese stewards who attended to our needs for food and drink lived, and slept, in some squalor, I thought, with a horde of cockroaches as their companions.

One end of the gun-room was partially screened off by a 'stand' of wooden lockers, wherein we kept our journals and sundry treasured private possessions. The 'holy of holies' behind these lockers was occupied by 'the Sub' and such other sub-lieutenants, Engineering or Paymaster branch, as might be on board, together with the senior group of midshipmen. This caboose was furnished with standard Admiralty-pattern arm-chairs, decidedly more comfortable than the settee and straight-backed chairs each side of the long table sufficing for the rest of us, who were usually about a dozen, for work and meals. Sleeping, dressing, washing were all confined within a congested 'flat' and bathroom amongst the Warrant Officers' cabins, two decks below the Quarterdeck. Royal Marine Bandsmen, one to every three or four Midshipmen, slung our hammocks each evening and lashed them up in the morning and, thankfully, assisted us in the care of our clothes and keeping us smartly dressed: never have my boots been so well polished!

Perhaps my group of fellow Ansons and I were more fortunate than others. I could not subscribe to the view that gun-room life in those years was harsh, certainly not in the three great battleships of which we had direct experience. Hard, yes, but not harsh. Discipline was strict and routine was rigorous and demanding. We were worked hard, whether under formal instruction, on watch, or in charge of the ship's boats on their innumerable duty trips around the harbour throughout the day and frequently much of the night. If we did wrong and merited punishment, this was meted out by stoppage of leave or of our monthly wine bill. The latter was not very serious, for being under age (twenty one years) King's Regulations and Admiralty Instructions (the Bible by which the Fleet was run) forbade us to drink spirits, so the loss of wine or beer was of no great significance. Only once in my nearly three years in gun-rooms can I recollect a midshipman being punished by being caned. These circumstances were very different from earlier generations.

Discipline was tightest in *Resolution* under Max Horton. Shortly after we joined, he decreed that 'the young gentlemen' of the gun-room lacked self-confidence. To help remedy this, a 'duty' midshipman would report to him at noon each day when in harbour to recount what was going on in the ship that day, what was going on in the port or country in which we happened to be (Malta, Turkey, Greece . . .), and finally, any major events in the world during the past twenty-four hours.

It was a nerve-shattering experience. The Captain's day cabin was 90 feet wide. He sat stern-faced behind his desk on one side. The 'snottie' stood on the other side, more than the length of a cricket pitch away from, to our eyes, this grim and threatening figure. Any hesitancy or mumbling was unacceptable, the report had to be loud and clear. The relief when the ordeal was over was enormous and, even more so, when word came that one was not required to repeat the performance at a later date. Looking back now on this particular episode, I am sure the end result was entirely salutary, and nothing did more to build up my self-confidence and ability to stand on my own feet.

The Fleet worked to a regular yearly routine; a short winter cruise in January–February, a spring cruise in March/April which included a large scale strategic exercise with the Atlantic Fleet, and two summer cruises from June to October separated by a short spell in Malta in August for replenishment with stores and provisions. To be away from the comparative restraints of that tight little island throughout the heat of the summer was a relief to all.

The start and end of each cruise were marked by major strategic and tactical exercises lasting two or three days. The whole Fleet was engaged, being divided into Red and Blue Forces. The exercises culminated in day and night battles between the opposing forces, in which massed destroyer torpedo attacks were a major feature. Strangely, in the light of subsequent history, submarines only occasionally played a significant role in these exercises and even when they did, the scale of 'casualty' or 'damage' imposed on their targets as a result of successful torpedo attack was totally out of keeping with reality.

This lack of appreciation of the submarine threat may be explained by the withdrawal in 1931 of the ageing Great War *L*-class submarines from the Mediterranean Fleet, to be replaced a year later by the new *R*-class submarines. Another factor was the safety rules which required all submarines to be on the surface at night, burning navigation lights, and taking no part in any of the exercises during dark hours. Apart from this serious lack of realism, the exercises provided for the surface fleet first-class training with existing armaments in *surface* action at sea, either by day or night. The threat from the air, other than carrier-borne aircraft, was never, apparently, seriously contemplated. The Royal Air Force was conspicuously absent from any simulated air attacks on the Fleet, but carrier-borne aircraft were realistically employed in attacks on the Fleet both at sea and in harbour.

When not exercising, ships dispersed in the spring for individual visits to chosen ports, along the French and Italian Rivieras, and in the Adriatic, Aegean and Eastern Mediterranean during the summer. The short winter cruise was generally to remote bays and anchorages around the coast of Greece, which provided, for those so inclined, wonderful wildfowl shooting (duck, woodcock and snipe). Admiral Sir Dudley Pound, when serving earlier in his career as Chief of Staff to the C-in-C, had compiled a comprehensive and detailed guide to the kinds of shooting to be enjoyed during the normal course of Mediterranean Fleet cruises – a 'Michelin Guide' to wild sport in the Islands and Highlands of the Mediterranean. It was a treasured and much valued handbook, passed from ship to ship, a few copies of which were still in existence after World War II.

The pulling (rowing) regatta in cutters, whalers and gigs, was the main event of the Fleet's assembly at the end of the first summer cruise, the second was concluded by a sailing regatta. This regatta always included a midshipmen's 'crash cutter' race in the few two-masted dipping lug 32-foot cutters that still existed in the fleet. This was a two-mile race starting with the cutters at anchor, masts down and awnings spread: 'on the gun', furl awning, weigh anchor, up masts and make sail. Having completed the first half mile, down sails and masts, out oars and row for the next half mile; then up masts and sail for a further half mile; and finally down sails and masts, out oars and pull to the finishing line. It was an exhilarating contest, testing both physical fitness and mental alertness, woe betide the slow witted or inattentive, when heavy yards and masts came crashing down, bruised bodies if not broken heads or limbs were the penalty.

Competition encompassed everyone's life. One had to be the smartest, cleanest ship, be first in everything – in Squadron or Flotilla General Drill, in Gunnery and Torpedo firings, in the Regattas; and, by no means least, in the endless round of Squadron, Flotilla or Fleet competitions for football (soccer and rugger), hockey, cross-country running and athletic sports. Ships' companies were never idle, there was always something going on and particular attention was directed to ensure that the gun-room inhabitants did not miss out on anything. We were not allowed to forget that our development into efficient officers and leaders was being constantly monitored, not only from within one's own ship, but from the very top.

Admiral's inspections were dreaded events. I, like most of my contemporaries, desperately feared being hauled out from my fellow midshipmen, who were assembled on the top of 'B' turret, to drill the ship's company of some one thousand men mustered on the fo'c'sle below. To my relief, I was never so selected. But the trauma of the two-day inspection never eased, ship's company and ship were inspected, from head to toe and truck to keel on one day; followed on the next by the General Drill and General Quarters, the former to prove the ship's ability in seamanship and the latter its efficiency in using its weapons. The ship's armament, whether main, secondary, high-angle, torpedo or close-range, and her offensive capability and ability to react quickly to any requirement or emergency were fully tested.

But, with the benefit of hindsight, little attention was paid to 'Damage Control', a subject so painfully learnt when World War II put all our training to the vital test. The overall drive towards fighting efficiency was a reflection of 'W.W.'s' emphasis on training the fleet to fight by day or by night, and to be instantly ready to meet any emergency. He stamped his personality everywhere and his words and actions were instantly noted throughout ship, squadron and fleet.

Observing the evolution of 'Away all boats' during his inspection of *Glorious* he stood, watching, behind a young lieutenant in charge of lowering one of the boats. Things were not going well. There was a muddle, confusion and tangled ropes, with the air full of four-letter words. This display continued for some time, until 'W.W.' stepped forward, tapped the lieutenant on the shoulder and pronounced his verdict, his deep, resounding voice carrying afar: "Young man, the measure of your language is the measure of your incompetence." That was all. Maybe from this distance it sounds pontifical but the effect was dramatic and widespread and we all absorbed the lesson.

This was not the only side to 'The Great Agrippa'. There were many occasions and examples of his ability to relax and enjoy the company of others, especially the young; frequently his guests on board added to the pleasure and variety of our lives. The author Maurice Baring was one such visitor. He seemed to enjoy the gun-room as much as the Admiral's quarters aft, to which he was wont to return, despite efforts to restrain him, by diving over the side, clad in his dinner jacket, from the deck outside the gun-room and swimming to the gangway aft on the quarterdeck. Another feat gaining admiration and esteem was his ability to balance a full glass of beer on top of his totally bald, egg-shaped head. Thus equipped, he would wager to make his way from gun-room to bridge when the ship was at sea at night, fully darkened, up ladders and past immeasurable obstacles without spilling a drop. No hand touched the glass until his objective was reached. He invariably won his bet, an outstanding and memorable achievement.

There was much to be learned culturally and historically from the many places visited during the Fleet's cruises away from Malta: the treasures and antiquities of Greece, Italy, Egypt were there to be seen if we so wished. The wonders of Venice, Cairo, the Acropolis in Athens, the Pyramids, the ruins of Knossos in Crete, of Baalbek in Syria, of Pompeii, were imprinted on my mind forever. Nearly every port visited, and even some of the remoter anchorages, provided opportunity for broadening the mind and learning that there was more to life than the usual 'run ashore' to sample and indulge in what the locals could provide in the way of 'wine, women and song'. The temptations towards the latter tended to be overwhelming, despite the good efforts of the ship's chaplain to whom was normally given the responsibility of arranging 'cultural' tours.

Malta itself was not lacking in a higher level of entertainment. Throughout the winter months, the Opera House in Valletta (sadly destroyed in the bombing of 1942) was home to top class Italian companies. The gun-room of *Resolution* took a box for one night a week for the 1932–33 season. But a night at the opera once a week was more than the average midshipman could afford; full evening Mess Dress (stiff shirts, white waistcoats and all) was an added burden and, in the end, the cost defeated the good intentions of improving our minds with something better than the bars, dance-halls and prostitutes of the lower end of Strada Stretta (The Gut).

'Showing the Flag' was a major object of ships' visits to ports around the Mediterranean. The ritual invariably included an 'At Home' for the resident British population and the big-wigs, military and civilian, of the local authority. Being before the days of the ubiquitous cocktail party, the usual form was the 4 pm to 6.30 pm *thé dansant* held on the specially prepared and be-flagged quarterdeck. French chalk was sprinkled on the sacred teak planking, and the Royal Marine Band purveyed 'Palm Court' music until the currently favoured foxtrots or waltzes took over. To my juvenile mind this was a ghastly form of entertainment, but one in which the midshipmen were nevertheless required to participate fully, particularly in providing dance partners for the more elderly and least attractive female guests. On the French and Italian Rivieras these latter seemed to predominate, young and attractive girls were conspicuous by their absence, or, if any were present they were monopolised by the Wardroom. I loathed the role of 'gigolo' to the elderly English expatriate population who so dominated proceedings.

At Corfu at the end of the first summer cruise 1932, the assembled Fleet was visited by Their Royal Highnesses, the Prince of Wales and Prince George. They arrived late one evening by Imperial Airways flying boat, escorted by the float planes (Fairey III F) of the 1st Cruiser Squadron and two R.A.F. flying boats. During the next two days, they inspected every ship of the Fleet. The Prince of Wales visited submarines and their depot ship, flotilla leaders, cruisers and above, while Prince George boarded destroyers and Royal Fleet Auxiliaries. Mediterranean summer weather blessed the visit, and with the few previous days given over to cleaning ship, it was ensured that not a blemish was visible anywhere in the fleet. I wrote in my Midshipman's Journal, "The ship (*Achates* of the 3rd Destroyer Flotilla) is now looking remarkably smart and the steel decks are really marvellous, polished until they could be used as a mirror!" As some recompense for all the 'spit and polish', a 'Make and Mend' was ordered on the afternoon of

HMS *Achates*. 3rd Destroyer Flotilla, 1932.

the first day, to be followed that evening by 'Splice the Mainbrace', an extra tot of rum all round.

On the afternoon of the second day the fleet sailed for Malta, their Royal Highnesses taking passage in the aircraft carrier, *Glorious*. For them a series of spectacular day and night exercises was laid on and there must have been some anxious moments in the minds of those in charge during the very first of these, a torpedo attack on the battle fleet by 18 Ripon aircraft from *Glorious*. To witness this Their Royal Highnesses were airborne in two Fairey III F aircraft. After the attack, as they were about to land back on the carrier, fog came down. The Prince of Wales's aircraft landed before *Glorious* was totally enveloped. It was some time before she ran clear and landed Prince George's aircraft, and her others.

The demonstrations of the fleet's fighting efficiency culminated in the most spectacular of all. A massed destroyer torpedo attack on the big ships, combined with full calibre firing from their 4.7 inch guns at battle practice targets suitably positioned to represent opposing destroyer forces. All was carried out at a speed of 28 knots, each ship being allocated 90 rounds of ammunition (an unheard of allowance in those days of economy), 30 for each of the two for'd guns and 10 to each aft, to be fired when attacking and retiring. With the destroyers attacking in line ahead formation and with the gunnery targets very fine on the bow, there was some danger in this highly realistic practice, ships 1½ cables (300 yards) apart, 28 knots, guns blazing, noise and smoke, but fortunately outwardly all went well.

But no-one had expected or anticipated the absolute internal shambles enacted by this fusillade from 'A' and 'B' guns firing at such a fine angle ahead. There was a scene of desolation on the mess-decks below; glass fittings broken, electric leads hanging in festoons, mess tables and stools overturned and lying about in confusion. Similar chaos existed on the fo'c'sle, where all the paint had been scorched, with everything stained yellow from cordite fumes, and one of the guard rail stanchions flattened by a shell, the copper from the latter's driving band was sprayed all over it. It was as near war as one could hope to get in peace time and, as such, most excellent training for guns' crews and control parties. For the rest of us it was a thrilling and realistic experience of action at sea – but without the danger from enemy retaliation.

We were back in Malta later that day, and so ended my three months 'destroyer time'. On the very next day, my fellow Ansons and I from the 3rd Destroyer Flotilla joined HMS *Resolution*, a different ship from the comfortable old *Ramillies*, but we found four other Ansons in the gun-room ready to welcome us. The reversion to 'big-ship' routine was easily effected, but I had had a sniff of small ship life which stiffened my thoughts about the future, though these did not weigh heavily!

Within a fortnight *Resolution* left Malta with the fleet for the second summer cruise which was to take her to ports in the Eastern Mediterranean, and then to Mudros in the Aegean for competitive gunnery firings. Barely had *Reso* arrived at Mudros, at the end of September, than she was ordered with the fleet repair ship *Resource* and four destroyers of the 4th Destroyer Flotilla to proceed to the east coast of Greece, north of Mount Athos. The region had been stricken with a severe earthquake and help was urgently required. *Resolution* arrived off the village of Ierissos thirty six hours after the initial shock and further shocks were plainly felt on board as the ship anchored. Landing parties were sent ashore immediately to assess the damage.

Ierissos itself and neighbouring villages within a few miles radius had been flattened, with many killed and injured. Some of the latter had already been evacuated by a Greek destroyer, but she did not reappear on the scene. No help was at hand, except what could be provided by the British ships, most urgent needs being medical aid, food and water.

A makeshift tented hospital was set up on open ground near the ruined village. Water was ferried ashore by launch to fill large canvas tanks erected near the beach, and within twenty-four hours the bakeries of *Reso* and *Resource* were daily supplying bread for 5,000 people, plus flour to be sent to adjacent villages, by mule or donkey. All had to be transported by ships' boats and landed across an open beach which was at times exposed to rough seas, everyone was kept exceedingly busy.

A worse task was to follow, digging out the already decomposing bodies from the ruins and burying them in hastily dug graves in a newly defined burial ground, the old village cemetery having been destroyed. There was no difficulty in finding the bodies, for the weather was hot, the smell of death everywhere and the stench horrific at times. With that phase completed, attention turned to building a line of wooden huts to house the survivors who had hitherto been existing in the open without any form of shelter. The line of buildings was naturally named 'Oxford Street', after Commissioned Shipwright Oxford of *Reso* who was in charge of construction.

By the fifth day, some semblance of order had been restored and, most importantly, the local people were emerging from their state of shock and beginning to show interest in doing something for themselves. Utter despair, inability to think or act, a total numbness, had been the immediate result of the disaster which had so suddenly and unexpectedly struck them. It took some days for this obliterating apathy to begin lifting and we were thankful to see the new mood developing. This fresh determination had become well established by the time *Reso* was ordered to return to Mudros, leaving *Resource* to continue the relief work, until the Greek authorities could take over.

The only happy by-product of all the desolation at Ierissos was the sudden appearance of Noel Coward from the hinterland. In khaki shorts, with a haversack on his back, he had been on a walking tour in Macedonia. Hearing of the disaster and that there were HM ships about, he had come to investigate. We gave him passage to Mudros, to stay with the C-in-C and to our joy he found the gun-room to his liking and its piano not too much out of tune, despite the alcohol frequently poured into it.

Although each cruise away from Malta began and ended with a few intensive days of tactical exercises, when ships were put through their paces for fighting a fleet action at sea, the cruises were mainly periods for relaxation. The remainder of the year, at Malta, was for routine docking and maintenance and, once that was accomplished, for weapon training by individual ships and by squadrons and flotillas. The routine was to sea on Monday mornings, back in harbour by Friday afternoons, gunnery and torpedo firings, by day and night, throughout the intervening days.

The British economy was in a bad way and so many restrictions were in force, 'economical' speed was the rule for the endless hours spent steaming up and down the practice areas for gunnery sub-calibre firings. It was dreary in the extreme for all concerned, but was deemed essential practice for the full calibre 15" and 6" 'shoots' which took place almost on a weekly basis. High Angle (H.A.) firings from the 4" H.A. armament against sleeve targets towed by Fairey III F Fleet Air Arm aircraft also featured regularly in the weekly programmes. Safety requirements precluded much realism and little skill was gained in the difficult task of shooting down attacking bomber or torpedo-carrying aircraft, as later years was to prove.

Torpedo firings, occupying less time, were more exciting. Even the great battleships took part, discharging one or two 21" 'fish' from the enormous torpedo 'flats' down in the bowels of the ship, and on completion there was always the daunting task of retrieving, by ship's cutter or whaler, the practice torpedoes, bobbing vertically in the sea. They were difficult to spot from afar and no easy object to capture and restore to the parent ship.

Little time was spent on anti-submarine practices. *The submarine threat was thought to be of little importance and so was largely ignored*, an attitude borne out by the insignificant part played by submarines in tactical exercises. Only in one, at the end of the spring cruise in 1933, did they feature largely.

Conversely, the potential danger from mines was not so overlooked, ships were constantly exercised in streaming paravanes as protection from moored mines. There were no specialised minesweepers in the fleet, but the 3rd Destroyer Flotilla of the new 'A' class, the first design since the Great War, was equipped with T.S.D.S. (Two Speed Destroyer Sweep), two paravanes towed from the stern of the destroyer, the width of the path swept narrowing should speed exceed 18 knots. It was a splendid scheme in theory, but a horror to operate, with the paravanes reluctant to comply with design requirements.

Ships were never idle and time went swiftly by, ships' companies being content with their lot. The Invergordon Mutiny in the Atlantic Fleet in September, 1931, which so shook the country, scarcely rippled the surface in the Mediterranean. Ships were, fortunately, well dispersed at the time, on their second summer cruise. Though the drastic and foolish pay cuts affected men abroad as much as those at home, time and distance helped to ameliorate the blow. *Ramillies* was at Alexandria, enjoying her visit, and I cannot recollect any comment whatsoever.

After the fleet had re-assembled in October for the annual sailing regatta (which occupied our attention far more than Invergordon) every ship received a visit from its Admiral or Senior Officer, bearing a stirring message from the C-in-C. The ships' companies were congratulated on their steadfastness and reminded of their duty, and of the need to reassure the nation that it could still have faith in the Royal Navy. As to be expected, nobody could have put this message across better than 'W.W.', when he addressed the ship's company of *Ramillies* on 23rd October.

In July 1933, attention for me and my fellow Ansons focussed sharply on the approaching examination in seamanship, to be held after the fleet pulling regatta in mid-August. The exam had to be successfully passed to qualify for promotion to Sub-Lieutenant and on the marks gained depended the eventual date of promotion to Lieutenant. It was a critical milestone and, as its date approached, trepidation increased, with a frantic swotting up of seamanship manuals and other sources of knowledge: the lessons and experiences of the past two and three quarter years had to be at our finger tips. It was an oral exam, ranging over every conceivable aspect of seamanship, conducted by a Captain and two Commanders, with marks also included for one's Journal, a record, suitably illustrated, that every midshipman was required to keep of daily events and items of interest and importance throughout his sea time. Maximum marks were 1,000, 90 per cent being required for the first class pass. In the event, with aroundabout 890 marks I obtained only a second class pass. I was content, but could not help wishing that the ten additional marks had not eluded me.

Within days, I was on board HMS *Brazen* of the 4th Destroyer Flotilla, bound for England to re-commission. Her Captain was Commander L.D. Mackintosh, son of the Mackintosh of Mackintosh, well known to my father in Inverness. It was a happy augury for a happy voyage in fair, summer weather. We passed Ushant in the early hours of a day at the beginning of September and soon, in the northerly breeze, the scent of the English summer countryside was in our nostrils. In a few hours we berthed at Devonport and I was on the night train from London to Inverness that evening. It was wonderful to be home again after two years and eleven months absence. The knowledge that I would be back on the treadmill of learning in less than three weeks, this time for the Sub-Lieutenant's six month course at the Royal Naval College, Greenwich, was of no consequence – though the length of my leave, after nearly three years abroad, was hardly in keeping with K.R. and A.I. which laid down a scale of a month for every year abroad, and was a matter that coloured my views in future whenever the question of 'leave' came up.

Chapter Five

Sub-Lieutenant's Training Courses

Many varied experiences were exchanged or boasted of when the Anson term of 1927–30 re-assembled at the Royal Naval College, Greenwich, in the autumn of 1933. Everyone had advanced from adolescence to manhood, dramatic changes in personality in some, new friendships formed, old ones dropped.

The magnificent, palatial buildings of the college were no shield in the ensuing winter against the cold and fogs, so prevalent close to the river. The chill percolated right through the ancient solid, thick, stone walls, these, paradoxically, a seemingly impenetrable obstacle to the installation of any form of central heating. The only warmth in our living quarters was a coal-fired stove in the sub-lieutenants' ante-room, where the main trade at the bar of an evening was a constant supply of 'hot toddies' as an antidote to streaming noses and hacking coughs.

Six months of intensive education were concentrated on Mathematics, Physics, English, History (general and naval), and French whilst grudging time was found for the briefest introduction to the Principles of War, outlined in the official 'Naval War Manual'. Its most telling point was its frontispiece, a photograph of a uniformed sailor, inscribed, 'The most important single factor', a lesson of widest application, never forgotten personally, but frequently ignored in some quarters.

The Sciences were essential ground-work for life in a Navy on the verge of enormous technological advance but they were not my strong point and I much preferred Naval History, especially that taught by Professor Geoffrey Callender, whose three volumes of 'The Sea Kings of Britain' had been the basis of all teaching of Naval History at Dartmouth. A small, pert, sprightly and energetic man, he enlivened and elaborated the whole subject with his extraordinary ability in keeping the class fully absorbed. He would end his lecture one day by breaking off abruptly in mid-sentence and the next week, next period, marching briskly into the classroom, adjusting his pince-nez at his lectern, he would carry on by completing the sentence exactly where he had left off before. He was confident his audience required no amplifying explanation. His teaching went far beyond a mere catalogue of naval battles; strategy, tactics, weapons, evolving designs of ships, command and communications, none were neglected; an essential supplement to the scant treatment otherwise accorded to the Principles of War.

The Captain of the college, Captain A.T.B. Curteis, an austere man with little sense of humour, or sympathy for high spirited youth, alarmingly announced one day that all sub-lieutenants were to parade before him in their newly acquired frock coats. In some trepidation we assembled, and to our relief it transpired that he was greatly dissatisfied with the 'fit' of these, as churned out by Messrs. Gieves, who held a virtual monopoly. Each individual was closely inspected and my frock coat was condemned outright as thoroughly ill fitting around the shoulders. I was not alone (Messrs. Gieves must have suffered grievously from loss of custom) in transferring my alleigance to rival naval tailors, Moseley and Pounsford of Portsmouth. The frock coat they then made lasted me my remaining thirty-five years in the Navy, being converted on my promotion to Captain when frock coats were no longer an item of uniform, into the regulation tail-coat for evening wear, a little tight round the chest, but otherwise still a perfect fit. After my marriage in 1946 I gained another bonus from 'M & P', albeit an expensive one: they proved most excellent ladies' tailors!

The bright lights of the West End of London were a natural attraction, as bees to nectar we craved the social life that went with them. But it was not that easily attainable, leave was restricted and 'late passes' strictly rationed, and with the main gates locked the obvious consequence was a test of initiative in scaling the railings surrounding the college and nefariously gaining entry to King William block wherein lay our cabins. Transport presented few problems; nearly every sub-lieutenant possessed his first car, inevitably second hand, for some, a terrible clapped out old banger which would never have passed the modern M.O.T., for others, the better class of sports car of the day. The Old Kent Road was an easy drive, by midnight traffic was virtually non-existent; the worst hazard an uncontrollable skid on wet and greasy tramlines. One of my more alarming experiences was ending up on the pavement between lamp-post and solid stone building, facing the wrong way and with a burst tyre.

The other occupants of the college, the R.N. Staff Course and those aspiring to higher qualifications in their professional specialisations (known as 'Dagger' courses), made no impact on, and had no contact with the sub-lieutenants. If there was a co-existent Senior Officers War Course, we were oblivious to it, and no doubt vice versa.

The Royal Military Academy, Woolwich, provided sparring partners for rugger and other forms of sport and it also opened the doors of its Riding School to those of us who wished to improve our ability on horseback. I had not ridden since Shetland pony days in early childhood and readily seized the opportunity; the instructors were fierce, the very opposite of the sleepy, docile mounts we had to goad into action, but great were the benefits of the weekly basic lessons.

Preparation for the inevitable exams which concluded the two terms was interrupted for me by a week in the Royal Naval Hospital, Chatham. An abscess in my left inner ear required an operation, painful, but I was in safe hands, the Surgeon Lieutenant Commander made a good job of it and I was soon fully recovered. Our paths were to cross in later years, again to my benefit.

The exams over, our General education now considered complete, it was time to turn to more professional matters. Satisfied with a second class pass, I was glad to move on in April to Portsmouth for the next round of Sub-Lieutenants' courses in the Gunnery, Torpedo, Navigation and Signals Schools, the then Shore Establishments *Excellent, Vernon, Dryad* and *Mercury.*

The summer (1934) slipped past quickly at HMS *Excellent* on Whale Island, man-made from a sandbank in Portsmouth Harbour, complete with its private zoo but not yet modern sanitation; earth closets instead of W.C.s. As befitting the Navy's premier Gunnery School, whose Gods were precise drill and impeccable attention to detail, irreverently termed 'gas and gaiters', the days were fully occupied with practice and theory. As well as many hours on the parade ground, there was gun drill for every calibre of gun from the mighty and thunderous fifteen inch down to the simple three pounder, the standard saluting gun carried in every ship above destroyer. The classroom provided the background theory for the control of all these varied weapons. Inattention or crass mistakes, by class or individual, received the invariable reaction of having to 'double round the island'. It was a mile or more, at more than a gentle trot, with strategically placed Gunners' Mates ensuring there was no slackening of pace. For the more heinous offences full equipment and rifles were an added burden. How we sweated that summer! Physical punishment it may have been, but infinitely preferable to the alternative of stoppage of leave.

It was time to take a decision about my future, for within six months these specialist courses would finish, some new appointment could be expected and it was appropriate to inform Their Lordships of any preference. I had long made up my mind that at all costs I would try in future to avoid battleships in particular, or any other large ships with a gun room. But putting my name forward to specialize in Gunnery, Torpedo, Navigation, Anti-Submarines or Signals, would be no guarantee of achieving this, likewise leaving it to chance and remaining a 'salt horse' (non specialist). The field was narrowed to either Fleet Air Arm or Submarines. My initial inclination was to the former, flying had always fascinated me, as it still does. But various personal reasons persuaded me not to pursue this, the alternative was to volunteer for service in Submarines. I had little knowledge of them, but the attractions of possible early command, of an independent way of life, and influenced by what I had seen of submarine officers during my previous three years at sea, all combined to sway me in this particular direction. Above all, it should ensure the immediate avoidance of 'big ship' life.

Accordingly, I tried my luck by putting in a formal application to the Captain of Whale Island, knowing full well that in the eyes of the Gunnery world submarines were beyond redemption. Little encouragement was shown but I progressed to a medical examination to prove fitness for service in submarines, without which my application could not be forwarded to Their Lordships.

I failed this first hurdle. My left ear was found suspect, from the operation undergone a few months previously in RNH Chatham, the Surgeon Commander (PMO) of *Excellent* declared me 'medically unfit' and so my application got no further. Whale Island may have been happy, but I wasn't. I bided my time until later in the year when I re-applied during the Torpedo course in *Vernon*, knowing *Vernon* had no PMO and my 'medical' would be carried out in *Dolphin*, the submarine base across the harbour, where I hoped for a more favourable answer. In the event all went well and a cursory examination of my ear revealed nothing untoward. My application to join submarines was duly forwarded.

We had an hilarious farewell to Whale Island, the tensions of the last few days of oral and written examinations were released at a final joyful guest night dinner in the Ward-room, where staff and students alike let their hair down. Appetites for fun and games were not satisfied when the bar closed at its normal time of 11 pm. A group, keen for further adventure, decided our target should be the large red statue of a lion, surmounting the entrance to the building known as West Battery, and that it be removed to the middle of the wide lawn in the centre of the establishment, for all to see come daylight.

It was a mammoth task. The beast weighed about a ton, we thought, and once freed from its mounting could only be lowered to the ground by the use of heavy blocks and tackles rigged over the roof of West Battery and anchored to the ground behind. A temporary halt was called to evade discovery by the Duty Officer, accompanied by a Petty Officer carrying the regulation oil lantern, passing on his routine middle watch rounds. They noticed nothing. At last all was accomplished, in the darkness of the night, and the lion awaited dawn in its new position, in the centre of the lawn.

As the light grew it was observed by a sentry, who promptly gave the alarm, arousing the Commander and reporting that 'the bear had escaped from the zoo and was loose on the lawn.' This was enough to excite the whole establishment, for the zoo and its inhabitants were a very treasured and closely guarded possession, the bear the most highly valued of all.

A price, of course, had to be paid for this prank. At the morning parade, the final before the establishment closed down for its summer leave period, it was announced that all sub-lieutenants' leave was stopped until the culprits owned up; they promptly did so. The penalty enacted was not severe, our leave was stopped until the lion was properly back in its rightful place on West Battery. It was a harder and heavier task than getting it down, but by tea-time the job was done. A very tired, exhausted and dirty group of sub-lieutenants were only too glad to get cleaned up and away on leave by evening, thankful indeed that Whale Island had treated the matter so lightly. Confidence was restored in the Gunnery World's sense of humour and willingness to accept so readily on this occasion, the ridiculous.

The remaining courses, Torpedo, Navigation and Signals, were largely uneventful, more relaxed, maybe, than Whale Island; and a personal boost to morale as I obtained first class passes at VERNON and DRYAD, strangely there was no qualifying examination for Signals. With second class passes already obtained for Seamanship, Greenwich and Gunnery, my 'full house' of two's and one's seemed about par. The only discordant note, in the last few weeks of 1934, was a summons by the Commander-in-Chief, Portsmouth, the redoubtable Admiral Sir 'Joe' Kelly, for our group to appear before him in person. In a few terse words he informed each sub-lieutenant he was either 'lazy' or 'rorty', quite what the latter meant no one was entirely sure, but the general tone was clear, we were a lousy lot! The end of term was near and not too much attention was paid to this castigation from on high so we went our ways unperturbed.

I was appointed to *Dolphin* in January 1935, 'for submarine training'. It was a much smaller establishment than it is now, concentrated mainly within the walls of the old, original Fort Blockhouse. Wooden huts, dating from the Great War, comprised the instructional area, the only buildings outside the ancient Fort whilst the adjacent 'Petrol Pier' was a reminder that the earliest submarines were powered by petrol engines, not diesels. Junior officers under instruction were accommodated in the ex-depot ship *Dolphin*, tied up inside the main jetty, no longer seaworthy and totally immobile, she was barely habitable; her decks leaked, and an oilskin over one's bunk was essential in wet weather. But we did not expect luxurious living conditions, the 'H' and 'L.50' class submarines forming the attached Fifth Flotilla provided practical experience.

The Officers Training Class (OTC) numbered eleven, two Lieutenants (E), one Warrant Engineer with previous service in submarines as an Engine Room Aritificer (ERA), and eight executive officers, six being term-mates (Ansons) straight from sub-lieutenants courses. Throughout the three month course, and in the final examinations, the Engineers were streets ahead of the others, reflecting the technical weight of the syllabus. At the end, our knowledge of submarines, their design, hulls, armament, propulsion and all their systems and equipment, were fully tested in written and oral examinations, the latter carried out in a blacked-out compartment of an L.50 class submarine. In total darkness one had to put one's hand on whatever valve, electrical switch or pipe, the examining officer decreed. It was a supreme test of one's knowledge of a submarine's internals.

A Guest Night in the Wardroom of *Dolphin*, with its usual accompaniment of string band in the gallery, five course meal with wines to match, provided a splendid opportunity to celebrate this major milestone, successfully passed by all but one of us. The night ended on a different note, the 'de-bagging' of the Instructional Staff First Lieutenant, an unpopular figure from his hard driving of his pupils of the OTC. He took it in good part. I was not to meet him again until many years later when I found myself his Chief of Staff when he was appointed Flag Officer Submarines. To ensure no lurking scars remained and that nothing was hidden between us, I quickly reminded him of this distant but crude episode. There was no problem, we got on well and my increasing admiration for him as FOSM (the late Rear Admiral B.W. Taylor, CB, DSC) banished all earlier perceptions.

Now qualified in submarines, with the magic letter (S) after my name in the Navy List, my pay increased by nearly 50 per cent, but for me, like most of my companions, this was not the real bonus. It was the prospect ahead, leading to the possibility (probability, if one kept one's nose clean) of early command while still a lieutenant. For those who married young a lieutenant's extra six shillings a day submarine pay (30p in modern coinage, and a mere pittance today) was a very real benefit, which was reflected then in the higher proportion of married junior officers serving in submarines than in General Service.

I had done well in the qualifying tests, written and practical, the last formal exams I ever had to sit, so had first choice of my next appointment. I now found another bonus of service in submarines, officers' appointments were controlled from Blockhouse, by a 'passed over' Lieutenant Commander (ex-submarine CO) on Rear Admiral Submarines' (RAS) staff, instead of by a remote and inevitably impersonal appointing authority within the Second Sea Lord's domain in the Admiralty. I had no hesitation in deciding where I wanted to go, the Fourth Submarine Flotilla on the China Station was the dream of every young officer: 'old China hands' never ceased to sing the praises of the Far East. Very promptly I received an appointment to HMS *Rainbow*, to join her at Hong Kong in May.

Chapter Six

The China Station, 1935–37

With three others of my training class (still all Ansons together) I embarked in the S.S. . . . , coal-fired and the most ancient of the P&O fleet. There were not many passengers on board as it was the beginning of the 'hot season' and few people were travelling out East. With some young cavalry subalterns rejoining their regiments in India, we virtually had the run of the ship to ourselves, too much, on occasion, to the liking of the ship's captain, saddled with the problem of keeping our high spirits under control; but he was no despot, and our few weeks on board were blissful.

The Mediterranean, with calls at Marseilles and Malta, was nothing new to me; but Port Said, Aden, Bombay, Colombo, Penang, Singapore, beckoned ahead, conjuring up the magic mystery of the East. A 'run ashore' at each was irresistible. Fortunately, stops were always for more than a few hours, the ship had to coal, a filthy operation, with everything smothered in coal dust, and so there was no inclination to stay on board. The teeming crowds thronging the quays and streets, the bazaars with their astounding variety of wares and merchandise, but also, in contrast, the poverty, the beggars, the cripples with their never ending cries for 'baksheesh' (money), my eyes were opened to a world not hitherto experienced. Only Alexandria in my Mediterranean years had given an inkling of what lay beyond.

Excursions ashore always ended in the most favoured 'watering hole' at whatever port the ship stopped, the Taj Mahal at Bombay, the Galle Face at Colombo, the Eastern and Oriental at Penang, Raffles at Singapore. The barren rocks of Aden were an exception and barren indeed.

We steamed steadily on into the Tropics; their cloying moist heat, the sudden change from day to brilliant, starlit night, and at ports of call the scenes ashore, the lives and ways of planters and other Europeans in contrast to the native population, the scents and smells, the lush green vegetation, all brought Somerset Maugham books vividly to life.

And so to arrive at Hong Kong in the early light of a fine May morning; what a harbour! The beauty of its surroundings, with the background of the Peak and the hills of the mainland, its vibrant, pulsing activity, it took one's breath away. Great passenger liners, ocean-going cargo ships of every nationality, smaller coastal steam-ships, heavily guarded against piracy, bustling ferries, hundreds if not thousands of junks and sampans, under oar or sail, many the only home for whole families; there scarcely seemed room for all on the calm surface of the water.

Lying quietly at her buoy off the Naval Dockyard was HMS *Medway*, depot ship of the 4th Submarine Flotilla, only a few years old, the first of a new breed of submarine depot ships specifically designed for the task. Hitherto all had been conversions from merchant ships of one sort or another, and thus, inherently, unlikely to be all that was needed. *Medway* was large and capacious, and provided unheard of comfort for the crews, officers and ratings, of attached submarines whilst every requirement for stores and provisions, armaments, repairs and maintenance, was lavishly met. She was indeed a 'mother ship' beyond compare, I do not believe her like afloat has been repeated in the Royal Navy.

Once on board *Medway* and back in uniform after the care-free weeks gratis P&O, I was directed to *Rainbow*, one of the four submarines lying in the 'trot' on *Medway's* starboard side. Nervously I crossed the planks between submarines and boarded her, it was 11 am, monthly pay day, time for 'up spirits', but also time for *Rainbow* to shift berth, in other words do what was called a 'trot fob'. The First Lieutenant, Lieutenant A.C.C. Miers (later Rear Admiral Sir Anthony Miers, VC, KBE, CB, DSO+) already well known throughout the submarine service as a very redoubtable, fierce and dynamic character, set me down in the wardroom with orders to guard the ship's company pay and prepare it for issue; meanwhile, he disappeared on to the bridge to carry out the 'trot fob'. I was left alone to wrestle with a vast quantity of strange Hong Kong dollars and sort them out into the right amounts for each man. 'Trot fob' completed, Tony Miers reappeared, I was then subjected to a rigorous interrogation of my antecedents. It became apparent that I was acceptable, largely, I think, because we both had connections with Inverness and its regiment, the Queen's Own Cameron Highlanders. Thus began my initiation into submarines, a period I have invariably referred to as, 'the best two years of my life,' a definition readily accepted some ten years later by my wife, and which I have maintained without detriment to our subsequent continuing years together.

Rainbow was a happy ship, reflecting the spirit that ran through the whole flotilla, they were cheerful, sparkling times, and life was gay (in the old meaning of the word. I abhor the way this small yet so expressive word has been usurped and utterly abused in modern language). Our captain, Lieutenant Commander J.E. Broome, had been in command for just over a month, artistic, a brilliant cartoonist (his drawings appeared regularly in the weekly glossy magazine 'The Sketch'), talented games player of the same calibre as his first lieutenant, it was inevitable that there was a clash of personalities between the two; they seldom saw eye to eye and at times were at daggers drawn. Despite this they were united in their efforts to make *Rainbow* the most efficient and smartest submarine in the flotilla; some task, with ten other lieutenant commanders in command, all vying for promotion and their 'brass hats', competition was severe.

Medway then supported twelve submarines, six 'O' class, five 'P' class

HMS *Rainbow.*

(*Poseidon* having been lost in 1931) and one 'R' class, *Rainbow*. The flotilla was strengthened two months later by the arrival from the Mediterranean of the three other existing 'R' class. All were large and somewhat unhandy, designed for ocean patrol work as a counter to Japan's growing naval might; living conditions on board were comparatively comfortable, there was even a small bathroom, complete with minute bath about four feet long, for the officers. I never heard of the latter being used for its rightful purpose, it consumed too much precious fresh water, and was of far greater value for stowage of other gear.

They were well armed submarines, with six bow torpedo tubes and two stern tubes; with re-loads for every tube, they carried a total of sixteen 21" torpedos. Some had an outfit of the newly introduced Mark VIII, others the older Mark IV, the former could be fired either 'straight' or '90° angled' to left or right. Power loading was provided for the six forward tubes, in use it turned the fore-ends into a nightmare of strumming wires and whizzing torpedoes, the average time to re-load a full salvo of six was seventeen and a half minutes, the best time ever achieved twelve minutes. It was a horribly noisy and extremely hazardous system, thankfully not repeated in immediately later designs. Being the balmy days of peace none of the torpedoes were fitted with warheads, but six of these latter were carried on board in a specially equipped magazine; moving them from there to the torpedoes was a slow and laborious evolution, which was, however, practised once a year when submarines carried out the drill of 'storing for war'. A four-inch gun, mounted well above the casing and manned through a separate gun-tower, completed the main armament. All submarines were well practised in use of this gun, from periscope depth to opening fire on the surface a good time was twenty to twenty-five seconds, rate of fire was of the order of seventeen rounds per minute, from which ten hits should be achieved on a target measuring twenty feet by ten feet at a range of one thousand yards.

HMS *Bruce*, ex-destroyer flotilla leader from World War I, formed part of this flotilla. She was specially converted for the recovery and carrying of large numbers of torpedos and was heavily in demand, acting as target ship for submarine attacks and picking up torpedoes fired in practice; as a measure of this the flotilla fired 459 torpedoes in 1935.

I became *Rainbow*'s '4th hand', with the duties of Navigator and Correspondence Officer. Fortunately navigation had always been one of my pet subjects, so I hoped it would present no major problems; the worst was finding time to keep up with the flow of weekly Notices to Mariners. Their contents had to be scanned for relevant corrections to the vast number of charts carried on board, in folios covering the western Pacific, from the Bering Straits in the north to Australia in the south, with much of the Indian Ocean as well so keeping them corrected was a tedious, painstaking task occupying many hours, which interfered badly with more pleasant pursuits unless accomplished during the night hours of one's turn, every third day, as Duty Officer on board.

Being Correspondence Officer was something totally new to me, Jackie Broome was as meticulous over the handling of official letters as he was on other matters when on the bridge or in the control room at sea. He insisted that, down to the last detail, everything must be exactly right. The Admiralty pattern typewriter was not conducive to this, an unreliable, unwieldy contraption if ever there was one. I quickly put *Rainbow*'s standard issue to one side and bought a second-hand 'Corona' portable, a delightful little machine, on which I soon became expert, albeit two fingers only. It served me for many years.

Soon after joining *Rainbow* the flotilla sailed for Wei-hai-wei, the normal base of the China Fleet for the summer months of May to September, thus escaping the heat and humidity of Hong Kong. It was a thrill to have responsibility for the safe navigation of the ship, and though still without a Watch-keeping Certificate I was soon allowed to keep watch on my own. Navigation was straightforward; none the less, there were hair-raising moments. Our route north, between China and Formosa, led through favoured fishing grounds off the east coast of the former; on these were many large junks, moving slowly and erratically under sail, whether fishing or not. They recognized no rules of navigation and on sighting a passing foreign vessel their one endeavour was to cut across its bows at as close a distance as possible, so that the horde of devils which they, traditionally, believed was always in close pursuit of their own craft would be cut off by, and transferred to, the other ship, whose bows they had so narrowly scraped across. In daylight it was not difficult to take appropriate action to avoid hitting them but by night they were an absolute menace, showing no lights, the first inkling would be a large sail looming out of the dark which made for some heart-stopping moments. We certainly learnt to keep a good look-out!

In fair weather the flotilla wended its way north, the submarines continuously 'leap-frogging' ahead of *Medway* to carry out day-time torpedo attacks on her. Most of these were dummy attacks, i.e. no torpedoes were actually fired which was useful practice, but providing no concrete proof that the attack would have been successful. Only the actual firing of a torpedo could give this but because torpedoes were expensive, and their loss unacceptable, occasions for firing them were restricted to areas and conditions when their recovery would be easy.

Rainbow dived routinely one morning to carry out an attack in this series but for some unknown reason a satisfactory 'trim' could not be obtained. As *Medway* approached and the attack progressed, *Rainbow* continued to flounder about with conning tower awash, half way between the desired periscope depth and the surface. Fury enveloped the control room, the class-room in *Dolphin* had not prepared me for anything like this. I stood transfixed, as inconspicuous as possible, beside the ISWAS, that antediluvian torpedo fire control instrument, trying to keep out of the line of fire as battle raged between captain and first lieutenant. This lamentable display of how things should NOT be done ended with some acid signals from Captain (S) in *Medway*, but no doubt, thus to be able to see a submarine throughout its attack, it was great entertainment to the flotilla wives, and others from the fleet, embarked in the depot ship for passage to Wei-hai-wei. Regardless of King's Regulations and Admiralty Instructions, and occasioned by there being no regular civilian form of transport to such a remote spot, this practice of *Medway* turning herself twice a year temporarily into a passenger liner was well established. What better use for a whole lot of empty submarine officers' cabins? But I doubt if it ever had Their Lordships' formal approval. There were many blessings for being at such a distance from London, with communications and the media not yet developed to their present state.

That first summer in Wei-hai-wei passed all too quickly, plenty of work, and when time permitted plenty of outdoor recreation. It was an ideal base for an extended period of intensive weapon training for the China fleet. On the doorstep of the Yellow Sea, with its kindly climate, there were limitless practice areas for surface ships and submarines, with virtually no interference from passing shipping, of any sort. The only drawback was the atrocious 'Asdic (sonar) conditions' which persisted throughout this summer; these put a blanket stop on any anti-submarine training by destroyers and sloops. The submarines benefitted; instead of hour after hour submerged, acting as the proverbial 'clockwork mouse' (target for Asdic training of surface ships), all time was spent improving their own skill with torpedo and gun. It was all day-time work, to sea at six am on four or five days a week, back alongside *Medway* twelve or so hours later. No training was carried out at night as submarines were forbidden to dive between sunset and sunrise. It was a serious flaw in their operational training, as later years were fatally to prove.

I revelled in those weeks which provided immense opportunities for the aspiring young submariner to learn his job, and I found the work thoroughly satisfying; the hours at sea were long, and work did not end on return to harbour, routine chores had to be caught up with and preparations completed for the next day's exercises, batteries charged, torpedoes re-embarked. Fortunately there were few social distractions nor disturbed nights, unless one happened to be Duty Officer sleeping on board one's submarine when wind and sea got up, causing the 'trot' of submarines to start moving, uneasily at first, then fiercely bumping against each other. Their design made them highly vulnerable to such buffeting, oil fuel was carried in their rivetted external ballast tanks, and unacceptable leaks developed if bumping became severe. The immediate remedy, the submarines cast off from *Medway* and, under the care of Duty Watch and Officer, crept away to previously allocated positions around her, where they anchored, and remained until the weather improved. On a dark night, probably raining, and with few navigational aids, it was no simple task to anchor accurately in one's ordered billet. If not satisfactorily done a curt signal from 'mother' soon told one to move to the correct spot. Such occasions placed much responsibility on junior officers, to an extent unusual in the Navy as a whole.

The week-ends gave complete relaxation: 'Black Friday' started the ball rolling, a weekly dance at the Wei-hai-wei Club so called because 'black ties' and long evening dresses were 'de rigueur'. But it only affected the few, those whose wives had managed to get to Wei-hai-wei, plus a few, a very few, girl friends who, closely chaperoned, had wangled their way to this remote island. For the rest, we were content with a wide range of recreational activities; hockey, football, tennis, and, from mid August onwards, some of the best snipe and duck shooting obtainable anywhere in the world.

The duck were to be found in a chain of lagoons along the coast of mainland China, some ten to fifteen miles to the east; a perilous journey, over primitive roads in a hired car of ancient vintage, was all part of the day's adventure. 'Pidgin' English sufficed for all communication and over the years the local population had got used to and accepted the strange ways of the 'foreign devils' carrying 12-bore guns, and, for a few dollars (the Chinese dollar then worth anything between one and two shillings, five and ten pence today), would take on any task; gun-bearer, beater, general factotum. They were delightful people, humorous, helpful, willing, adding greatly to the day's enjoyment.

The snipe, like the duck, were migrating from their breeding grounds in the far north to warmer climes for the winter, they broke their journey in the province of Shantung after crossing the Yellow Sea and for a few short weeks were widespread wherever the ground was cultivated; fields of soya beans alternating with strips of maize were especially favoured. Local knowledge was essential to a successful day's shooting, the Chinese peasants, cultivating the fields for some distant landlord or warlord, were only too willing to co-operate, and gladly accompanied one all day for a few dollars payment. It was exciting shooting, the snipe, as always, were difficult targets as they zig-zagged away; but great care was required. There were hidden hazards, always the possible Chinaman, with his horse, mule or donkey, working out of sight behind a line of maize. Numerically the day's bag was never astronomical, perhaps twenty to thirty snipe for two guns; a welcome addition to the breakfast menu in the ward-room mess next day. In complete contrast to the daily round at sea throughout the preceding week, they were days of absolute freedom, only occasionally marred by mishap or accident. One such incident involved an American officer, from the U.S. Navy's summer base at Chingwangtao, some forty miles along the coast to the west who had joined us for the day. He was not particularly careful, with one shot he bagged a Chinese peasant, a donkey, and the snipe at which he had fired. Fortunately the two former at long range, so they were not seriously hurt and the usual fee of a dollar for every pellet closed the incident, but we did not invite him to come shooting again.

At the end of August *Rainbow* departed for Hong Kong, to spend the next three months in dry-dock. It was her turn, in common with the rest of the flotilla, to undergo work on her main ballast tanks; the rivets to be replaced by welding, and other alterations made, to reduce the likelihood of leaking oil fuel. I stayed behind in Wei-hai-wei, joining the Spare Crew in *Medway*, with few duties other than augmenting the routine watch-keeping roster; a tedious and unexciting time, with appearances on the depot ship's quarterdeck as Officer of the Watch few and far between. Fortunately it did not last long, the Third and Fourth Hands of the Flotilla were a lively lot, given expression at that time by a craze for practical jokes. Thereby, the Fourth Hand of *Orpheus* and I incurred a degree of displeasure by our making the Commander of the depot ship, an earnest, staid Gunnery Officer, an 'apple-pie' bed; a very successful one, too, but unfortunately we were betrayed by the Wardroom Chief Steward, who had spotted us sneaking out of the Commander's cabin. I was promptly sent packing back to *Rainbow* in Hong Kong: no punishment in reality, apart from missing a few days' shooting. I took passage in another 'R' class submarine, *Regent* bound there for routine maintenance and docking. She, also, was a very happy ship and it was a joy to be at sea again in a submarine, if only for the five day passage to Hong Kong.

Rainbow, stripped to her bare bones, lay in the bottom of a dry-dock in Kowloon, across the harbour from Hong Kong and its Naval Dockyard. She was in the hands of contractors, whose Chinese workmen swarmed all over her, the re-building of her Main Ballast tanks proceeding apace; an experienced team of Admiralty overseers supervised the work, but ultimate responsibility for the final answer of a clean and properly working submarine remained with her crew. There was plenty to occupy them fruitfully and Tony Miers saw to it they were never idle, but with 'Make and Mends' more often the rule than the exception, football, hockey, water polo – in fact any sport – became as important to us as the refitting work and routine maintenance. As the chaos on board gradually evaporated, the painting out of internal compartments became top priority. It was astounding how quickly normality returned once the major jobs were finished, the Chinese workmen wasted no time and their zeal was impressive. An eight hour shift was eight hours working, and no tea breaks. Re-embarking the main battery was completed in under two days, five to six days was the norm in an English yard.

When *Medway* with her 'chickens' and all the wives returned from the north the pace of social life exploded. There began an unending round of cocktail parties, dinners and dancing as there were many attractive girls in the Colony and young bachelor officers were welcome. If one's nose was clean, and cards were correctly played, attendance at three different cocktail parties an evening was not exceptional, with, if still sober, dinner and dancing to follow at 'The Grips', the Hong Kong Hotel. It was the age of genuine cocktails – Manhattens, Martinis, Sidecars, White Ladies – and hostesses vied with each other in producing the most exotic. Straight drinks; whisky, gin, brandy, were reserved for the realm of the male establishment, the clubs and officers' messes. Most things were paid for by 'chit', so ready cash was no problem, the day of reckoning arrived at the end of each month. It was a hectic life and temptingly easy to 'burn the candle at both ends', leading to dire physical and financial consequences; but for the majority of junior officers their captains and first lieutenants kept a sufficiently restraining eye on their behaviour for such things to get out of hand.

Christmas Day 1935 was celebrated in the normal naval way of those times. *Rainbow* still lay at the bottom of Cosmopolitan Dock in Kowloon, so we had our own celebrations totally apart from the rest of the flotilla, a short church service on the dockside, followed by rounds of the crew's quarters, and then a mammoth lunch, with guests, in the palatial colonial style house accommodating the officers. The festivities were too much for me. I had not yet learnt discretion and the ability to say 'No' to the overwhelming generosity of the ship's company, so the innumerable tots of rum offered to the youngest and most junior of the officers brought disaster. Lunch had barely ended before I was 'out' for the next eighteen hours, with a ghastly hangover to follow. I have never liked rum since. 'Splice the Main Brace', that excuse on special occasions to double the daily tot of rum to the lower deck, and the only opportunity for officers to partake, meant nothing to me in future.

Thankfully, early in the New Year *Rainbow* was afloat again, and soon once more at sea with new Main Ballast tanks and, for the starboard engine, a replacement Vulcan clutch; the latter a troublesome peculiarity of her

'O' 'P' and 'R' class submarines alongside HMS *Medway*, Depot Ship, Hong Kong 1936.

class, but essential if ever the diesel engines were to be used for going astern. Few C.O.s had much faith in this use when manoeuvring or berthing, reaction time compared to using the electrical main motors to go astern was slow and the engines could never be guaranteed to start first time. But if all worked well the diesels produced tremendous astern power.

Conditions at sea were totally different from the balmy summer days at Wei-hai-wei. The North East Monsoon was blowing strongly, the seas were rough, but Asdic (sonar) conditions were good, so all effort was concentrated on A/S (anti-submarine) training for the destroyers and sloops of the fleet. *Bruce* had a well-deserved rest from recovering practice torpedoes – the seas were too big anyway for the latter to be picked up – and submarines reverted to the boring role of 'clockwork mouse'; a target for the surface ships' Asdics.

Respite from this daily grind, early to sea and late back to harbour, soon came. The flotilla left Hong Kong for the regular cruise to the southern parts of the China station, to Malaya, Borneo, Singapore and, less frequently, to the Dutch East Indies and the Philippines. The flotilla was not always all together, submarines were dispersed to show the White Ensign in harbours and anchorages inaccessible to *Medway*.

The Rajang River in Borneo was *Rainbow's* first port of call. In company with HMS *Decoy* of the Eighth Destroyer Flotilla we gingerly felt our way up river through mile after mile of mangrove swamps, eventually, when the

HMS *Rainbow* alongside HMS *Decoy*, Rajang River, North Borneo.

muddy waters became too shallow for further safe navigation, *Decoy* dropped anchor and *Rainbow* berthed alongside. There was nothing to be seen but the mangrove swamps and the backdrop of rain forest stretching into the far distance, with faintly visible away to the north Mt. Kinabulu, the highest mountain in North Borneo. There was no noticeable habitation, the occasional crocodile or fish-eagle the only signs of life. It seemed a strange and remote place to be visited by two of HM ships, the ulterior motive, it was believed, was to assess the worth of the Rajang River as a potential naval base in the event of war with Japan. Though this did not weigh heavily, everyone in the fleet was very conscious of Japanese aspirations for expansion.

A smart, white launch bearing the District Commissioner appeared from up-river, and a happy liaison was immediately established with this representative of the distant Government. He gave us freedom to roam ashore where we liked throughout our four day stay, and also bore an invitation for a limited number of officers to attend a ceremonial 'curry tiffin' in a Dyak 'long house' some miles further upstream. The Dyaks were the native population, living in scattered settlements, each centred on a 'long house' which accommodated all the families making up the particular clan or tribe. Though not long cured of their head-hunting habits, we were assured they were friendly people, and so it proved to be.

I was fortunate to be amongst the lunch-party, which was a memorable occasion and not only for the meal itself. This was a gargantuan curry based on chicken and fish, rice cooked to perfection, all augmented by a variety and choice of sauces, chutneys, spices, fruits and nuts, the like of which I have never since experienced. But it was not only the munificence of the banquet that claimed attention, the setting and surroundings were rivetting. A wide and gently sloping ladder had led us to the living quarters in the long-house, all on the raised or upper floor whilst on the ground below roamed dogs, pigs, hens, ducks, all the livestock, supplemented by a few tame monkeys. We sat on rough, wooden benches, set beside tables running down the centre of the long-house, itself more than the length of a cricket pitch, behind, on each side were the separate cubicles for each individual family making up the tribe. The elders, male and female, seated amongst us, acted as our hosts, fluent English was non-existent, but most had a few words and it was remarkable how sign language sufficed to keep everyone happily engaged in makeshift conversation. We were waited on by young girls of stunning beauty, topless and clad only in colourful sarongs fastened about their waists. We were fascinated but swiftly brought back to earth, if and when our eyes could be persuaded to look elsewhere to examine the interior decorations, or, when leaning back, one's head made physical contact with the latter. The rows of mast-like wooden pillars supporting the roof ran close behind our backs, each and every one was decorated with a string of human heads, dried and shrunk to the size of a monkey's; trophies no doubt from past affrays with rival tribes – *long* past we hoped – but weird and ghoulish in the extreme. Head-hunters they indeed had been, and they were proud to show us the results, but how the human skull, with all external features intact, had been shrunk to such a diminutive size, remained a secret. Alcohol played no part in the proceedings, but completely satiated by all we had seen and consumed, not even the crocodiles on our return trip down river could raise a spark of interest.

Rainbow rejoined the flotilla at Singapore but her stay there was overshadowed by the suicide of her Engineer Officer, a young and promising Lieutenant (E) who had earned the liking and respect of all in his few months on board. His death seemed utterly pointless, but life had to go on. *Rainbow* was suddenly ordered to 'Prepare for War' and be ready to sail within forty-eight hours for a 'make-believe' war patrol.

Embarking torpedoes, fuel, water, stores, provisions were in themselves routine drills which presented few difficulties, other than finding room on board for the vast quantity of the last two (an insoluble, continuing problem as later years were to prove). A major bottleneck had first to be overcome. Moving the six warheads from their magazine half-way between fore-ends and control room and fitting them to the torpedoes already on board, in the torpedo stowage compartment, was itself a mammoth task which held up all movement in the front half of the submarine and until completed, little else could be done. It was the smaller details which then took the most time and care, arming warheads with pistols, having primed the latter with detonators, learning, checking and counter-checking recognition signals. No one had previous first hand experience of such matters, and the

Chinese junk crossing bow to cut off pursuing devils.

instructional manuals were not always all that explicit. We had to fumble our way forward with care, but it was a realistic exercise, extending depot ship and submarine to the full.

The flurry of activity was over within the forty-eight hours and *Rainbow* at once sailed for her Patrol Area in the eastern approaches to Singapore. This was a block of the South China Sea about thirty miles square which had been allocated to us, the only landmark, on its western edge, the Horsburgh Lighthouse sticking out of the ocean like a solitary phallic emblem.

We believed we already had considerable expertise in the use of torpedo or gun when attacking targets from submerged, but such expertise had only been achieved by a degree of artificiality in the practices or exercises involved. Seldom was there the chance to relate prowess in these fields to the wider, less easily defined, problems of how best to conduct an operational patrol under the sort of conditions that might exist in war. What we were now to undertake should give an inkling of these, or so it was hoped.

In the event, the so-called War Patrol lasted only four days, no guidance was given as to how it should be conducted so it was left to common sense, with safety paramount. Daylight hours were to be spent dived, with the opposition represented by the very occasional appearance of an RAF flying boat, or a 'target' ship passing through the area. From sunset each day to sunrise the next, *Rainbow* was to be on the surface with navigation lights switched on, in effect, 'peace' was to reign throughout the hours of darkness. The training value of the four days was thus cut by half, or more, safety regulations stultified any likelihood of achieving worthwhile realism in the simulation of war conditions. Not that anyone then had any clear idea, let alone experience, of what war would be like; and there was no doctrine, nor instructional handbooks, to advise.

Despite these shortcomings there was, in the end, much benefit for all on board. The daylight hours, submerged, gave ample scope for 'Watch Diving', instead of the almost invariable 'Diving Stations', much of the time coping with the difficulties of keeping accurate Periscope Depth in the rough seas prevailing. Officers of the watch experienced the tedium, and eye strain, of protracted vigil on the periscope and everyone suffered the discomforts of long hours submerged in hot tropical waters, without any form of air conditioning or cooling to alleviate the humidity and heat. We were all 'makee-learns' (pidgin English for the unitiated) in such aspects of submarine life, even to those with many years behind them of service in submarines it was a novelty. We in *Rainbow* were fortunate to gain this training, not all the submarines of the Fourth Flotilla were as lucky. I myself, by no means uniquely, never had another chance to absorb these essential lessons before World War II was on us.

There followed an interlude of fun and games at ports up and down the west coast of Malaya, we learnt much of the life of the rubber planters and how it helped the export trade of Scotch whisky! Then *Medway* and her flotilla headed back to Hong Kong. It was a hard flog into the teeth of the N.E. Monsoon, blowing at its strongest and rough seas quickly dispelled the enervating effects of leisurely and balmy tropical days and nights. The submarines themselves did not escape a severe battering, minor damage to casings (the light deck plating), particularly abaft the conning tower, where large sections went adrift, gave plenty of repair work to depot ship and dockyard on arrival at Hong Kong.

Before leaving for the usual summer training period at Wei-hai-wei, *Rainbow* took part in a combined operation with troops from the Army garrison in Hong Kong. With *Bruce* the aim was to land parties of soldiers at night in a remote area of the New Territories, *Rainbow's* participation being mainly to act as a navigational aid and guide to the raiding force. On a very dark night we led *Bruce* through a long, narrow, tortuous channel, with no buoys or lights to assist navigation. The land on either side was barely visible and, years before the advent of RADAR, the only aid to safe passage was our 10 kc/s ASDIC set, so transmitting continuously on this, we slowly felt our way past numerous rocks and hazards, with *Bruce* following closely astern. It was a novelty fixing our position by ranges and bearings obtained by Asdic. The operation ended successfully, with both ships landing their parties as planned, *Rainbow's* using her collapsible ten-foot canvas BERTHON boat, normally carried in the after casing. The soldiers suffered the discomforts of such an uncomfortable and unwieldy form of transport,

HMS *Medway* with her brood, China 1938.

but apart from this the exercise was a good demonstration of how a submarine could navigate safely at night, close in-shore, and land a raiding party, using Asdics if need be.

The summer of 1936 was much as the previous year. Four or five days a week at sea, the same constant round of practice attacks on the inimitable *Bruce*, mostly dummy attacks, but firing torpedoes every week, sometimes singly, occasionally in full salvoes, straight or ninety-degree angled, and if not practice torpedo attacks, then gunnery practices. In these particulars we were trained to a very high pitch.

To be in harbour over the week-ends was sacrosanct, all ships were fully occupied with routine maintenance, sport and recreation. Football, hockey, tennis, water polo, swimming, sailing; there was scope for every interest, and everyone was encouraged to participate actively. The island of Wei-hai-wei, on long lease to Britain from China, was blessed with a wealth of playing fields and despite the severe winters of snow and ice, with the sea often completely frozen, the hard, gravel pitches were beautifully maintained, their fast and true surfaces provided a more thrilling and exhilarating game than on grass. I was fortunate to have graduated to *Rainbow's* hockey team, with occasional appearances for the Flotilla. I never ceased to be amazed by visiting Indian Army teams, who always played in bare feet!

Preparation for the Flotilla, Squadron and Fleet pulling regattas filled any spare moments, and for rowing enthusiasts there was the bonus of a genuine 'eight' borrowed by *Medway* for the summer from Hong Kong University. There were problems in handling this delicate craft, particularly in getting it in the water from its safe stowage on *Medway's* boat deck and back again. It was not suited to the rough hurly-burly of depot ship life, being so much more fragile than the loads the cranes and derricks were used to. Once safely launched, and manned, not easily done from a ship's gangway, it was a joy to be experienced, speeding so smoothly across the calm waters of the anchorage. I was lucky to be amongst the chosen few who formed its crew. The style of rowing was so very different from the crudities to which we were accustomed in service boats. I doubt if it served any useful purpose in improving our chances in the forthcoming regattas, but it provided a fascinating thrill and experience, and we were the envy of those sweating their guts out in cutters, whalers, gigs, as they trained for the races ahead. Sadly, it was a 'one off' experiment. The difficulties of handling the 'eight' on board *Medway* were too great, and it did not feature again in the four remaining summers that Wei-hai-wei remained available for the China Fleet's training and recreation.

In August the Flotilla visited Chingwangtao, at the western end of the Yellow Sea, for a welcome mid-term break from the intense activities of Wei-hai-wei. I had four of the best days of my two years on the China Station, a visit, in the company of two other Third Hands, to Peking, as it was then called. It was a marvellous insight into the very heart of China, the Forbidden City and the Temple of Heaven exemplifying past glories. In complete contrast were the dirty and muddy streets of mean one-storey buildings, comprising all the bazaars and shops purveying a most fabulous range of goods concentrated there from all over Asia; silks, furs, jade, silver, china, each had their own street. There were no motor cars and a complete absence of the internal combustion engine, instead thronging masses of people, rickshaws, beasts of burden from camels to donkeys. The scenes, and wealth and variety of merchandise, were almost incredible. There was a different atmosphere to the night life; the bars, restaurants, dance halls, 'honky tonks', which all seemed to remain open all night, were coloured by the presence of innumerable White Russians, sad remnants of the Russian Revolution, eking out a meagre existence selling anything, themselves included.

Back in Chingwangtao, there was scope for entertainment and excitement too. A day's excursion to the Great Wall of China, within easy reach to the north where it ended its twelve hundred miles on the coast, was essential; surely, from its age and sheer length and size, it could well rank as one of the Wonders of the World. Beyond it lay Manchukao, or Manchuria, now in the hands of the Japanese, we were encouraged by our Chinese guide to express our distaste of this from the top of the wall.

Out riding early one morning amongst scattered trees, in beautiful flat open country to the north of the town, my companion and I suddenly heard the crack of rifle shots and of bullets whistling overhead. We were caught in the fierce crossfire between a gang of smugglers and the local police and customs officials. Beating a hasty retreat, it was a salutory reminder that war and peace were never far apart in the China of those days, we were glad to return to the ship unscathed, and were more circumspect as to where we went riding thereafter.

Before returning to Hong Kong at the end of the summer, *Medway* and her flotilla visited three very different ports, their only similarity being that they were all under Japanese control. Port Arthur, in Manchukao, no longer had the importance attached to it in the early years of the century, when it was the main Russian naval base in the Russo-Japanese war. All that now remained were the decaying fortifications and a rather dirty, seedy, run-down commercial port. Kagoshima, in the very south of Japan, was totally different. Japanese officialdom, so evident at Port Arthur, was absent and the people themselves were courteous and friendly, wherever we went we were made welcome. My red hair and very white skin seemed a source of special attraction to the Geisha girls who bathed us in the communal baths. Everything was spotlessly clean, even the brothels so hygienic they might have been part of a hospital. Things were cheap; an invoice, anonymously inserted in the Scrap Book in *Medway*'s Wardroom, attested to this. It read: '2 Girlie – 1 hour – 15 yen' (the yen then being worth about one shilling and sixpence, or seven pence modern currency).

At the third port of call, Keelung in the north of Formosa, Japanese officiousness and red tape reigned supreme. It was not an enjoyable visit. Three sailors from *Medway*, ashore on leave and creating no problem or offence, were severely beaten up and incarcerated by Japanese police and although soon released, the matter became a major diplomatic wrangle between London and Tokyo. 'The Keelung Incident' was not finally settled until Japan formally apologised in April 1937.

The tail-end of a typhoon caught us while on passage from Japan to Formosa, never had I seen such mountainous and confused seas with enormous waves bearing down on *Rainbow* from every direction. Her bridge was like a half-submerged rock for all of twenty-four hours, but she rode out the storm better than many a surface ship. A woodcock sought shelter and safety in a corner of the bridge for two days, then it was gone, no doubt continuing its southerly migration.

The winter of 1936–37 passed quickly, the social life in Hong Kong was even more hectic than twelve months before. I had made more friends, and took more part in all that was open to any active young man, there never seemed to be a moment of spare time. If we were not at sea on training exercises, there were parties ashore galore. We were happy, life was fun, everything was enjoyed to the full. Football, hockey, rugger kept us fit, there was horse-racing, the 'flat' at Happy Valley, where the Chinese betted madly, and steeple-chasing at Fanling in the New Territories, also riding with the Fanling Hunt, a pack of fox hounds which hunted a 'drag' over the countryside around Fanling. There were not many fences to jump, but the terraced fields and unexpected Chinese graves on the hillsides provided plenty of obstacles. A battalion of the Seaforth Highlanders had joined the

Japanese cruiser *Asigara* in Hong Kong 1937. Subsequently sunk by Cdr. Hezlet in submarine *Trenchant* 1945.

garrison in Hong Kong, bringing into my orbit some old family friends from Inverness and the Highlands: under their tutelage I learnt how to drink whisky.

By the end of April 1937, *Medway* and her flock were again northbound, for the summer at Wei-hai-wei. It was the last I was to see of them on the China Station, for *Rainbow* was left behind, refitting in the naval dockyard. Her junior officers, together with those from two other submarines in the yard, lived in a modest house at the very top of The Peak, the highest part of the island, habitat of the wealthiest of the civilian population. It was convenient, being adjacent to the ancient cable car railway station at the top, with its bottom just outside the dockyard, but that was about all that could be said for it. Throughout the summer the house was shrouded in cloud, with humidity and dampness twice what they were at sea level so clothes, shoes, boots grew fungus at an appalling rate. The only relieving feature was 'Prince', a Dalmatian dog on temporary loan. His antics were a constant source of amusement, even his insatiable fondness of port, and a glass carelessly left within reach of his long and curling tongue was emptied in a flash.

In July came the news of my relief's appointment, Lieutenant D.S.R. Martin, and he in person followed early in August. In anticipation of our time on the Station coming to its normal end, another Third Hand and I had earlier put in a formal request to be allowed to find our own way home.

Wei-hai-wei harbour 1936. HMS *Medway* submarine depot ship (right).

The Admiralty had approved, and refunded us the cost of what would have been the normal passage fare by P&O line via Suez. Accordingly, we had booked to travel home eastwards, by Canadian Pacific liner to Vancouver, across Canada by rail, and finally by C.P. liner again to Southampton.

The last few days in Hong Kong were a haze of farewell parties, amidst frenzied efforts to cram all worldly possessions, the accumulation of two years bargaining around the shops and bazaars of the Far East, into hastily acquired cabin trunks and camphor wood chests. Nobody but the Chinese could have provided the latter so quickly and cheaply. Suddenly I was beset with a major crisis in the shape of an excruciatingly painful abscess in my right ear. There were grim visions of being sent to hospital and missing the ship I had been booked to sail in. By the greatest of good fortune, the naval Ear, Nose and Throat specialist then in Hong Kong was the self-same Surgeon Lieutenant Commander, C.B. Nicholson, who had dealt with my other ear three years previously in Chatham hospital. He saw the problem sympathetically, and treated my ear so that I was able to sail as planned.

In mid-August we left Hong Kong in the Empress of Russia, coal-burning and one of the more elderly of the Canadian Pacific fleet. Our first stop was Shanghai, two days before the surprise Japanese attack on it. The Chinese population were already aware of impending events (no one else was), and were evacuating the city in large numbers, on foot, by rickshaw, handcart, pram, any form of transport available. It was an amazing sight, a mass migration of people and their belongings and we never learnt what had so

Officers' Club, Wei-hai-wei, 1935.

suddenly triggered it off, two days before actual hostilities. It put a stop to any thought of 'seeing the sights' in Shanghai, and there was some apprehensions on board as to whether we would get safely away.

In the event we sailed on schedule, but none too happy about the next two ports of call in Japan – Kobe and Yokohama. The Japanese port authorities were very reluctant to allow us naval officers, now three of us, ashore. Perhaps we ourselves were partly to blame as we were unwilling to co-operate in the endless questioning and form-filling and in the latter we deliberately confused matters. At Kobe in answer to a question on the form, we had given the names of the submarines we had served in (*Rainbow* and *Olympus*) but at Yokohama, on an exactly similar form and in answer to the same question, we had put down a different name, *Medway*, our depot ship. This created consternation and furious discussion amongst the officials, who on comparing the respective forms had discovered the discrepancy and clearly found it very sinister; in consequence we were kept on board and saw little of Yokohama, but had no regrets for the trouble we had caused Japanese officialdom.

The voyage through the Inland Sea of Japan was strikingly beautiful and that across the Pacific calm and peaceful; but we were unprepared for the sudden drop of temperature as we neared the Canadian coast. It plummeted from over 80°F one day to under 50°F in a night, winter clothes were all in baggage labelled 'Not wanted on voyage'. On reaching Vancouver its comparative warmth was very welcome.

It was a rush to get all gear disembarked and on to the trans-Canada train, already with steam up, waiting alongside the 'Empress of Russia's' berth. Time also had to be found for acquiring some further essential luggage. Canada was 'dry' and alcoholic drink could only be purchased at Government liquor shops on production of a valid licence. The thought of four days in the train with nothing to drink was unbearable – but we had no licence. Thankfully, the First Officer of the 'Empress of Russia' was aware of our plight, he lent us his licence, directed us to the nearest liquor store, and saw us on to the train with only minutes to spare.

In the greatest comfort we travelled across Canada, breaking the journey for two days at Lake Louise in the Rockies. The spectacular scenery of the latter, the unending wide horizons of the prairies, the lakes and woods of eastern Canada, they imprinted memories which have lasted all my life and which I have always longed to refresh (and fifty years later have done so!)

At Quebec we joined the 'Empress of Britain', the proud 'flagship' of the Canadian Pacific Line. Within five days we were in Southampton on a gloriously fine September morning; and so to a six week's marvellous leave at home in Scotland, where my 'pride and joy', a twelve horse-power, two seater Lea Francis car awaited me. It had safely survived two years life with the Army, on loan to my elder brother, and was almost what I was most looking forward to!

Chapter Seven

First Lieutenant's Time, 1937–39

After my time as Fourth and then Third Hand in *Rainbow*, I hoped I would be 'elevated' to First Lieutenant for my next job. Reflecting on those past two years, I had learnt much and believed I had not incurred any lasting adverse reports, in spite of a couple of occasions when Jackie Broome threatened to send me back to General Service; occasions of minor importance I thought, when I had failed to meet the standards he required. His threats were salutary, and in the end his final report, on his leaving *Rainbow*, flattered me.

In the autumn of 1937, the formal appointment arrived, to HMS *Lucia*, depot ship of the Second Submarine Flotilla, as 'Spare Crew First Lieutenant'. The Flotilla (of two mine layers and three 'S' class submarines) formed part of the Home Fleet and, when not accompanying the latter on its routine Spring, Summer and Autumn cruises, was based in the West Country, at Devonport. *Lucia* was an ancient, coal-burning, ex-German cargo liner, captured in the early days of the Great War and converted to the role of submarine depot ship; although nothing like as comfortable and as well-equipped materially as *Medway*, such resources as she could provide were adequate for the few submarines she supported. But it was not a happy Flotilla, as had been the Fourth and amongst junior submarine officers it was known as 'The Punishment Flotilla'. Quite why is hard to explain as neither discipline nor routine was unduly repressive. Devonport, with Plymouth and the whole of Devon and Cornwall behind it, was an attractive base. Perhaps the trouble lay in the Flotilla being too much at the beck and call of the Home Fleet; the submarines were the 'dogsbodies', regarded almost wholly as targets for Anti-Submarine (A/S) training and given little scope to develop their own offensive potential.

Spare crew life was boring, there were two spare 'Jimmies' (first lieutenants) anyway, and so even less for each of us to do. Prepared to go to almost any lengths to achieve more exciting duty, we prayed, longed, that sickness, injury or new appointment would overtake a first lieutenant in one of the attached submarines, so that, at least, one of us could step into his shoes. But it was not to be for the whole winter of 1937.

The little wooden, coal-burning Drifter, HMS *Mist*, belonged to the Flotilla and on cruises provided diversion from more humdrum duties. By

Second S/M Flotilla Spring Cruise 1938 – visit to Portuguese S/M school. Lt. Cdr. Bolus in centre. He was later lost in command of *Thetis* in 1939. Author on his right.

custom she was manned by members of the spare crew and commanded by the spare crew First Lieutenant. She got no marks at all for cleanliness, and being apt at sea to behave in a somewhat drunken fashion she was invariably referred to as 'the Drifter PIST.' No sooner had I joined the Flotilla than I was told to take command and follow *Lucia* from Portland to Plymouth; making barely seven knots when flat out, progress was utterly dependent on winds and tides and with no gyro and the magnetic compass a law unto itself, navigation presented a host of problems; battling through the Race off Portland Bill into the teeth of a strong westerly blow, we seemed to be going backwards most of the time. But it was a proud moment when we eventually berthed near *Lucia* in the South Yard of Devonport Dockyard. It was the last we saw of her, for shortly she was ordered to join the Reserve Fleet; after a major clean-up operation she was reluctantly accepted.

The spare crew Commanding Officer was Lieutenant Commander Sam (G.H.) Bolus, an already experienced submarine captain. Seldom have I met a more sympathetic man; he understood so well the frustrations of being relegated to 'spare crew' and, like us all, wanted nothing more than to 'belong' to or 'have' his own submarine. He and I got to know each other very well, especially through the occasional day at sea together, in one of the Flotilla's submarines, when we were given a practice 'run' in our respective roles as Captain and First Lieutenant. How delighted he was when appointed, in April '38, to command one of the new 'T' class submarines, *Thetis*, then building at Cammell Laird's at Birkenhead. Little did any of us forsee how tragically this would come to an end on 1st June 1939.

The Home Fleet, as usual, went south for its spring cruise in 1938, *Lucia* spending most of it berthed alongside the South Mole at Gibraltar. Unexpectedly, there arrived a German submarine depot ship and her half dozen or so small attached U-boats. They berthed close astern of *Lucia*, who was deputed to act as 'host' ship. It was the first contact between the two submarine services since Germany had broken her treaty obligations and embarked on building up an underwater fleet. We were suspicious of their presence. German surface warships had already demonstrated their unwelcome support of General Franco in the lingering Spanish Civil War, and were well known to frequent the waters off the south coast of Spain; but a force of submarines, what were they doing?

Visits were exchanged between the two flotillas and, as submariners, much common ground was found. A formal wardroom guest night dinner was held on board *Lucia* for the German flotilla, attended by the U-boat captains and many other officers. In the midst of what was proving a friendly, even hilarious, evening, the Germans were suddenly recalled to their ships and within the hour the whole flotilla had sailed, with a rousing send-off from their hosts of earlier in the evening. Thus ended a fleeting contact between two future enemies. But why the sudden departure? The reason became clear the next day, Germany invaded Austria, and presumably the flotilla had deployed to meet possible eventualities in case of hostile international reaction.

This encounter, at first hand with men who manned the German U-boats provoked much thought and discussion. Primarily, they were fellow submariners, nobody regarded them as Nazis – one hardly knew the word in those days – nor had we any deep forebodings of Hitler's insatiable demands for power and territory, or of the potential consequences. The opposite view was vividly illuminated for me personally a few months later. *Lucia* and her flotilla were on the summer cruise, at Torbermory in the Isle of Mull. On a Sunday morning Bill King (Lieutenant W.D.A. King, first lieutenant of *Narwhal*) and I walked across the island to have lunch with an old family friend who owned the adjacent island of Ulva. It was a hot summer's day and we were glad to reach the ferry and our final destination, where we were liberally entertained by our hostess, a widow who had lost her husband in the Great War. Encouraged by a good lunch, towards its end we were extolling the praises of the Germans we had met a few months earlier in Gibraltar. It was a blunder of the first order. Rising in wrath from her chair and seizing the stick without which she could not walk, she threatened to belabour us out of the house unless we retracted such benevolent views. We found it prudent to do so! It was a dramatic outburst, the older generation castigating the younger, yet appealing to them to come to their senses and open their eyes to the dangers ahead; it had its effect. For the first time, I began to think seriously about the ominous clouds gathering over Europe. I revised the views so readily and easily formed at Gibraltar, and I believe Bill King did likewise.

To my joy, my days in the spare crew had ended in May 1938 just before the flotilla left Devonport for its summer cruise. I was appointed First Lieutenant of HMS *Seahorse*. The 'S' class were superb, easily handled submarines, even if less comfortable and more cramped internally than what I had been used to.

My captain was 'Flick' Currie (Lieutenant F.B. Currie), just coming to the end of his first year in command. He and I had shared many dawn adventures during the past winter, pursuing in his genuine two-man wild-fowling punt the flocks of widgeon and other duck frequenting the creeks across the harbour from Devonport Dockyard; complete with a fearsome gun, whose one pound charges we made up ourselves, it gave us many hours of stealthily paddling through icy waters, but seldom ending successfully. I could not have been more pleased than to become his 'No. 1'. Quietly spoken and of few words, he was an able submarine Captain, who had the trust and respect of his crew. *Seahorse* was a happy ship.

There was little change when, all too soon, 'Flick' Currie was relieved by Lieutenant Commander R.H. Dewhurst, known as 'Dogberry' to all. A very different personality from his predecessor, just back from time in General Service after his first year in command, he was bursting with energy and talk, keen to impress with his overwhelming breadth of knowledge, and to pass it on. A bustling, energetic figure, he saw to it that there was no falling off in standards.

From Tobermory we visited Scapa Flow in the Orkneys when it was high summer and beautiful weather. This famed naval base of the Great War bore little evidence of its past strategic value, or possible future use in a similar role. The only relics were the few remaining stranded hulls of the scuttled German High Seas Fleet, those not yet salvaged for scrap. *Seahorse* received an invitation from Metal Industries, the salvage firm, to visit the last of the battleships they were hoping to raise. She rested upside down, her upperworks on the sea bed of the Flow, her bottom, lying like a great whale, a few feet above the surface of the water. It was simple to get on board, an air-lock in her double-bottom led into the interior, dimly lit throughout. It was easy to move from compartment to compartment, but eerie to visualize what it had been like twenty years before, the sea had left few traces of its long presence. Metal Industries said that each of us could take a souvenir and like most, I was satisfied with a thick, grey, earthenware cup from a mess-deck, standard German issue no doubt, but nothing like the quality of 'mess traps' provided in the RN. The Coxswain and Chief ERA of *Seahorse* had grander ambitions; making their way to the Engine Room, they successfully removed from its mounting one of the main engine-room telegraphs, a hefty contraption of solid brass weighing all of a hundred pounds, and worth a deal more. They hoped ultimately to mount it in *Seahorse*, exactly where goodness knows! It went far beyond Metal Industries' definition of 'souvenir'. After struggling with it back to the air-lock, they were relieved of the trophy and thanked for their efforts in salvaging such a valuable item. A disappointing, but perhaps inevitable end to great initiative. I was glad, though, not to have to wrestle with finding a place for it in an already over-crowded submarine.

Later in the year, in September 1938, in an atmosphere of increasing international tension, the Home Fleet gathered for its autumn cruise at Rosyth in the Firth of Forth. The situation blackened as Germany continued to threaten Czechoslovakia and the Fleet was ordered to deploy to its war stations. The submarines of the Second Flotilla had sailed in advance, to take up positions in the outer reaches of the Firth, for practice dummy torpedo attacks on the strongly escorted heavy units of the Fleet as they passed on their way to Scapa Flow and Invergordon.

It was a familiar type of exercise, but everyone was aware that, possibly in a few days, the worsening situation could change all the circumstances. What was now 'practice' could become 'real'. This added a special flavour to the normal procedures. Everyone was that little more taut, keyed-up, keen to do well, whether in submarines below the surface, or in the destroyers protecting the heavy ships.

Seahorse had dived, obtained a good 'trim', and was patrolling her ordered position when the Fleet hove in sight as expected, with its large A/S screen of destroyers ahead and on either side of the big ships. We were well positioned on the starboard bow of the force, for a straightforward dummy attack. All went well until, at periscope depth and penetrating the screen to get to a firing position at close range, the Captain, on the 'attack' periscope, took a quick bearing of the target, then swung round for an 'all-round' look to see where the escorting destroyers were. I saw a look of horror flash across his face as he ordered, 'Down periscope. Flood Q. Sixty feet. Shut watertight doors.' Clearly it was a moment of crisis. Slowly, oh, so slowly it seemed, the needle on the depth gauge crept round as *Seahorse* started to gain depth. Then a sudden deafening roar of sound, like an express train passing close overhead, with simultaneously a more ominous rumbling noise as the submarine shuddered slightly; then silence, utter and complete. At sixty feet we took stock. All compartments reported everything correct, there was no internal damage and watertight integrity was unimpaired. Neither periscope, however, could be moved, they were jammed fully down. *Seahorse* whilst submerged, was sightless.

We remained at sixty feet, firing a succession of yellow smoke candles to warn surface ships to keep clear and when judged safe to do so, we surfaced. But all was not straightforward, the upper conning tower hatch could not be opened. Access to the bridge could only be gained via the gun-tower hatch. All then became clear; both periscope standards had been knocked over, with one lying across the upper hatch to the conning tower, thus preventing it being opened. There was no other apparent damage.

At his final look through the periscope the Captain had realized *Seahorse* was right in the path of a destroyer, HMS *Foxhound* of the Sixth Destroyer Flotilla, and was in imminent danger of being rammed; hence the flow of

HMS *Osiris* – (unidentified location).

emergency orders. We were fortunate to have had time to get deep enough to avoid serious damage, or worse, but perhaps unlucky in that the top of the periscope standards was only just clipped by the blades of *Foxhound's* starboard propeller. Had we been a foot deeper we would have escaped unscathed. The only damage to *Foxhound* was to her propeller. She had not detected us on Asdics and was unaware until later of our presence, only knowing her propeller had struck something.

To put two of His Majesty's Ships out of action at such a crucial time was not popular. *Seahorse* crept back ashamedly to Rosyth to have her bent periscopes removed and the bridge cleared of debris, and then returned to Devonport for the necessary and more lengthy repairs. It meant several weeks in dock, the trauma of Munich was long past before the submarine was again fit for sea.

I said farewell to *Seahorse* in April 1939, on being appointed First Lieutenant of Reserve Group 'B' Submarines, attached to HMS *Dolphin* at Fort Blockhouse in Gosport. My year had been happy, but I was ready to move on, and not sad to leave the Second Flotilla. I looked forward to finding many old friends in *Dolphin* and her Fifth Submarine Flotilla.

There were two such groups of submarines at Blockhouse, classed as in 'Immediate Reserve', they were berthed out of the way at the Petrol Pier. The main jetty was kept for the 'boats' of the running flotilla. Group 'A' consisted of *Oberon*, *Otley* and *Otway*, the latter two being 'rejects' from the Royal Australian Navy. *Osiris* and *Oswald*, lately returned from the Fourth

Flotilla in China, formed Group 'B'. Each group had a CO, a First Lieutenant, Third and Fourth Hands, an Engineer Officer for each 'boat' and a crew two thirds the strength of the normal 'O' boat complement. It was sufficient for normal maintenance in harbour, and adequate for one submarine from a group to have the occasional day at sea in the local submarine exercise areas, thus providing sea-going practical experience for the training classes from the submarine school in *Dolphin*. The two groups worked closely together, to make up, if need be, any sudden or unexpected shortage of manpower in specialist categories. If longer periods at sea were required, crews were temporarily brought up to strength from the Fifth Flotilla spare crew.

My Captain was Lieutenant Commander R. Sheridan-Patterson; he had retired from the Navy in the early thirties, after his first submarine command, and had been recalled from the Retired List for further service when the international scene worsened in 1938. He was a wise old bird, who never interfered in the running of the group, but was reliably at hand for advice and help if needed. At sea, he was a different man, always in complete command, unhurried, never flustered, he inspired confidence. In assessing the tactical situation whilst carrying out an attack from submerged, and in use of the periscope, he was a wizard. For him, the ISWAS and more recent sophisticated torpedo control instruments, were superfluous; he had the mathematical ability to solve all the problems in his head, and, what's more, he gave a running commentary of how he was doing it as the attack progressed, so that others could learn from him.

An obvious fondness for the pleasures of life, which had, from his own accounts, been given free rein during his years ashore, never interfered with, or detracted from, his remarkable qualities and ability. I could not have wished for a more capable yet kindly CO; he was one in a million and, as I was later to realize, there was no-one better with whom to go to war in a submarine whose crew included many reservists, who, like him, had had recent experience of civilian life.

Joe Cowell (Lieutenant P.J. Cowell), was the First Lieutenant whom I relieved; little did we foresee that twice in the next ten years was I to take over from him again. We spent hours in the wardroom of *Osiris* that first morning, he talking volubly and endlessly in explanation of the working of the group, very different from that monosyllabic senior midshipman who had temporarily controlled our lives in *Revenge*'s gun-room on my first going to sea nearly nine years earlier. I did not reveal that I recognized the same person. Mid-day had long gone and my tongue was hanging out, desperate for a drink. I wondered why the delay. On suggesting it was time to put the matter right, he replied, 'Oh, I thought you were teetotal!' I disillusioned him, and from then on the turnover went smoothly. No-one else has ever made that mistake, and he did not repeat it!

The new job was very different from being No. 1 of a running boat, but my task was immediately eased by finding that the Coxswain of Reserve Group 'B', Chief Petty Officer Nicholls, had been Second Coxswain of

Rainbow when I had been in her three years before. Likewise, the then Coxswain of *Rainbow*, Chief Petty Officer Tallyn, was now 'Drafting Coxswain' in Blockhouse, and her Chief Stoker, Hawkins, was 'Drafting Chief Stoker'. Friends in high places indeed, who helped to solve the many problems that arose in keeping two old 'O' class boats in running order, with only two thirds crew between them.

Despite the limitations of being 'in reserve', life was not always confined to Gosport, Spithead and the Solent. By the end of April *Osiris* was on her way to a very enjoyable few days in Belfast, and from there south for a week at Gibraltar. Her crew for this prolonged absence from Blockhouse was made up to full strength by 'borrowing' from the spare crew and other Reserve Groups.

Returning from Gibraltar, *Osiris* called at Falmouth in order to carry out special trials in the deeper waters of the western end of the English Channel. The trials were to test a new type of submarine recognition signal, a form of grenade designed to be fired from the Underwater Signal Gun, as fitted in every submarine, at depths down to three hundred feet. On rising to the surface the grenade would fire a combination of coloured lights. The regulation smoke candles, white or yellow, were hitherto the only reliable means of identification when submerged, though Asdics and hydrophones were available for communication – of a sort.

The trial began in fair weather, with *Osiris* steadily increasing depth and firing grenades at each stage, three hundred feet was reached, all having gone successfully. It was the maximum depth for the trial, near the limit for *Osiris*, probably deeper than she had ever been and the hull was protesting, with audible creaks and groans. A sudden cry of alarm from aft, from the motor-room, reached the control room. A one-inch rivet in the port main motor cooler had blown out and sea water at full diving pressure (about 140 lbs./sq. in.) was cascading over the main motor switchboards, these were entirely open, without any form of protection or covering. As I dashed aft through the engine room I saw Petty Officer Haddleton, the Petty Officer, L.T.O. (senior Electrical rating), frantically pulling the port main motor starting switches, whilst simultaneously kicking out, across the gangway behind him, the starboard switches with his feet. The switchboards were a frightening sight, short circuits everywhere, vivid blue flashes from great slabs of copper, on the verge of melting, all sustained by a solid jet of water spouting from the bowels behind the switchboard, and spraying everywhere as it hit the interior of the hull above. Fortunately, the drenching helped to quell incipient fires. Quick action in dropping the main battery fuses, forward of the control room, cut off all electric power, and once the inlet valve to the main motor cooler had been shut, matters were again under control. Using emergency procedures *Osiris* surfaced hurriedly. She returned in slow time to Portsmouth, spending several weeks in the Dockyard for the necessary repairs to switchboards and cooler.

It was a disturbing experience, revealing a serious design fault not unique to the 'O' class, in that the main motor coolers, when in use, were open to the full pressure of the sea, and at great depths could not be guaranteed to withstand this. The consequences could have been very much more serious, even disastrous and it was reassuring that members of this motley, scratch crew had reacted so promptly and correctly.

The summer months passed quickly. Life at Blockhouse was full of fun and there was ample time for relaxation and recreation. There were many friends around, some from my days in China, others acquired since. We were well aware of the peace-time risks involved in our profession, but fully determined to enjoy life down to the last drop in the bucket. Increasingly, however, we could not fail to take note of the ominous international outlook. None of us had joined submarines with any thought of ever having to to go war; other reasons had persuaded us to volunteer but those conscripted thought no differently. That we might now, soon, find ourselves engaged in actual war added a new dimension to our lives. There was no ducking the fact that life would become more dangerous; in case the worst came about, make the best of the present, that was the general reaction.

High spirits therefore generally permeated the wardroom, but these were blighted entirely and suddenly on Thursday, 1st June 1939. It was a guest night, normally the excuse for especially cheerful, if not rowdy, behaviour. In the course of dinner senior officers present were seen to get up and leave and word quickly went round that *Thetis* at sea for her trial dive from her builders, Cammell Lairds at Birkenhead, had failed to surface. The evening's gaiety came to an abrupt end, people gathered in anxious groups awaiting further news. We knew that, whilst building, *Thetis* belonged to the Fifth Flotilla and that Captain (S) (Captain H.P.K. Oram), was attending the trials. As the news worsened and the final tragedy became clear, we were powerless to do anything but speculate on the cause, and grieve, most of us had friends on board. It was not so very long since, in *Lucia*, I had said goodbye to Sam Bolus, *Thetis*'s captain, and I knew well the other officers on board. Freddie Woods (Lieutenant F.G. Woods), one of the only four survivors out of more than a hundred on board, was a particular friend, dating from Hong Kong days. I saw much of him later and, although outwardly he continued, always, to show a very brave face, he never got over the dreadful experiences of that fateful disaster. His inner self completely changed. At Blockhouse it was weeks before life returned to normal.

The summer wore on, blessed with idyllic weather, but the clouds over Europe grew blacker and blacker. It was not until the end of July that the threatening outlook had any marked effect at Blockhouse. Summer leave was advanced but travel abroad was banned, people really began to sit up and take notice. Donald Pirie (Lieutenant D.A. Pirie) and I had intended a fortnight touring by car through the Vosges mountains in France, our main purpose gastronomic. We had spent hours planning this, at week-ends with his lively family at their new home in Lymington, appropriately named 'Great Swallows', or whilst sailing in their beautiful little yacht *Wapipi*. It was a bitter blow to give up all we had devised.

Sailing in *Wapipi* in the Solent, 1939.

Sailing in *Wapipi* in the Solent 1939. *Wapipi* was built by Morgan Giles (Teignmouth) and designed by Laurent Giles for Commander Pirie, first war submarine commander. *Wapipi* was last seen in the Med. in 1970, owner unknown.

More urgent matters soon prevailed, mobilisation, with all ships in reserve being brought forward for service. Reservists came streaming into Blockhouse, and in no time at all Reserve Group 'B' was 'kitted up' to full complement, with a mixed bag of old submarine hands, straight from many years of 'civvy street', individuals every one of them; but all were cheerful, keen and ready to accept their changed circumstances. *Osiris* commissioned formally on 2nd August, as did the other submarines in the Reserve Groups, and I, remaining as her first lieutenant, relinquished all duties I had hitherto had with *Oswald*. A week later all ships brought forward from Reserve had assembled in Weymouth Bay, to be reviewed by His Majesty King George VI. The next two days at sea were occupied with elementary diving exercises, before *Osiris* returned to Haslar Creek and *Dolphin*.

Hectic days, extending well into the nights, followed, as all the submarines based at Blockhouse competed in the rush to store for war. The congestion on and around the main jetty was horrific; stores, provisions, spare gear, torpedoes, warheads, ammunition all piled up, as submarines queued up to berth under the two available cranes. Orderly confusion was the only possible description.

Late one evening after dinner, I was standing on the fore-casing of *Osiris* as she embarked torpedoes. The Instructional First Lieutenant (Lieutenant E.P. Tomkinson), who had become a great friend during the past months, was idly standing on the jetty, surveying the scene, having little to do with all the activity born of that period of crisis. He made some ribald remark and I turned to reply, leaning with my hands on the wire guard-rail running along the casing. Alas, the wire had been disconnected, which I had not seen in the dark. To the amusement of all I went neatly head first into the sea, fortunately no harm was done other than a wet uniform. My cap remained on my head throughout, its inside and my hair stayed bone dry! It was the only time I ever suffered the indignity of falling off a submarine's casing, or, not altogether unknown for others, off the narrow wooden plank connecting one submarine to another.

'Tommo' Tomkinson was, by any account, a very remarkable man; large of stature, friendly, overflowing with high spirits and vitality, his intelligence, knowledge and vision were outstanding. Never at a loss for words, nor slow to speak his mind, he also invariably saw the lighter side of things and could be guaranteed to introduce a jovial note into the most serious problem or outlook. His cheerful contribution to life reached everywhere in Blockhouse. I believe his qualities of leadership ranked amongst the finest ever produced by the submarine service, his friendship was a blessing I treasured. As war looked more and more inevitable, his tongue-in-cheek, light-hearted, summing-up of how we should meet it, 'No medals, no tombstones', became our catchphrase.

Three days later we sailed for a five-day mock war patrol in the southern North Sea, between the Thames Estuary and the coast of Holland. Representing the potential enemy, German U-boats, we were supposed to

Review of the Reserve Fleet by H.M. The King, Weymouth August 1939. HMS *Osiris*.

provide a target for our own surface and air A/S forces, broadcasting our presence by surfacing and making a signal whenever we had carried out a dummy attack on passing merchant ships, of which there were many. In the event we were never located or hunted, which did not bode well for any future war against Germany, but at least, the exercise provided very good training value for *Osiris* and her bunch of officers and men so hurriedly assembled together. It helped immeasurably in shaping them into something approaching an efficient crew.

After this, *Osiris* had a quick two days in dry-dock in Portsmouth Dockyard to check on propellers and under-water fittings. Then a final two days at Blockhouse before sailing for Gibraltar on 27th August 1939, with ultimate destination Malta. At noon that day she was formally transferred from the Fifth to the First Submarine Flotilla. The passage to Gibraltar provided time to change the all-pervading peace-time mental outlook into something stiffer, to meet the different conditions of what now seemed inevitable, the actual outbreak of hostilities. This was a difficult transition, because no-one had any experience of what these conditions would be like, nor were there any guidelines to provide advice. Training in such matters had been virtually non-existent and reliance had to be placed on imaginative common-sense. The omission was remedied, some time later, by the issue of a document called 'Submarine Principles', (SMP) a collection of foolscap sheets tacked together and containing hints and tips on how to conduct a submarine war patrol in enemy waters, collated and distilled from the knowledge of the older generation who had had Great War experience.

Ship's Company, HMS *Osiris*, Lt. Cdr. Sheridan-Patterson centre of row seated, author on his right, Malta 1939.

Up-dated in the months and years ahead, as current first-hand experience was fed into it, it became a very valuable guide.

At eleven o'clock on the morning of the third of September 1939, a fine, sunny, warm day, *Osiris* was on the surface, ploughing her way through the Sicilian Channel, when, some distance north of but within sight of the Italian island of Pantellaria, there came the fateful signal 'FUNNEL - GERMANY' – a signal that was to change our lives for nearly six years. When decoded it meant simply 'Commence hostilities with Germany'. Up to that final, dramatic, moment everyone had hoped it would never happen, no-one on board was a warmonger wanting war. Apprehensively, all eyes turned towards Pantellaria, would Italy back her ally? Nothing occurred to disturb that peaceful Sunday morning and *Osiris* continued steadily on her way to Malta, relieved at least that we were not yet embroiled with a second foe.

Malta, when *Osiris* berthed there next morning, was bereft of HM ships. The Mediterranean Fleet, that age-old bastion of British policy in that strategic Sea, had deployed to all quarters of the globe. The First Submarine Flotilla, under Captain P. Ruck-Keene, with its depot ship and its 'S' boats, had already left for home waters. *Osiris* was soon joined by *Oswald* and *Otway*. The three 'O' class submarines appeared to be the only White Ensign warships in the whole of the Mediterranean capable of offensive action, if needed. It was a sombre picture.

Chapter Eight

At War – The Early Years, 1939–41

For the last months of 1939, life in Malta was little troubled by the war afflicting all the United Kingdom. There were, naturally, restrictions on former peace-time freedoms and liberty, such as censorship of news and mail, but the main problem for the crews of the three elderly 'O' class submarines based there was, in one word, BOREDOM. There was no Mediterranean Fleet to call on their services for anti-submarine (A/S) training nor, in return, to provide targets for practice torpedo attacks by the submarines themselves. Long periods in harbour prevailed, only alleviated by the occasional day at sea in the calm waters off that still tranquil island, for what was commonly referred to as 'independent exercises', a means of ensuring, at least, that the submarines remained reasonably proficient in the basic practices of their trade.

Malta's own 'local defence force' of three or four ocean-going trawlers called up from Hull's fishing fleet, hurriedly armed and converted into A/S vessels and commissioned under the White Ensign with their erstwhile crews of horny-handed deep-sea fishermen, took advantage of such occasions to try their hand at hunting submarines instead of fish. Their lack of previous training required the most elementary practices, but at least these gave them a grounding in their new role even if they did little to enliven the routine dives of the 'clockwork mice' involved.

In harbour the submarines berthed alongside Manoel Island in Sliema harbour. Accommodation for officers and men was hard to come by, the former found a well-furnished house on the waterfront opposite to where the submarines lay, which acted as a comfortable wardroom mess whilst the latter were billeted in Fort Manoel, an old and largely derelict Army barracks, the forerunner of the subsequent home of the Tenth Submarine Flotilla. With no depot ship, or shore base equipped with equivalent facilities, the submarines had to 'make do' for day-to-day existence and routine maintenance, improvising on what they could devise or scrounge from any handy source, falling back on the resources of the Naval Dockyard when all else failed. But the latter was several miles away, on the far side of Malta's Grand Harbour, and transport to and fro, whether by land or sea, was never easy to obtain and always time consuming.

Innumerable bars along the Sliema front helped to wile away the dreary evenings, with the fleet absent they touted eagerly for custom and the crews of *Osiris*, *Oswald* and *Otway* were a godsend to them. *Osiris* had its favourite, 'The Dun Cow', and it saw many beery and noisy occasions which I often seemed to join, with the current songs of 'Roll out the Barrel', 'Hang out the washing on the Siegfried Line' echoing across the waters. At that stage of the war the breweries of Malta still produced beer that was palatable, and cheap. This was the very reverse of conditions in later years with Malta increasingly under siege, when beer was almost unobtainable and what there was was barely drinkable.

As time went by and news filtered through of what our submarines were achieving in the North Sea, and the casualties they were sustaining, it became ever harder to accept with equanimity the very passive role which enveloped the three 'O' boats. Life was as quiescent as though they were back in reserve at Blockhouse, excepting that now they were fully manned and nominally supposed to be ready for war-time operations. The latter seemed a long way off and there were no signs of Germay's Axis partner, Italy, engaging in any form of hostilities. It was not surprising that to some of the reservists in the ships' companies, abruptly rousted from their peaceful civilian occupations at the end of July, the need for their call-up became questionable and they began to ask that they be returned to the United Kingdom and be de-mobilized. With my fellow first lieutenants, Jimmy Prowse in *Oswald* and David Wanklyn in *Otway* – Jimmy an old friend from China days and 'Wanks' whom I had briefly got to know in the Second Flotilla and at Blockhouse – we had to use all our persuasive powers to allay such feelings, but they remained a latent source of irritation and frustration until a more active role for these three ageing submarines eventually transpired. *Otway* was the first to find such relief, recalled home to England by the end of the year, surplus to the needs of the Mediterranean and because of difficulties in the provision of spare items of equipment, she being, with the ill-fated *Oxley* lost at the very beginning of the war, a unique hybrid design pre-dating the 'O' class. So *Osiris* and *Oswald* were left on their own, virtually, as far as any offensive action could be visualized, the sole heirs of the once great Mediterranean Fleet.

I had much sympathy with the feelings of the reservists and I found it particularly exasperating to be so isolated from active participation in the war, whose early months were later to be dubbed 'the Phoney War' though it was far from this for those constantly at sea, actively fighting it. I pestered my captain, 'Sherry P', to find us some more active employment, and every time a Confidential Admiralty Fleet Order (CAFO) appeared calling for volunteers for some special party or operation I formally applied to have my name sent forward. Invariably all to no avail, in his kindly way 'Sherry P' turned down all my pleas and applications, telling me to 'bide my time, the war would be a long one and I would get all the excitement I wanted'. How right he was, the wise old bird.

The tedium was relieved when *Osiris* and *Otway* spent from early October to November in Alexandria. We were on our own, tied up at No. 6 gate in the commercial port, all living on board but with easy access to that

ancient, yet modern and very civilized, city. At least it was a change of
scenery from Malta, but the daily round of life on board was hardly any
different, and though the fleshpots ashore were more varied and exciting
than those to be found in Malta, I found little to attract me ashore. But the
cinemas and restaurants, as yet untouched by the consequences of war,
provided entertainment on a par with the best of pre-war Paris, the likes of
which were now unobtainable in most of Europe. My clearest recollection is
of seeing the recently released film 'Gone with the Wind', in a cinema more
lavishly comfortable than any I had ever experienced at home.

Osiris was back in Malta by mid-November, for routine docking and
maintenance in the Dockyard, which saw out the rest of 1939. New Year's
Eve was wildly celebrated in the Sliema Club and briefly the war was
forgotten. But then it was back to the same old routine of keeping up
appearances of being at war. Thrown back on our own resources for finding
relaxation and recreation, I developed a lasting liking for the Maltese people
and their island, something that had never blossomed in my three years
there as a midshipman. I explored the island in long walks at the week-ends.
The more I saw the more I liked, a sentiment growing to admiration in the
harsh years which they shortly had to endure.

There were changes on board throughout the winter, mainly amongst the
officers. At the end of November Bill Jewell (later Captain N.L.A. Jewell),
Third Hand and Torpedo Officer, level-headed, athletic and the very
staunchest of companions and supporters whose good humour never failed,
had returned home for further advancement with an appointment as a First
Lieutenant. His relief was not of the same calibre, straight out of the egg
with no sea-going experience, and much more devoted to his young,
attractive, blonde wife than to acquiring the tricks of the trade as a
submariner. She had cleverly wangled a passage to Malta and took *Osiris* by
storm, whose crew through the circumstances then dictating their lives had
become an entirely 'bachelor' collection of men, quite unused to the
frequent presence on board of a scantily clad female. It soon became plain
that neither of the two were suited to the demands of submarine life in
wartime and in due course his place was taken by Lieutenant J. Raban-
Williams, who, newcomer though he was, fitted much more happily into the
close-knit family we had become. The 'Chief', our Engineer Officer Joe
Blackeby (Commissioned Engineer J. Blackeby) with years and years of
submarine experience behind him, firstly as an Engine Room Artificer
(ERA) and then as a Warrant Engineer Officer and later Commissioned
Engineer Officer, was recalled home for an appointment where all his
accumulated knowledge and experience could be put to better use. We
could not have wished for a better relief, newly promoted Warrant Engineer
Uren, younger and less sure of himself but also with years of submarine
experience.

By far and away the most significant change took place in the spring of
1940. Word was that no submarine commanding officer should be over the

age of thirty-five; in the light of the stresses and strains being experienced on war patrols in the North Sea and Norwegian waters at that time perhaps such guidance was justified, but for us in *Osiris* it struck a cruel blow. 'Sherry P' was over age and had to go. By April he had been relieved by Lieutenant Commander J.R.G. Harvey. 'Ginger' Harvey, like his predecessor, had retired from the Navy after qualifying for submarine command and had been recalled for active service when war broke out, after several years on the beach. A former Navy boxer, brave as a lion, excitable, he was a totally different kettle of fish from 'Sherry P', lacking much of the latter's wisdom and sympathetic understanding. We adapted to his different approach and manner but another aspect was less easy to accept, as became blatantly obvious to me and others in the control room on our very first dive with 'Ginger' in command. Once we were under water he had only the vaguest idea of what was happening around us on the surface of the sea as revealed through the periscope. If ever the submarine expression of 'lost in the box' applied to anyone it certainly applied to him in full and I have never stopped wondering how on earth he got through his 'perisher'. It was a worrying change from the quiet expertise of 'Sherry P', whose constant coaching over many months of how to carry out a successful torpedo attack now stood me in good stead. I found myself not only trying to keep the submarine at its right depth and looking after its trim (the first lieutenant's traditional roles when dived) but also assisting a more-often-than-not bewildered captain as he tried to sort out the true situation above us. Things did not augur too well for the future, should war descend on the Mediterranean.

A future that by May 1940, was increasingly fraught with menace. Germany's overwhelming supremacy in the land battles then raging in Norway and France gave every encouragement to Italy to become more belligerent. A consequence was the resuscitation of the Mediterranean Fleet as battleships, cruisers, destroyers began to assemble at Alexandria. *Osiris*, in company with the 28th Anti-Submarine Group, her friends the Hull trawlers, left Malta on the 9th May to join the Fleet and on arrival in Alexandria on the 13th found she was back amongst former friends, the depot ship *Medway* and the Fourth Submarine Flotilla from China, now re-named the First. An intensive period of training at sea followed, devoted mainly to giving the destroyers much needed experience in hunting a submarine, but very occasionally finding time for *Osiris* to get in a dummy torpedo attack or a practice gun action. We were very rusty and needed these desperately.

Of the five officers who had commissioned *Osiris* in that long ago August of 1939, only two now remained; our navigator – a seasoned and stalwart RNR lieutenant, C.A. Pardoe – and myself. During our winter of enforced idleness in Malta, with time heavy on his hands, Pardoe had gladly jumped at the chance of being lent to the Contraband Control Service, operating to restrict sea-borne trade with Germany. His tour of duty as a Boarding

Officer took him to the Dardanelles, whence he returned to Malta on board an ancient, rust-ridden Bulgarian tramp steamer, whose cargo of hides and dried figs was condemned as contraband and impounded in the Lazaretto on Manoel Island. It was still there years later. His lurid tales of Bulgarian customs and habits, gastronomic and sexual, enlivened our lives for months, adding flavour to our otherwise humdrum existence. He was also a very skilled navigator and when *Osiris* was at sea her geographical position was never in doubt.

The port of Alexandria had changed out of all recognition from its state in the autumn of 1939; with a massive boom across its entrance and its waters now crowded with warships, including a French squadron of cruisers, it had been transformed into Britain's main naval base in the Mediterranean, displacing Malta which was regarded as too vulnerable should war with Italy come about. Oddly, as far as *Osiris* was concerned, one feature in the harbour remained constant; invariably, as she passed through the boom returning from a day's exercises or a longer period at sea she was greeted by a little family or 'school' of three porpoises who, cavorting around her bows, would then escort her to her berth. They were to welcome her on every occasion of entering Alexandria harbour that I knew of in 1939 and 1940. They did not appear when we left harbour. How long the porpoises continued their strange greeting I do not know, but I cannot recollect seeing them in later years when in a 'T' class submarine. Perhaps there was some peculiarity in the sound of *Osiris*'s diesel engines or underwater noise she generated, or pressure waves from her uniquely shaped bows, which so attracted them. To have one's safe return to harbour faithfully marked in such a welcoming, friendly fashion seemed to cast a spell or aura of good luck around *Osiris*; alone of her class she continued to survive, until towards the end of the war when increasing mechanical failures finally took their toll, and she was reduced to being sunk by our own side, to serve as a 'bottomed' target for A/S training off the East African coast.

As the war clouds in the Mediterranean loomed ever closer, *Osiris* left Alexandria on 31st May for a precautionary operational patrol. She was in the Aegean off the North coast of Crete when Italy entered the war on the 10th June; for us, at last, the 'Phoney War' had ended and we could hope for offensive action, and also expect to be subject to attack. Depth-charges were still an unknown quantity, but much had been heard at second hand of their unpleasantness as reports from the home-based flotillas slowly percolated through to *Medway* and her now assembled First Flotilla of 'O', 'P' and 'R' class submarines.

This first patrol yielded no excitement, nor did *Osiris*'s second patrol from the 29th June to 23rd July, off the Dardanelles and in the eastern approaches to the Gulf of Athens. Neutral shipping gave ample scope for dummy torpedo attacks whilst maintaining dived patrol off the Straits of Gallipoli and everyone learnt from the difficulties of keeping accurate course, depth and trim in the fiercely fluctuating currents and changing densities caused by the constant flow of fresher water from the Black Sea, through the Dardenelles out into the Mediterranean. It was all useful 'intelligence' for future patrols, but enemy ships were conspicuously absent.

After two weeks in Alexandria *Osiris* sailed on 4th August for her third patrol, this was to be in the southern part of the Adriatic and hopes were high that it would be more productive. It was suspected that the entrance to the Adriatic, through the Straits of Otranto, had been mined by the Italians, but *Osiris* diving deep, passed through without any untoward incident. In the patrol area all, including the weather, was peace and calm and of enemy shipping there was little sign, though a fast-moving unidentified vessel forced *Osiris* to dive hurriedly during the night of the 13th/14th August. Two nights later came a more realistic encounter, when on the surface not far off the Italian coast a cargo ship was sighted and *Osiris* closed to attack. It was a brilliantly clear moonlit night and it was quickly seen that the ship, of about 3,000 tons, was in ballast, with her propeller thrashing round half out of the water. Despite the target's obvious shallow draught torpedoes were fired but no hits were obtained, so *Osiris* resorted to the use of her gun and closed to a decisive range of a few hundred yards. Inevitably she was sighted by the target who thereupon tried to ram her, dodging this *Osiris* opened fire, with the first round the crew immediately lowered the lifeboats and abandoned their ship, leaving it steaming aimlessly. It proved difficult to sink and *Osiris* could do no more than continue to pump shells into it from close range, aimed at its water line and propeller and rudder. It was before the days of flashless cordite as far as *Osiris*'s outfit of ammunition was concerned, so the night was rent by brilliant flashes of gunfire and much noise. This Brock's benefit was within easy distance of the coast and continued for nearly two hours but evoked no response from the enemy so once the ship had been stopped and was listing heavily *Osiris* withdrew from the scene, satisfied that it was sinking. The remainder of the patrol was as quiet as the weather, but some success had been achieved and *Osiris* was in happier mood when ordered to leave the Adriatic and return to Malta for a quick routine docking.

On arrival there on 24th August, things were found to be very different, frequent daylight air raids on the island were proof indeed that war in the Mediterranean had really begun. The Italian bombers came over at a great height, tiny silvery specks in the clear blue skies. For one of these raids *Osiris* lay alongside a wharf in the dockyard, apparently their target, and it was fascinating to watch from her bridge as they pursued a steady course overhead, undeterred by furious fire from Malta's ack-ack batteries. Of 'Faith', 'Hope' and 'Charity', the three ageing GLADIATOR fighters which was all the RAF then possessed in Malta, there was no sign, they had done their best in the initial weeks of the bombing and were now all too frequently unserviceable. Fortunately, the bombers' aim was never very accurate and on this occasion the nearest bombs fell on the playing fields of the Marsa, well over a mile away. As time went on and the raids became more dangerous we learnt it was prudent to take cover when the sirens sounded their dismal warnings.

The air raids were not the only signs that life had become more dangerous; the first casualties in The First Submarine Flotilla occurred, with five submarines, including *Oswald*, our old sparring partner from Reserve Group days at Blockhouse and the past winter in Malta, failing to return from early patrols. At the time we in *Osiris* were unaware that the Flotilla had been hit to this extent and we remained blissfully undismayed. It was the Flotilla staff back in *Medway* in Alexandria who initially bore the brunt and had the sad task of reporting the submarines missing and writing to next-of-kin. Looking back on those days it is now plain that the 'O', 'P' and 'R' class submarines were a highly unsuitable design for the submarine war in the Mediterranean; which, coupled with a lack of realistic operational training for war, brought about the disastrous losses in the First Flotilla in the first few months of hostilities.

Osiris left Malta on 9th September with orders again to patrol the southern part of the Adriatic, specifically to attack shipping now known to be plying between ports on the East Coast of Italy, e.g. Brindisi and Bari, and harbours on the coast of Albania. This traffic was vital to the Italian army which had recently invaded Albania and was menacing Greece. Once in the Adriatic, the situation was astonishing and portrayed a fantastic change from *Osiris's* last experience. A constant stream of ships, a few large liners, obviously acting as troopships, many smaller cargo ships, some escorted, some not, were encountered as they made the short trip across the Adriatic, fully laden east bound, empty and in ballast west bound. The excitement aroused by meeting such a variety and number of potential targets was exhilarating, only to be matched by immense frustration as *Osiris* failed again and again, for one reason or another, to complete a successful attack.

Eventually, success was achieved one afternoon. A west bound line of three small ships, empty and riding high in the water, presented themselves on a plate. Conditions for attack were perfect and *Osiris* steering an opposite course and from ideal range, prepared to fire a salvo of ninety degree angled torpedoes. But there were anxious moments before they were finally sent on their way as it required much prompting from the Torpedo Control Officer and myself before 'Ginger' Harvey could be persuaded to set the DA (Director Angle) on the periscope and give the order to fire. This hesitation was due to his attention being diverted as the crucial moment approached by his suddenly spotting an escorting destroyer on the far side of the line of ships. Taking account of the light draught of the targets the torpedoes were set to run at as shallow a depth as practicable, but there were no heartening sounds of explosions at the time they should have hit. Downcast faces and disappointment were widespread as realization dawned that yet again, apparently, the attack had been unsuccessful. Then, within a further minute, an unexpected loud 'bang' startled everybody, the periscope went up for 'Ginger' to take a quick look, which immediately became more protracted as with eye glued to the eye-piece, he excitedly proclaimed that we had hit the destroyer on the other side of the convoy. There was relief and rejoicing all round; not only had we broken our 'duck' but we had removed the immediate threat of retaliation. Subsequently it was learnt that we had indeed sunk the Italian torpedo boat *Palestro*.

Shortly afterwards orders were received to return to Alexandria, and on the first of October *Osiris* was safely back alongside *Medway*, content that some of the events of her last two patrols had, at last, been in her favour and that the many dreary months of waiting for action were a thing of the past.

It was my last patrol in *Osiris*; while in Alexandria a signal came through to say that I was to join the 'perisher' (Commanding Officers' Qualifying Course, COQC) starting at Blockhouse the following January and that passage home was to be arranged as soon as possible. Impatient though I was to do my 'perisher' – my contemporaries in length of service in submarines were either ahead of me, already doing the course, or had become casualties of war – it was a sad moment when I said 'good-bye' to *Osiris*. Her crew, the majority reservists and much older than me, had weathered all the trials and tribulations of the long, weary months before Italy came into the war, meeting the inaction with stoic acceptance, and they had finally proved themselves on operational patrols, which at last had brought some excitement into their lives and justified their long exile from home.

I had learnt at first hand a very great deal about human relationships, but not very much about the more specialized art of wartime submarining; for the latter I had behind me only the experience of a few operational patrols – which did not even include the sound of a depth charge. But as a counter to this lack of exposure to the real thing, however, I had had, above all, the benefit over many months of the wisdom and teaching of 'Sherry P', with, in a different way, the example of 'Ginger' Harvey, whose courage would take him anywhere, only marred by his inability to interpret correctly what he saw through the periscope.

After a few weeks kicking my heels in *Medway* came the happy day when I finally left Alexandria by train for Suez, a blissful journey, whatever one may have heard or thought of Egyptian railways. The port of Suez was crowded with shipping; troopships, cargo ships, all engaged in the endless, vital task of supplying Wavell's Desert Army, but, perforce, with the Mediterranean barred to them, having to accept the long voyage to and from England around the Cape. The whole place pulsed with life and I felt a very small cog in a very large machine, but all went smoothly and I was soon embarked in the MV *Britannic*, in earlier years a top class passenger liner plying the North Atlantic routes between England and N. America. Now painted a sombre grey all over and stripped of all luxuries in her conversion to troopship, it was hard to imagine that she, and her sister ship *Georgic*, the then largest diesel driven ships in the Merchant Navy, had been the pride of their owners, the White Star Line. Only the 'O.C. Troops' had the comfort of a state-room to himself, for the rest of us, fortunately not many, we were crammed three or four to a cabin and I was lucky to have congenial companions in the three-berth allocated. Of the hundred or so passengers on board most were Army wives and children being evacuated from Cairo to Durban and Capetown, and of the few naval officers nearly all were submariners returning to England for one reason or another. We were a happy bunch, except for one unfortunate suffering from DTs and on whom we were expected to keep a watchful eye. He should really have been a hospital case and when the bar was open – the ship was not yet 'dry', as troopships became later in the war – it was quite a problem restricting his intake. Apart from this our time was entirely free, with so much feminine company on board, of which we had been starved for months, there was no difficulty in finding occupation and entertainment.

One serious shipboard romance evolved. Alistair Mars, fellow submarine first lieutenant lately of *Perseus* of the old Fourth Flotilla in China and new First Flotilla at Alexandria, and now homeward bound for the same 'perisher' as me, worked swiftly as was his wont and by the time the ship reached Aden he was engaged to the prettiest girl on board, nursery-governess to an Army family. At our next port of call, Mombasa, lightning arrangements were made for their marriage in the Cathedral and he did me the honour of asking me to be his best man. Although there were few present, barely noticeable in the vast emptiness of the Cathedral, it was a moving occasion. The remaining weeks of the voyage home, with calls at Durban and Capetown, must have been a wonderful honeymoon, seized in the middle of a deadly war.

Britannic had sailed from Suez within twenty-four hours of embarking her passengers, forming with some other empty troopships a small, valuable but vulnerable convoy, to be guarded throughout the voyage down the Red Sea by the eight-inch gun cruiser HMS *Kent*. She was a lame duck, unable to steam faster than seventeen knots having been hit in the stern by an Italian torpedo while on some operation in the Mediterranean and now going elsewhere for repairs, she was considered adequate to ward off any possible attack from Italian naval forces still actively alive and posing a threat from their base at Massawa in Eritrea. At night, with the ship darkened and all scuttles shut, conditions on board were purgatory; designed for the cool of the North Atlantic the ship's ventilation system could not cope with the heat of the Red Sea, and with no air conditioning and a total of only three fans throughout the whole of the accommodation, it was a wonder that no-one was prostrated by heat exhaustion. We were indeed glad when, once well clear of the Red Sea, the convoy dispersed and ships proceeded independently. The rigid conditions were somewhat relaxed and the nights became more tolerable.

Brief calls at Durban and Capetown saw the end of almost idyllic conditions akin to peace-time cruising, with the disembarkation of all the Army families. At these two ports the welcome and hospitality showered on the ship and its occupants was beyond belief, apartheid had not reared its ugly head and South Africa was a firm ally, committed to the battle against Nazism. But for us remaining on board as *Britannic* ploughed her way northwards after once more crossing the Equator, the regime had to adapt to our return to the war zone, emphasized at one stage by the temporary return of HMS *Kent* as a protection against surface raiders. We slept at night in warm clothing, with life-belts and a water-tight torch immediately to hand, ready for a quick dash on deck should the worst happen. It was the only time during the war that while at sea I constantly felt anxious, no doubt because we were a fat, juicy target and there was little we could do to avoid action or defend ourselves. How brave were the men of the Merchant Navy who endured this year in, year out, suffering frightful casualties throughout more than five years of war.

Fortunately, the farther north we got the more the weather closed in, with heavy overcast skies and poor visibility favouring our safe passage for the last three days of the voyage, when passing through the more dangerous areas where attack was most likely by either U-boat or those long range airborne predators, the Focke-Wulf aircraft. The few naval officers on board helped to man the ship's totally inadequate anti-aircraft armament of ancient Lewis guns mounted in the wings of the bridge and along the boat deck. It was cold work, for none of us had clothing suitable for watch-keeping on an open deck in the North Atlantic in December; there were a few scares, when the ship had to alter course to avoid the reported positions of particular U-boats, but of the dreaded Focke-Wulfs we saw no sign and it was a relief to all when we finally rounded the north of Ireland and arrived at Liverpool, in good time for all formalities to be got through and to be on leave for Christmas.

I was in London a few hours after we had docked in Liverpool, to report to Flag Officer Submarines, whose wartime headquarters had moved from the Firth of Forth area some months previously and were now established, for the duration of the war, in a requisitioned block of flats known as Northways, in Swiss Cottage, north-west London. Northways was the hub around which all submarine life revolved throughout the remaining years of the war; it was the focal point for all decisions affecting the strength and size of the submarine service, the deployment of flotillas, depot ships and individual submarines, and it exercised day-to-day direct operational control of home-based submarines at sea on war patrol. It also controlled the careers of all submarine officers, and it worked very closely with HMS *Dolphin* at Blockhouse who continued as the drafting authority for all ratings and had responsibility for all initial submarine training.

On arrival at Northways I was immediately ushered into the presence of the great man himself, Max Horton, who in a lengthy interview then cross-examined me closely on every conceivable aspect of submarine operations, equipment, weapons and, by no means least, welfare, as experienced in the Mediterranean. The intensity and persistence of his questioning I attributed to my being the first submarine officer of some seniority and experience, little as mine was, to have returned from the Mediterranean since Italy had entered the war six months previously, and to have had actual patrol experience of the conditions pertaining in that particular theatre of war. It was a daunting forty minutes and at first I could not help remembering those long-past but frightening noon-time reports to the Captain when I had been one of his midshipmen in *Resolution* in 1932. It was the first time we had met since those days and he did not reveal if he remembered them; I did not remind him. But his questioning was friendly and my nervousness soon vanished. I came away immensely heartened and impressed by his all-pervading depth of knowledge of submarines, their weapons and equipment, and by his understanding of the problems and difficulties faced by those who manned and operated them. It was a totally inspiring experience, underlining how very, very fortunate was the submarine service to have him leading it throughout the crucial years of 1940–42, perhaps far more than was widely realized at the time. From then on I would have done anything he asked me. That he went on to win the Battle of the Atlantic, without which the final Allied victory in Europe would never have been possible, only emphasized the immense and total grasp he had of fighting the under-water war, and his leadership was beyond compare. I like to think that, stemming from that interview, came my early return to the Mediterranean some six months later as a budding CO, due to the opinion he may then have formed.

Released from Northways with orders to report to Blockhouse in mid-January for my 'perisher', I went on my way rejoicing at the thought of nearly three weeks' leave. A quick visit to Gieves to get some warm uniform and then the night train from Euston to Inverness; trains seemed to be running much as I remembered them despite the 'blitz' and though it took some persuasive talking to acquire a sleeper at such very short notice, all was made smooth when I recognized from earlier years the friendly face of the sleeping car attendant, who, quite unjustifiably, seemed to regard me as some sort of hero. And so to all the relaxation that home and Scotland could give me.

War-time rationing had hardly as yet affected the north of Scotland and air raids and bombs were still a phenomenon, only to be experienced on exceptional random occasions where special targets existed. Life was comparatively peaceful, food was still plentiful, and it was easy temporarily to forget the war; but the loss of virtually the entire 51st Highland Division at St. Valery in France after the evacuation of the rest of the British Army from Dunkirk was a deeply felt and enduring memory. Many families I knew personally were affected and it brought home to every town, village, crofting community and the remotest glen in the Highlands and Islands the reality of war and its sadness, but also a determination to see it through to its final end.

I was back amongst more vivid realities on arrival at Portsmouth on my way to *Dolphin* for my 'perisher'. The city had suffered a very heavy air raid the night before, and the train from London only got as far as the Town station, instead of going on as usual to the Harbour. As I left the station, viewing with dismay and some apprehension the scenes of chaos around, wholesale devastation, smoking ruins, hose-pipes snaking everywhere, a damaged City Hall, there was a deafening explosion nearby and a large lump of metal clanged against the wall beside the pavement six feet from where I was standing. A delayed-action bomb (UXB), of which there were still a few about, had gone off. I wasted no further time 'goofing' and hurried on to HMS *Vernon* where, to my relief, I soon got a boat across the harbour to *Dolphin*, where all was peace and quiet, untouched by last night's depredations except for a few incendiary bombs which had been rapidly dealt with.

Joining up with the other four 'perishers', a mixed bunch as regards age and seniority but all experienced submarine first lieutenants, Harry Winter, Mike St. John, Tommy Catlow, Alastair Mars, none were strangers to me, we were introduced by our 'Teacher Captain', Lieutenant Commander H.P. de C. Steel, to Reggie Darke (Rear Admiral, retired), the Captain of *Dolphin* for the whole of the war. He was shrewd and kindly, though a stickler for the rules and never to be taken lightly – only a fool would try to pull the wool over his eyes – and he gave us some wise words of encouragement after which we were entirely in Pat Steel's nurturing hands.

The course lasted five weeks, two at Blockhouse after which we moved to HMS *Cyclops* at Rothesay on the Clyde, depot ship of the Seventh (Training) Submarine Flotilla, for the remaining three weeks. It was intensive, high pressure work, in the attack teacher ashore in Blockhouse for the theory behind the tactics of carrying out a torpedo attack and initiation into the handling of the submarine, and then at sea in *Oberon* of the Seventh Flotilla for more advanced work and where all we had learnt in the safety of the attack teacher ashore was put to the acid test afloat. Opportunity was also found for practising gun actions and for instruction in the wider aspects of operating submarines in war. Occasionally we were interrupted at Blockhouse by air raids or a sudden call to take up duties to repel an expected invasion by German forces, and I also found time to enquire into what had happened to my beloved 3-litre Bentley, left in one of the wardroom lock-up garages when I had 'gone to war' in *Osiris* in August 1939. All I could discover was that the garages had been cleared on the outbreak of war for the stowage of submarine spare gear and the car had been dumped on the playing fields. Alas, clearly it was no longer there, but more of this anon.

During our three weeks on the Clyde the Captain of *Oberon* (Lieutenant Commander E.F. Pizey) must have had his heart in his mouth on many occasions as the embryo student CO, temporarily in charge of his treasured submarine, floundered about trying to get into the right position for a successful attack, submerged by day or on the surface at night; but Bertie Pizey and Pat Steel had a wonderful 'modus vivendi' and neither of them ever appeared unduly disturbed or flustered. Between them they got us all successfully and happily through the course. It had been an enjoyable and light-hearted five weeks.

By the end of February we were formally declared to have qualified for command of submarines, and with a short address from Captain S/M Seven (Captain R.L.M. Edwards) we went our separate ways. 'Sluggy' Edwards's final parting advice, 'Knowledge is the key to Life', delivered in his deep, sonorous voice, seemed particularly appropriate to our survival in war ('know your enemy') and his words have remained with me ever since.

Chapter Nine

First Commands, 1941–42

With the 'Perisher' successfully behind me, my thoughts and hopes naturally began to look ahead to the day when I might get command of an operational submarine, but first I had to have an apprenticeship in command of one of the small 'H' class submarines belonging to the Seventh Flotilla and normally engaged full-time on training duties. There were no immediate vacancies available at the end of February 1941, so my fellow 'perishers' were relegated to the humdrum appointment of 'Spare CO', either in *Cyclops* at Rothesay on the island of Bute in the Clyde, or at one of the other bases dotted round the country devoted to the anti-submarine training of the ever growing number of corvettes, frigates, destroyers, so desperately needed for the Battle of the Atlantic. Spare COs were held ready to step in and take command should any existing CO go sick or not otherwise be available to go to sea.

But even this did not seem to be coming my way. I received a telephone call direct from Northways in London, it was explained there was a sudden and unforeseen shortage of experienced first lieutenants in home-based submarines and, it was emphasised, with *no* reflection on how I had done in the 'Perisher', I was being temporarily appointed as No. 1 of *Otway*, then refitting at Newcastle-on-Tyne. It would only be for a fortnight or so. Obviously, there was no option and so I found myself back again with the old and decrepit 'O' class, and who was to be my Captain, none other than 'Ginger' Harvey again. It was like old times, but *Otway* in dry-dock in the middle of a long refit, and Newcastle suffering nightly air raids, was not my idea of life post-'Perisher'. Fortunately, it did not last long and in under two weeks I was back as one of the spare COs in the Seventh Flotilla.

Cyclops, swinging endlessly round her buoy in Rothesay Bay, was a peaceful haven despite the constant comings and goings of her attached submarines. She was old, uncomfortable and none-too-clean, without any of the modern frills and facilities which *Medway*, *Forth* and *Maidstone* provided as fully equipped submarine depot ships. Nevertheless, she fulfilled an essential task of looking after a mixed bag of ancient World War I 'H' and 'L' class submarines and such others as *Oberon*, no longer regarded as fit for operational patrols and hence consigned to training duties only. The wardroom was a contrasting mixture of young submariners itching to get on and get to sea operationally and of the depot ship's officers, largely the 'old and not-so-bold'; called back from retired life to serve through the duration of the war, they were quite content to see it out in a 'quiet number' unlikely to move from its moorings in a sheltered bay on the Firth of Clyde.

Rothesay itself had little to offer in the way of recreation or relaxation. Its life generally seemed to be run by its landladies, who had normally depended for their livelihood on summer holiday visitors and although these had now dried up, they had a stranglehold on everything that went on, extending to the extortionate charges they tried to levy on those in the flotilla fortunate enough to have a wife or sweetheart able to accompany them. A long and involved railway journey, culminating in an infrequent ferry service from the little port of Fairlie on the other side of the Clyde, did not add to Rothesay's attractions or accessibility. Relationships with the 'locals' tended, in consequence, to be strained but were prevented from reaching abysmal depths by the daily presence on board of the heir to the Marquis of Bute, sole owner of the whole island. Enrolled as one of the depot ship's watch-keeping cypher officers, with a subordinate rank in the RNVR, and always on hand when the wardroom bar was open, he was able to pour oil on troubled waters, and was often called on to do so.

The little 'H' boats of the Flotilla were scattered around ports and harbours on the West coast of Scotland and in Northern Ireland, such as Tobermory, Ardrishaig, Campbeltown, Londonderry. They seldom saw their mother ship and led a hard life. Living on board permanently under very cramped, crowded and uncomfortable conditions, with only the most primitive washing and laundry facilities, their crews saw the rough end of things but never allowed their standards to drop; moreover, they never served together for long, being constantly subject to the disruption of drafting changes as individuals moved on, vital links in the ever-moving chain of officers and ratings passing through the training machine. They were given an essential breath of the sea in the Seventh Flotilla, and then moved on to become the crews of the increasing numbers of new 'T', 'S' and 'U' class submarines now beginning to pour out of the country's submarine-building yards.

My first venture in command nearly ended in disaster. After twiddling my thumbs as one of the spare COs in 'Cycle-box', as *Cyclops* was generally known, I was suddenly sent to Campbeltown to take temporary command of H28 whilst her captain, Lieutenant L.W. A. Bennington, attended an investiture in London and had a few days well-deserved leave. Ben was a very old friend, a 'sparring partner' of many a run ashore in the old days of the Second Flotilla, in the piping times of peace, and I was delighted to take over from him, albeit temporarily, what I knew would be a well-run and happy ship. We sailed the next morning, a Saturday, for Londonderry, from where for the next week H28 was due to act as 'clockwork mouse' for the Escort Forces based there. Our voyage across to Lough Foyle was uneventful, apart from having to ask our escort, a World War I 'S' class destroyer under the command of Lieutenant Peter Gretton, RN – later to become one of the most successful and efficient Escort Force Commanders in the Battle of the Atlantic – to sink a floating mine which had passed horribly close down our side. By evening H28 was safely secured alongside, up river in the heart of the city, but not until a strong flood tide had given me a few heart-stopping moments as it threatened to sweep us under the Craigavon Bridge as we strove to turn in the narrow channel and face downstream.

I was glad to have the Sunday as a quiet day in harbour, to take stock of my first command and to learn our orders for the next week's exercises. That evening we dropped down river and secured to a mooring buoy in Lough Foyle, off Moville, to be all ready for an early start on the Monday morning, 10th March.

By 4 a.m. H28 was under way, proceeding northwards down Lough Foyle, heading for the A/S training exercise areas in the open sea. It was a dark but clear night and, as was customary in the narrow channels of Lough Foyle, ships under way were showing navigation lights. About fifteen minutes later there were seen, fine·on H28's starboard bow, the navigation lights of a steamer proceeding up-channel, on an almost directly opposite course to H28; to those on the latter's bridge it appeared that, although the steamer was on the wrong side of the channel ("keep to the starboard side when going with the flood tide!"), if she held her course she would safely pass down H28's starboard side. Suddenly the very worst happened. Only a few hundred yards distant the steamer altered course violently to starboard, heading across H28's bows, rather than straight at us. It was immediately obvious to me that a collision was inevitable, but there was a fleeting chance to ensure that we would hit her rather than she plough straight through our slender hull. H28 went 'full astern' but there was not time to take all way off the submarine before our bows crumpled into the port side of the steamer, about twenty feet abaft her stem. It was a sickening, frightening moment as H28 shuddered and reeled back, my mind overwhelmed by a sense of total catastrophe, for which I, and only I, could be responsible; quickly relieved as reports from below indicated there was no internal damage and the submarine's watertight integrity was intact and no-one had been hurt. But our bows were bent and the front doors to the torpedo tubes were inoperable, and clearly we were not fit for sea and for the planned week's exercises. With our tail between our legs we shamefacedly returned up-river to Londonderry to await further orders for our repair.

There I made contact with our adversary, the S.S. *Lairdsbank* of the Burns Laird Line. She had been on her routine nightly run between Glasgow and Londonderry and was undamaged, barely aware that there had been 'an incident'. To this day I believe that she had never really seen H28 and had made her crucial alteration of course solely to regain her correct side of the channel, unaware of how close she came to running down and sinking a British submarine. It was a merciful escape for H28 and all on board her.

The next day orders came to sail that evening for Belfast, and on arrival

H43

there the following morning H28 was taken in hand for repairs in the shipyard of Harland and Wolff. On 16th March Ben returned from London, to reclaim his precious but now battered command. Fortunately, we saw things alike, that H28 had survived we viewed as a cause for celebration not for recrimination. It took more than a few days to complete all the formalities of the Board of Inquiry into the collision, so we had ample opportunity for happy days and nights exploring the pubs and bars of Belfast. Our 'runs-ashore' together were reminiscent of more carefree days in the past than of what was to come to Belfast in the future.

But soon I was summoned to Northways, to give my account of events, there were no dire or lasting consequences and I heard that my next appointment, to command H43 in mid-April, would stand. Meanwhile, I could go home on leave, in a final interview Max Horton briefly adjured me "not to do it again". So ended my first venture in command of a submarine, how lucky I was, things could have gone, or been, so much worse, and no doubt had it been peace-time the matter would have been treated differently. I could only hope and pray that I would never again be confronted by similar circumstances. To this day recollection of those vital, crucial moments in Lough Foyle gives me the shivers.

H43 was in the final stages of a major refit in Sheerness Dockyard when, on the 14th April, I relieved Lieutenant J.S. Huddart in command. Johnnie, who had been in *Orpheus* in the Fourth Flotilla in China when I was in *Rainbow*, never allowed life to lie too heavily on his shoulders and our turnover was completed in a matter of minutes. He had other pressing

Admiral Max Horton (right) and the First Lord of the Admiralty Mr A. V. Alexander, 1942.

engagements in mind, doubtless in pursuit of the fair sex. Sadly, it was the last I was to see of him, within the year he had been lost when in command of *Triumph* in the Mediterranean.

Sheerness Dockyard, with years of experience behind them, were past masters in the art of refitting small submarines, but they ran into trouble with H43. Preliminary sea trials appeared satisfactory but mechanical problems in her diesels then developed, which delayed by a week the final completion of the refit; there then followed days spent 'wiping', de-gaussing and noise-ranging, essential measures to be taken before venturing wider afield into the Thames estuary and beyond, where bottom-laid German magnetic and acoustic mines were a permanent dangerous threat.

Eventually all was pronounced satisfactory and on 11th May H43 left the dockyard for good, moving across to Southend-on-Sea to join a convoy of merchant ships sailing that evening for Methil, the convoy assembly point on the Firth of Forth. There were no excitements during the passage up the East coast through 'Bomb Alley', the weather remained fair, and H43 met no problems in steaming quietly along on the surface, keeping station astern of the long, straggling line of ships, constantly herded, chivvied and rounded up by the mixed escort of destroyers, trawlers and motor launches. The forty-eight hour trip gave everyone on board a wonderful opportunity to settle down, get to know their submarine and exercise essential drills, even if diving was precluded except in the event of an emergency encounter with the enemy. Luckily the latter never occurred. The nearest we came to it was when, off the Yorkshire or Northumbrian coast, an elderly Avro Anson of Coastal Command returning from a reconnaissance flight over the North Sea suddenly appeared out of the clouds directly over the convoy; every gun, rifle, rocket-launcher throughout the long line of ships immediately opened fire wildly, regardless of the aircraft being plainly British. Rumour subsequently had it that it came down in the sea some way off the track of the convoy and its crew had been picked up by one of the escorts. Whether this was true or not, H43 and her, as yet untrained, crew had witnessed a prime example of how 'trigger happy' those in the East Coast convoys could become. It was salutary.

From the Firth of Forth onwards, for the long journey through the Pentland Firth round the North of Scotland, to Tobermory in the Island of Mull whither H43 was bound, we no longer had the 'protection' of a convoy and sailed independently, but under the escort of an A/S Trawler, HMS *Jason* whose primary task was to ward off possible attack by 'friendly forces'. All too often these were inclined to be oblivious of the fact that a submarine steaming peacefully on the surface in those waters need not necessarily be a U-boat to be set upon immediately. It was accepted practice that no Allied submarine be allowed to make surface passage between ports around the United Kingdom unless under the close escort of a surface vessel; experience had shown how very essential it was to have such safeguards.

By the time H43 arrived at Tobermory, late on the evening of Friday, 16th May 1941, her ship's company, officers and men, had advanced from a bunch of largely raw, untrained submariners leaving Sheerness a week earlier into a well-drilled and efficient team now capable of all that would be required of them in their impending role of 'clockwork mouse', or even, if need be, in meeting the demands of an offensive operational patrol. It was remarkable what had been achieved from a few days at sea under the prevailing conditions of war, though undisturbed by any form of active hostilities. I could not help feeling satisfied by the transformation that had taken place.

Tobermory was the base from which Commodore, Western Isles, imposed his dynamic and iron will on every newly commissioned ship – destroyer, frigate, sloop, corvette, trawler, motor launch – about to join the Western Approaches Command; in a matter of a few weeks they were turned into disciplined fighting units fit and ready to play a full part in the Battle of the Atlantic, that never-ending war against the U-boat. He had a reputation for the unorthodox, any emergency drill or surprise evolution was liable to be sprung on the new arrival, at any hour of the day or night, and woe betide those caught napping or unprepared. It was enough to scare the daylights out of any young and inexperienced C.O. It was therefore with some trepidation that I berthed H43 alongside HMS *Western Isles*, the very headquarters of the redoubtable Commodore (Vice Admiral (retired) Sir Gilbert Stephenson), known to all who passed through his hands as 'The Terror of Tobermory'.

In the event, I had nothing to fear. He knew little of submarines and of how they functioned, and provided that *without fail* they met all that he required of them for the training of his surface ships, he largely left them to their own devices. Normally they were entirely in the hands of a comparatively senior submarine commander, responsible for all submarine affairs which he ran from the ancient, tiny depot ship *Alecto*, a relic of World War I if ever there was one, but still adequate for looking after the two or three 'H' boats allocated to the Western Isles training task. At the time of H43's visit *Alecto* and Commander Robin Gambier were absent, somewhere on the Clyde for *Alecto's* routine maintenance and docking; thus I suddenly found myself SSO (Senior Submarine Officer), totally unexpected and something I had never imagined. To make sure I was on the right 'wavelength' with the Commodore, I invited him to walk through H43. To the surprise of his staff, and me, he accepted and it was an exhilarating and eclectic half hour, ensuring a happy future relationship.

No sooner was his inspection over than H43 was detached to Oban for the week-end, to re-fuel. It was strange to see an ordinary road-tanker drive on to the jetty to deliver the diesel fuel, but in *Alecto's* absence it was the simplest way to replenish and it gave submarines a welcome break from the rigours of Tobermory. No-one would claim that Oban was the most exciting of ports to visit, but it opened its doors hospitably to the very few HM ships that ever had occasion to berth alongside its neat and tidy jetties, still redolent of the fish that in days of peace were their main 'raison d'être'.

For the next two weeks H43 was totally involved in the regular training routine followed by the ships 'working up' at Tobermory. At sea from Monday to Friday, with long hours dived in the exercise areas to the west of Mull, whilst being 'hunted and attacked' by an endless succession of embryo escorts, who made full use of the lengthy daylight hours of those summer months. There was scant relief when darkness brought proceedings to a temporary halt, barely time to retire to a remote anchorage in the south-west corner of Mull to recharge batteries, before off to sea again for the next day's round of exercises.

We were too busy to be bored and time passed quickly, the week-ends alongside *Western Isles* in Tobermory were uninterrupted by the Commodore and we were permitted to relax. H43 had been joined by another 'H' boat, whose captain was my fellow 'perisher', Mike St. John. We found time for some hilarious days, and evenings, ashore together, ably abetted by Rosie Gambier, who, in her husband's absence, was determined to see that we would not fail for entertainment ashore in Tobermory, whether this be trout fishing in the local lochs or wilder parties throughout the long evenings in her hospitable home where she maintained 'open house' to all and sundry.

There was a flurry of excitement at the end of May, coinciding with a week-end in harbour. It started badly with the devastating news of the sinking of HMS *Hood*. Her sudden loss was a blow of staggering severity felt throughout the whole Navy, for she had epitomised so powerfully and glamorously everything that had gone into our upbringing and training. But, bitter though the blow was, it was immediately succeeded by the ferment of the hunt for her destroyer, the German battleship BISMARCK. There was even a moment when it seemed as if the two little 'H' boats from Tobermory would be deployed operationally on a patrol line to try to intercept her, but wiser counsels prevailed and it was soon decreed that for everyone at Tobermory A/S training should have priority and would continue as planned. I was not alone in feeling some sense of relief.

Early in June I had another telephone call from Northways, my relief was on his way and would be at Oban shortly. I was to join the large mine-laying submarine *Rorqual* at Devonport, for passage to Alexandria where I was appointed as one of the spare COs in the First Flotilla. It was thrilling news, with the added bonus of being told there would be time for a few days leave at home in Inverness before joining *Rorqual*. I was a happy man as I turned over H43 to my successor; to be going back to the Mediterranean was all I could wish for, for at that time it was where the war, for British submarines, was at its height and I wanted desperately to be in the thick of it.

Rorqual, when I joined her in Devonport, was temporarily home after a successful year in the Mediterranean under the command of 'Dogberry' Dewhurst, my former captain in *Seahorse*; with many fruitful minelays to her credit, she now had a new crew under Lieutenant L.W. Napier. We had a tranquil passage to Gibraltar, dived by day, on the surface at night and it was comforting to be once more on board a modern submarine fully equipped and trained for offensive operations, with, moreover, more space and better living conditions and food than the 'H' boats could provide.

After a brief pause at Gibraltar to embark vital stores for a Malta increasingly under siege – the main load was ammunition for the few RAF fighters that could be kept functioning on the island – life on board changed perceptibly. There was a natural reappearance of heightened tension, the stresses and strains concomitant with *Rorqual*'s return to being an integral part of the struggle raging throughout the length and breadth of the Mediterranean. Everyone on board was just that little bit more on their toes, on the 'qui vive'.

Malta vividly brought home just how much the war had intensified in the last six months; though the worst of the air bombardment by the German Air Force was yet to come, it was plain for all to see that there were likely to be very sticky times ahead. But the island was still an active base for offensive operations directed against the flow of supplies crossing the Mediterranean to maintain Rommel's armies in North Africa. A small striking force of cruisers and destroyers would be stationed there occasionally, whilst, more permanently, the number of 'U' class submarines grew steadily, soon to become the Tenth Submarine Flotilla. 'Shrimp' Simpson, his submarines and his small and highly dedicated staff were already having an effect out of all proportion to their small numbers on the enemy's vital supply lines across the central Mediterranean. To meet their needs Lazaretto on Manoel Island had now grown into a submarine base of immense significance, which in itself meant that in due course it became a major target for the Luftwaffe. During *Rorqual*'s fleeting visit I was lucky to be able to pick the brains of so many successful COs and to learn of their methods and techniques. It was inspiring to meet again old friends such as Dick Cayley (UTMOST), 'Wanks' (UPHOLDER), 'Tommo' (URGE), Teddy Woodward (UNBEATEN), Tony Collett (UNIQUE), but I missed the chance of seeing my Anson term-mate Johnny Wraith (UPRIGHT); he was out on patrol, adding to the flotilla's continuing record of success. He continued to serve in the Mediterranean until lost in *Trooper* towards the end of 1943, sadly our paths never directly crossed and I was never able to see him.

A week later *Rorqual* reached Alexandria and was reunited with the First Flotilla and *Medway*. I found I was the junior of three spare COs, the others being George Reynolds, who had been in China with me, and Ben Bennington, more recently seen in H28 in Belfast. Though we continually vied with each other whenever there seemed to be the slightest chance of a CO going sick or needing a rest, we remained on close and friendly terms, each with his own particular duty in the depot ship. I was especially lucky in being detailed off to be the full-time assistant to the Flotilla's Staff Officer (Operations), working in *Medway*'s palatial Operations Room, which was in effect the nerve centre of all Allied submarine operations in the Mediterranean. It was directly and closely linked to the staff and headquarters of the Commander-in-Chief. It was a wonderful opportunity to be at the very heart of things and learn accordingly; fleet operation orders and directives, intelligence reports of every description, individual submarine's patrol orders and their subsequent detailed patrol reports, a constant flow of signals, in essence all the paperwork lying behind what the submarine actually achieved at sea, all was there for my education. There was a colossal wealth of information to be gleaned from every conceivable source, I was fascinated by it all and time never hung heavy on my hands. In addition, the Staff Office was the place where the COs of submarines in from patrol gathered daily and exchanged views and gossip. I gained much from being privy to all this and was encouraged by my boss, 'Hairy' Browne, and the SO (O) (Lieut. Comdr. H.C. Browne, lately CO of *Regent* in the First Flotilla) to play a full part in everything that went on.

I had been engaged on this enthralling job for about two months, by which time I knew well all the COs of the Flotilla and their exploits, when, one morning in mid-October a signal arrived from Captain (S) Ten in Malta saying he required immediately a CO to take command of *Thrasher*, who, though belonging to the First Flotilla, was at that time lying in Malta, replenishing between patrols. 'Hairy' Browne handed me the signal and told me to take it in to Captain (S) One (Captain S.M. Raw) who would decide which of his three spare COs he would send. 'Hairy' also told me to be sure to see that a bottle of champagne, in actual fact the very last on board in the wardroom, was delivered to the Captain's cabin whilst I was there with the signal. It duly arrived just as Sammy Raw was about to give his decision, which, to my delight, was that I was to go. How great a part that bottle played in his making up his mind I know not, but we wasted no time in opening it. As an omen of good fortune I got hold of its cork and still have it with me.

After dark that night I boarded a Sunderland flying boat of 201 Group, RAF at its base in Aboukir Bay. By midnight we were winging our way towards Malta; keeping well clear of land it was an uneventful flight, and for me, the sole passenger, an unexpectedly comfortable one. Just as dawn was breaking we smoothly came to rest in Marsa Scirocco, Malta.

I was in Manoel Island for breakfast and then met 'Shrimp' Simpson who explained that Joe Cowell, *Thrasher*'s present captain, was in need of a rest and, as she was required to go on patrol within a few days, he had no option but to ask Captain (S) One to send a relief. Our turnover was quickly effected, though not without some embarrassment. Joe felt that he had been unnecessarily sacked, and it was fortunate that, together, we could recall the happier occasion when I had relieved him as No. 1 of Reserve Group 'B' at Blockhouse a few months before the war.

Joe had a lucky 'break' that night; he was a passenger in the same Sunderland that had brought me from Alexandria, now continuing its onward journey to Gibraltar and eventually England. Whilst taking off from Marsa Scirocco one of its four engines fell off, bringing it to a nerve-shattering and undignified halt. Fortunately, there was no other serious damage, nor was anyone hurt, and once the engine had been replaced it was able to try again. This time all went well and Joe got safely back to England.

Events had moved so fast for the few days around the 12th October 1941, the date when I was formally appointed in command, that I was more than thankful to have a week in harbour to catch my breath and come to terms with what had hit me. *Thrasher* had commissioned in the spring of 1941, completed her work-up at home by mid-June and joined the First Flotilla in early July. She should have been in prime fettle, but she was not. Her crew had become unsettled by lack of success on the patrols so far carried out in the Mediterranean and her one notable exploit, the rescue of Allied soldiers, mainly Australians and New Zealanders, and a few Greek civilians from the south coast of Crete in the third week of July, an additional 78 people living on board for a few days, had not alleviated their concerns. They were unhappy and I could see the first task was to weld them into an efficient and contented team.

Built by Cammell Lairds at Birkenhead, *Thrasher* was one of the last batch of "T" class to have rivetted as opposed to welded pressure hulls and she was one of the very few with Sulzer 2-stroke diesel engines – which proved virtually trouble free for this, her first, commission and ran as smoothly and quietly as a pair of sewing machines, in contrast to the clattering, noisy

HMS *Thrasher* going on patrol from Alexandria, 1942.

4-stroke engines of Vickers or Admiralty design in most of the other 'T's. With six internal and five external torpedo tubes and carrying a total load of seventeen 21" torpedoes, and a very effective four-inch gun, she had a formidable armament. Quick to dive, easy to handle, I thought her a superb submarine; in the months ahead I grew very fond of her and her crew, establishing with the latter a relationship that has endured in the case of some individuals for over fifty years.

On the evening of the 20th October 1941, *Thrasher* slipped from her berth alongside Lazaretto and headed out to sea for her fifth Mediterranean war patrol. It was a momentous occasion. I knew her crew would be summing me up and wondering if I was up to it and would bring them a change of fortune; inwardly I was nervous and anxious, but very much aware that this must never be allowed to show and that an appearance of complete confidence was essential. Fortunately, our orders were straightforwardly simple, conduct a patrol off Benghazi, a major supply port for the German and Italian armies in Libya, and sink what shipping we could – but be economical with torpedoes, which were in very short supply. It was lucky that *Thrasher's* previous patrol had been in that same area and that she had gathered an invaluable amount of information about the Italian minefields laid to defend the port, and the 'swept channels' leading through them; so we were well briefed as to where best to patrol to intercept shipping and where not to trespass because of known or suspected minefields.

From 23rd October to 5th November constant watch was kept on the approaches to Benghazi; shoal water, minefields, surface and air anti-submarine patrols were the day-to-day hazards, compounded by a low lying

Self in command of *Thrasher* 1942, taken on board *Medway*.

desert shore bereft of identifiable marks as aids to navigation, apart from "3 palms conspic." shown on the chart on the coastline south of Benghazi. The dome of Benghazi Cathedral was the other exception, by far the most conspicuous object to be seen through the periscope. We soon established that the main swept channel to and from the port ran on a north-westerly line, exactly 311 degrees, from the cathedral. Daily a force of Italian minesweepers came out from the harbour and swept to seaward along this channel, for twelve to fifteen miles; nearly daily also *Thrasher*, from the opposite direction, having spent the night further off shore on the surface re-charging batteries, slowly advanced down the channel towards the harbour, dodging the motley collection of sweepers whilst not straying into the minefields on either side. The latter were clearly discernible when operating the Mine Detection Unit (MDU) fitted to the submarine's Type 129 Asdic set. I was not usually in favour of using the MDU or convinced of the reliability of the contacts it reported – too often they just served to scare one – but in the particular case of this patrol where it consistently picked up the minute echoes from mines and delineated the extent of the minefields, the value of its carefully directed and modulated transmissions far exceeded any possible danger arising from their being intercepted by the enemy. Our very lives depended on its use.

The constant playing of a game of 'cat and mouse' with the enemy's anti-submarine and minesweeping forces, the accuracy of navigation required, the avoidance of detection, in generally calm and therefore to us unfavourable weather conditions, was all of immense training value to everyone on board *Thrasher*, not least to me in using the periscope when enemy vessels were within hundreds of yards.

But this game never produced any targets worthy of attack by torpedo or gun so *Thrasher* had to look elsewhere. On the 28th October whilst patrolling well to seaward of the end of the swept channel a large (800 ton) three-masted Italian schooner was encountered, sailing slowly towards Benghazi; deciding it was big enough to warrant a torpedo, one was fired from close range at what seemed to be such an easy, simple target. This was the first torpedo I had ever fired in anger, and of course it missed. But it must have passed close to the target and its track been sighted, for great alarm and confusion was apparent on board. All sails came down with a run, boats were lowered, the crew abandoned ship and started to pull furiously towards distant Benghazi. I was a bit suspicious; it was all too reminiscent of how the crews of 'Q' ships in World War I were trained to behave whilst trying to deceive an enemy submarine, so the target was closely inspected through the periscope before *Thrasher* surfaced and disposed of it with an economical nine rounds from her gun. The sixth round exploded the schooner into a violent conflagration. There seemed no doubt that it was carrying a cargo of petrol or similar fuel.

There were two more opportunities for offensive action during the patrol but they brought no success. A convoy of small ships sighted at night on 1st

November escaped unscathed. On 2nd November an Italian CROTONE class minelayer, a small, shallow draught craft already spotted on several occasions, presented itself as too tempting a target to be ignored, whilst it moved slowly and spasmodically apparently reinforcing the existing minefields. Under ideal conditions for a submerged torpedo attack *Thrasher* stalked her quarry and from within easy range fired two torpedoes, they either missed or ran under the unsuspecting target. There was an ineffective reaction, the minelayer suddenly coming to life and charging wildly around, dropping thirteen depth charges, none at all close so we got off lightly in our baptism of fire, the first depth-charges we had experienced.

No more encounters with the enemy occurred beyond the daily sightings of patrolling aircraft and A/S (anti-submarine) or minesweeping vessels, and on 8th November *Thrasher* returned to Malta, for further work by the dockyard on the firing mechanism of her external torpedo tubes, which had been empty and out of action since early October. My superiors seemed content with the way this patrol, my very first, had been conducted, except that they told me I had been too profligate with torpedoes. None of the targets I had attacked were worth the expenditure of such valuable weapons. For myself, I had gained much in confidence from being so constantly in contact with such a variety of enemy forces, and where necessary evading them, and I felt happier about my crew who throughout some tense and trying times had met every turn of events impeccably.

During our post-patrol stay in Malta, Max Horton (Admiral Commanding Submarines) came out from London to see for himself how his submarines were faring in the Mediterranean. 'Shrimp' Simpson fixed it that most of his Tenth Flotilla were in harbour for the few days of the great man's visit and took steps to see that the three submarines of the First Flotilla (*Trusty, Thrasher* and *Rorqual*) also present, were equally included in the festivities, meetings and proceedings. It was a great three days and Max Horton's words of encouragement, which included a special message from Winston Churchill, gave our morale a tremendous boost. I have not forgotten how he adjured 'Shrimp' to treat his submarine captains with the same care and attention accorded to winners of the Derby. We enthusiastically latched on to this new role of being 'Derby winners'.

Sam MacGregor, 'Shrimp's' Engineer Officer, utterly imperturbable and unflappable, but quite unapproachable at breakfast, was the bearer of some good tidings for me personally. It will be recalled that during my 'perisher' I had learnt that my treasured old Bentley had last been seen dumped on the playing fields at Blockhouse. Sam, himself one of the greatest of Bentley enthusiasts, had been Senior Engineer in *Dolphin* when war broke out and he now told me that he had found my car abandoned in September 1939. He had rescued it and had arranged with an old lady living in a house on the outskirts of Fareham that it be lodged for the duration in a wooden shed in her garden. This slip of good news, so strangely at odds with all the trauma and destruction of war currently afflicting Malta, shone like a ray of sunshine; how typical it was of Sam to prosecute to a successful end whatever needed to be done to cope with any particular situation, forseen or unforeseen. In sterner ways he proved this again and again in the testing days ahead for the Tenth Flotilla.

After embarking a party of Yugoslavs who had flown in from Egypt the night before, as fierce and frightening a gang of desperadoes as one could ever wish not to have to meet on a dark night, *Thrasher* sailed from Malta on 22nd November bound for the Adriatic. Her orders were to land her passengers in two separate operations on the coast of Yugoslavia, and to attack enemy shipping as and when opportunity offered.

Diving deep through the Straits of Otranto on 24th November we reconnoitred the next day the approaches to the port of Brindisi. Heavy rainstorms prevented much being seen in the morning, but in clearer weather in the afternoon a small convoy of three ships was attacked, the leading ship being torpedoed and sunk. Further attacks on the remaining ships, which had stopped, were thwarted by the arrival of A/S forces from Brindisi. Though they hunted around assiduously their intermittent depth-charging was never close enough to worry *Thrasher*, who quietly withdrew from the area, crossing over the Adriatic with the intention of carrying out the first of the two special operations after dark the following night.

In this operation, two agents were to be landed; the leader, Stanislav Rapotec, was one of the bravest, toughest and most loyal men I have ever met. He was a 'Mihailovich man', a royalist, and thus unfortunately on the losing side of all the various factions engaged in resisting the German occupation of Yugoslavia. He survived the war and some hair-raising, incredible exploits, but he was never allowed to return finally to his native country. He became a successful artist and made his home in Australia.

In the event, just as Stan and his partner were on the point of getting into their canoes to go ashore, an urgent signal was received cancelling the entire special operation and ordering *Thrasher* to leave the Adriatic and establish a patrol line with the submarines of the The Tenth Flotilla in the Gulf of Taranto. Continuous gales, mountainous seas and overcast skies inhibited accurate navigation and the exact whereabouts of our consorts on the patrol line were an unrelenting problem, let alone our own position vis-a-vis the enemy minefields known to have been laid to guard the approaches to the main Italian naval base of Taranto. The patrol line had been formed to intercept heavy units of the Italian fleet expected to be leaving or returning to their base. The weather was so adverse that periscope watch by day could not be kept and most of the time had to be spent deep, whilst at night it was a question of heading into the seas at slow speed whilst trying to keep binoculars as dry as possible and maintain a good look-out. Even the 'Ursula Suits', oiled waterproof jackets and trousers, the brainchild of George Phillips, captain of *Ursula* at Blyth in the early days of the war and the forerunner of the present day popular 'Barbours', could not be guaranteed to keep one dry under the constant deluge of water cascading over the bridge. The 'bird-bath', rigged in the control room to trap the flood of water coming down the conning tower, was always in use. In the circumstances it was not surprising that no contact was made with the enemy.

It was a disappointing end to a patrol that had started auspiciously and had promised much, had we been allowed to remain in the Adriatic. For those embarked for the special operations it must have been more than frustrating. I had nothing but praise for their cheerfulness and their readiness to co-operate in any way with the running of the submarine during their enforced and prolonged stay on board. They must have been glad when they could see the light of day once more and get out of their crowded, damp quarters on *Thrasher*'s return to Alexandria on the 13th December.

The year 1941 ended with little in the way of Christmas or New Year holidays and there was much gloom all round. *Prince of Wales* and *Repulse* had been sunk by the Japanese who seemed to be carrying all before them, Singapore looked to be the next casualty, there was stalemate in the Western Desert and the German-Italian stranglehold on surface operations in the Mediterranean seemed tighter than ever. Only the submarines were carrying the war to the enemy.

On Christmas Eve *Thrasher* passed southbound through the Suez Canal and on the morning of Christmas Day she entered a dry-dock at Suez for routine maintenance and quick 'bottom-scrub'. Once the dock had been pumped dry all on board could settle down to the customary festivities, but the precaution was taken to batten down all but one of the hatches, the only access from or to the submarine being via the conning tower, at the top of which was a trustworthy sentry with orders to allow no one on deck, lest he fall into the bottom of the hard, concrete dock. Everyone made the most of this brief respite from the war and of their saved up 'tots' in celebrating Christmas Day in these peculiar circumstances. I was greatly relieved that my worst fears of some untoward accident never materialised, by next day everything on board was back to normal.

My earlier anxieties on taking over command had been dispelled by the end of the year and I felt confident that the ship's company, under the firm hand of the Coxswain (CPO Lamport), were solidly behind me and were capable of anything likely to be asked of them; except for illness or some unforeseen 'drafting' crisis they were likely to remain together for the rest of the commission, perhaps another year. But this last point did not apply to the officers, amongst whom there was constant change with first lieutenants and third and fourth hands ever on the move, to take up new appointments to fulfil the needs of an expanding submarine fleet, and to fill the gaps caused by increasing losses. Since October four new third hands and fourth hands had joined. Lieutenants I.S. McIntosh, J.N. Elliott and A.G. Davies and Sub-Lieutenant R.P. Fitzgerald. Ian McIntosh, as yet barely recovered from his epic voyage in an open lifeboat across the Atlantic as a survivor from a ship sunk by a German surface raider, in due course relieved Peter Roberts as No. 1. Bill Elliott had joined for special training, coming straight into submarines with three other officers from being destroyer first lieutenants, an emergency measure to offset a forecast shortage of No. 1s and hence potential submarine COs. In time he relieved Ian as No. 1 and both he and Reggie Fitzgerald saw out the commission.

Thrasher returned to Alexandria in time to sail for her next patrol on New Year's Day 1942. Once more she was destined for the Gulf of Taranto, having to make a surface dash into the teeth of a north-westerly gale to get there by the 6th January, to form a patrol line with the Polish submarine *Sokol* and *Unbeaten* both from the Tenth Flotilla. Nothing was seen of the reported force of an Italian battleship, cruisers and destroyers and after three days of patrolling in southerly gales, execrable weather, we were released with orders to patrol an area covering the south-eastern approaches to the Straits of Otranto, a move that brought good fortune.

Soon after midnight on the 9th/10th January, as *Thrasher* patrolled on the surface across the likely route of shipping moving north or south through the eastern part of the Ionian Sea, the cry of "Captain on the bridge" had me there in a flash. One of the look-outs had sighted two dark shapes just visible on the northern horizon and the officer of the watch had already altered course towards them. The night was stormy with boisterous seas but a fitful moon suggested there might be enough light to complete an attack submerged on what, as we closed the range, could soon be seen to be a southbound heavily laden merchant ship of about 5,000 tons, with a smaller escorting vessel zig-zagging across its track about a thousand yards ahead of it. Accordingly *Thrasher* dived when in a favourable position, but almost immediately the moon chose to disappear behind dark storm clouds and nothing could be seen through the periscope, nor could the target's H.E. (hydrophone effect, i.e. noise of propellers) be heard clearly enough to aim torpedoes. Therefore the only course to retrieve this mistake of thinking a dived attack would be practicable, was to allow the target to pass, then surface and set off in pursuit and to gain a position far enough ahead from which the attack could be completed on the surface.

It was exciting work. Whilst keeping the two ships clearly visible through binoculars and remaining far enough off to ensure that they did not see us, at full speed we slowly overhauled them, the merchant ship on a steady course, the escort ahead weaving widely from side to side. After two hours *Thrasher* had reached a favourable attacking position on the target's starboard bow and she turned in on to a firing course, slowing down to avoid getting in too close. As it was, the escort, at the right-hand extreme of its zig-zag pattern, passed only six hundred yards ahead of *Thrasher* who, practically stopped, kept bows on to her. I held my breath, thinking it inevitable that we would be seen, but no – not as yet. As the escort moved away, turning on to the left-hand leg of her weave, I concentrated attention on the merchant ship, coming along steadily for a close range shot on a broad track. Two minutes later the escort belatedly sighted us and, firing an alarm signal of a brilliant white Very's light, started to turn towards us; hurriedly fining up the angle of attack to a sixty degree track there was time to fire four torpedoes, though the prevailing sea and swell, coupled with our slow speed, only just sufficient to maintain steerage, made aiming difficult. By now the escort was heading our way at speed but as we dived there was the satisfying sound of the torpedoes hitting the target, to be followed by confirmatory 'breaking-up' noises as it sank. The escort's counter-attack was no worry, none of the twenty depth-charges it dropped being close, and although it hunted around for two hours it never got near us.

On the 16th January we were ordered back into the Gulf of Taranto to form a patrol line with *Upholder* and *Una*, twenty-five miles further into the Gulf than before. This time the weather was kinder, but again there was no contact with the enemy. The only noteworthy incident was communicating by Asdic, when submerged, with our neighbour, *Upholder*, at a range of eight miles. There was not often an opportunity to use the Asdic set for under-water signalling (S.S/T as it is known) between submarines, but favourable conditions on this occasion showed how useful it could be, not only for passing messages between the two submarines, but also for confirming their geographical positions relative to each other. Apart from this chatting to *Upholder* there was nothing to relieve the monotonous patrol. After four such days *Thrasher* was recalled to Alexandria, arriving there on the 25th January. Bad weather had persisted throughout the patrol, the barometer never rising above 1000 millibars between the 5th and 23rd, and but for our success on the 10th it would have been a dreary and dispiriting three weeks. We were lucky to have had that one fleeting opportunity.

Since her days in the building yard a small colony of rats had lived in comparative peace and harmony on board *Thrasher* but as their numbers increased they became a more obtrusive nuisance. Their depredations on stores and provisions were becoming more evident, and then there was 'Fred'. He regularly travelled the length of the submarine inside the ventilation trunking, poking his head through the 'punkah-louvres' and willingly accepting the tit-bits offered him in each mess that he visited, but now grown so fat that he could no longer get out. He was tolerable, but one night, lying on my bunk fully dressed except for my boots – only half asleep, as always in anticipation of the nerve-shattering cry of "Captain on the bridge" – I became aware of an unusual, sharp pricking sensation on one of my feet. Switching on the reading lamp at the head of my bunk I spied a half-grown rat sampling my left big toe; totally engrossed in this he failed to notice that I was awake and about to take action. Being comparatively agile in those days I was able, by a sudden, quick 'jack-knife' movement, to grab him by the tail and like lightning I was out of my cabin, up the conning tower one-handed and he was over the side of the bridge in an instant. What passed through the minds of those on watch in the control room and on the bridge I have no idea, probably that the skipper had gone off his head. I immediately enlightened them as to the true cause of my mad rush to the bridge, and subsequently decided it was time to get rid of these 'passengers'. So when in harbour alongside *Medway* the submarine was shut down and fumigated for twenty-four hours. We never saw a rat again, nor smelt or discovered any trace of them, not even Fred. Had they in some way become aware of their impending fate and evacuated the submarine in time? Nobody will ever know.

Chapter Ten

Thrasher at War, 1942

By the early months of 1942, the Mediterranean Fleet had been so reduced by war losses and by despatch of much of its strength to counter expected Japanese advances in the Indian Ocean that it no longer controlled the central Mediterranean, that area so vital to the Axis powers for the transport of troops and supplies for their armies in North Africa. The Italian fleet, while still 'in being' and remaining very much of a threat, was not the sole arbiter of who controlled these waters, the German and Italian air forces reigned supreme. Without the use of airfields in Cyrenaica, that bulge of the North African coast immediately to the east of Benghazi, the RAF was powerless to provide the fighter cover essential for the operation of surface units of the Fleet aimed at disrupting the constant flow of enemy traffic from Italy and Greece to North Africa, with Tripoli in Libya the main port. Neither had the RAF itself the strength for offensive maritime operations, and so it was that the submarines of the First Flotilla based in Alexandria and of the Tenth Flotilla in Malta bore the brunt of attacking this traffic. The Eighth Flotilla based on *Maidstone* at Gibraltar was, as yet, barely in existence.

The small U-class submarines at Malta were ideally placed, having the main enemy traffic routes virtually on their doorstep. The larger submarines of the First Flotilla were mostly 'T' class, but with a few surviving 'O', 'P' and 'R' class, and had a much longer distance to go in order to find their targets, involving five or six days on passage to and from their patrol areas. For the submarines of both flotillas the standard routine was dived by day, on the surface at night, and nothing significant would be achieved unless they patrolled in the enemy's most heavily guarded waters. They could never allow themselves to be detected, either by being seen or heard, until they had declared their presence by firing torpedoes, with the then almost inevitable retaliation from an angry enemy. Success depended on luck, reliable prior intelligence, good anticipation of enemy movements and the attacking skills of the individual CO. We knew what we were up against and how crucial it was that attacks on the enemy's shipping be pressed home regardless of the strength of escorting forces. The dangers, the stresses, the strains of this deadly type of warfare were obvious to us all, and I do not believe that there was anyone who did not experience fear at times. But there was not one of us who were not proud to be likened to 'Derby Winners' and I was fortunate to have the finest of them amongst my friends, to share their experiences when we were in harbour together, to celebrate their triumphs, and when at sea to co-operate if we were in adjacent patrol billets, or, on unhappy occasions, to mourn their loss.

With the drama of her last patrol and its unexploded bombs firmly behind her, *Thrasher* left Alexandria at the end of March for the Gulf of Sirte, with the main object of intercepting the convoys of small ships known to be running between Tripoli and Benghazi. Her passage was rudely disturbed on the second night by an unprovoked attack by a Sunderland flying boat on anti-submarine patrol off the Libyan coast. A sudden stream of tracer bullets from a dark sky was the first indication, to be followed by two heavy explosions as we hurriedly dived. The over-eager perpetrator of this assault, which fortunately caused no damage, had been slightly off course and was oblivious to the bombing restrictions covering *Thrasher*'s ordered route. Only on our return to harbour three weeks later, when the crew came on board to present us ceremoniously with a 'hookah' as a pipe of peace, were they convinced that they had not sunk, or at least damaged, an enemy submarine.

For most of the patrol the weather was kind, with cloudless blue skies, moonlit nights, calm seas slightly ruffled by a gentle breeze. These were ideal conditions, and a welcome change from the gales and tumultuous seas of the previous patrols throughout the winter. There was plenty of excitement, small escorted convoys to be pursued and attacked, constant enemy activity ashore, at sea, and in the air. Exceptionally, *Thrasher* came to the surface in broad daylight on two occasions to make long, sustained runs to get ahead of convoys of laden ships bound for Benghazi. In the extreme visibility, provided an unremittingly good look-out was kept, there was no danger of being caught by surprise. Aircraft escorting the ships could be observed from long range, at such distances they would not sight *Thrasher*, and I found it exhilarating to be in hot pursuit of the enemy under such conditions, and thoroughly enjoyed every moment on the bridge as we gradually overhauled the target and worked our way into an attacking position. The Gulf of Sirte was the only patrol area where I experienced suitable conditions for such tactics, elsewhere, the submarine's position would have been quickly compromised and it was only on the rarest of occasions that operations on the surface by day were justified.

I also found opportunity to develop the technique of attacking at periscope depth by moonlight. This was a method we had not been introduced to on my 'perisher' but 'Tubby' Linton, captain of *Truculent*, had told me that in good moonlight there was sufficient light through the large 'search' periscope of a 'T' boat for such an attack to be perfectly feasible. It could be just as accurate as using the small 'attack' periscope in daylight, and there was less chance of torpedo tracks or periscope being sighted. It became a favourite tactic of mine.

But once, near the start of this patrol, it could have ended unhappily, even disastrously. Two small ships in ballast escorted by a small torpedo boat were encountered one night, but firing torpedoes at them was immediately seen to be impractical because the outfit of torpedoes in the tubes were all old Mark IVs, which had been set before loading to run at depths suitable for a force of cruisers which *Thrasher* had a day previously been ordered to intercept. Depth settings too deep for the present targets could not be altered without withdrawing the torpedoes from the tubes, which was a laborious and lengthy process. The convoy was too tempting a target to let go by and in the circumstances I decided to use the opportunity to go through the motions of a submerged attack by moonlight. Conditions were ideal, it was a bright moonlit night and *Thrasher* was perfectly placed to run on the surface until she was well ahead of the convoy, then to dive and carry out her dummy attack. All went according to plan until the final stages, the escorting torpedo boat, zig-zagging broadly a mile ahead of the two ships, had been safely passed and no longer posed a problem so the periscope went up for a last look. To my horror, instead of the two ships, all that was visible was a close-up view of the side of the torpedo boat gliding past a few yards away, with the half-naked body of an Italian sailor smoking a cigarette and leaning on the guard rails abreast the first of the ship's two funnels. 'Stoker just come on deck for a breather' was my immediate thought as I hurriedly lowered the periscope and ordered *Thrasher* deep. Fortunately, he did not seem to have noticed the periscope staring at him and there were no repercussions. But it was a lesson to me: never think the escorts are safely past and can be ignored. It vividly reinforced Pat Steel's oft repeated dictum that nothing was more essential than the frequent 'all round look'. Presumably, the torpedo boat had suddenly decided to leave its position ahead of the convoy and take a sweep astern and in doing so had fortuitously passed over the fore-casing, which was deep enough not to be hit. I had failed to spot its unexpected movements, nor had our very alert and attentive Asdic operator heard its approach. We were very lucky not to have had the periscope standards knocked off.

Before the patrol ended, *Thrasher* was ordered to form a patrol line with two submarines from the Tenth Flotilla, to intercept a convoy bound for Tripoli from Italy. The weather had worsened with a south-easterly gale blowing up, bringing with it dust storms from the deserts of North Africa, which reduced visibility to only a mile or two. Nothing was seen of the convoy, though the peace of the afternoon and evening of the fourteenth of April was disturbed by the sound at regular intervals of distant explosions, gradually getting nearer. They were taken to be the occasional depth-charges dropped by the escorts of a convoy in the vain hopes of scaring off attacking submarines, a well-known Italian practice. Attempts were made to communicate by S.S/T with *Upholder* who should have been about eight miles away in the next door billet, but no contact was made. Post-war information suggests that she may have been sunk about this time by an Italian torpedo boat, but the explosions, as we heard them, were not in the sort of pattern indicating a submarine being hunted. They were mostly single, at long intervals.

The mystery of *Upholder*'s end around this time must remain open. Two or three days later we intercepted a signal from Captain (S) Ten in Malta to *Upholder* informing her that at such and such a time she was bearing . . . degrees . . . miles from the outer end of the swept channel into Malta, which conformed to an earlier signal ordering *Upholder* to leave patrol to arrive off the swept channel at the time specified in the second signal. This has always led me to believe it likely that *Upholder* made it safely back from patrol to the approaches to Malta and was then mined.

In any event, however her loss was incurred, it was a most grievous blow to both the Tenth and First Flotillas; soon to be compounded by the failure of *Urge* to arrive at Alexandria after sailing from Malta in early May, when the relentless bombing of the Luftwaffe forced the Tenth Flotilla to evacuate their base at Lazaretto. Within a month the two leading 'aces', Wanklyn and Tomkinson, of the submarine war had gone. It was hard to accept such a blow, and I personally had lost two more great friends, to be added to the toll the war was exacting from all those I had grown up with pre-war.

After being ordered to return to Alexandria and while on passage along the Libyan coast, *Thrasher* had a brief but spirited gun action with a large motor-driven barge. No definite result could be achieved before accurate fire from shore batteries forced her to break off the action and dive. We were back alongside *Medway* on the 22nd April and could reflect on a patrol full of incidents and in which, in two separate attacks, two ships had been sunk. They were not large in tonnage but were heavily laden with supplies for Rommel's armies, massing in Libya and soon to launch a devastating drive towards Egypt.

Thrasher's next patrol, in two weeks' time, took her back into the southern Adriatic, for what should have been a fruitful hunt for enemy ships but turned out to be thoroughly frustrating. There was no lack of potential prey, but attacks went wrong, aborted by the escorts, by unforeseen alterations of course, or by the range being too great. After a succession of such incidents it was a relief to find an easy, straightforward target, an unescorted heavily laden ship, southbound a few miles off the Italian coast. It was a simple attack and three torpedoes were fired from close range, of which two hit and with no escorts about I kept the periscope up to observe the effect. What I saw was devastating, the ship totally disintegrating and disappearing in a matter of seconds in a welter of dirty foam, so shattering a sight that I had forcibly to remind myself that we were engaged in a very brutal war and that such things must be, if we were to win, at whatever cost in ships and lives.

There were new faces in *Medway* when *Thrasher* arrived back in Alexandria on the 28th May. Sammy Raw, as Captain (S) One, had been relieved by Captain P. Ruck-Keene, affectionately known as 'Ruckers', as solicitous for those in his charge and as determined to wage war on the enemy as his predecessor, and a man of tremendous drive and initiative.

Captain (S) Ten with some of his staff and the remaining four U-class submarines, all that was left of the valiant Tenth Flotilla, had also arrived in Alexandria from being bombed out of Malta and were attached to *Medway*, to be given every welcome and facility that could be offered.

Our usual rest period was cut short, for all available submarines had to be at sea again by the 8th June, to take up positions in the Central Mediterranean to cover the passage of a critically important convoy from Alexandria to Malta. Operation 'Vigorous', as it was called, involved the whole Fleet and units of the RAF, and was co-ordinated with a similar convoy being run from Gibraltar. As expected, the Italian battle fleet sallied forth from Taranto to try to attack the westbound convoy. Only one submarine, P35 of the Tenth Flotilla, under the command of Lynch Maydon (Lieutenant S.L.C. Maydon), was lucky enough to get off a long range shot, 'winging' one of the battleships. For the rest of us we had two hectic days tearing about mostly on the surface, in frantic endeavours, in the light of a stream of conflicting reconnaissance reports from aircraft, to best position ourselves to intercept such a thrilling target. From the bridge of *Thrasher* I saw the masts and tops of the Italian battle fleet legging it for home at high speed. It was a tantalizing sight but they were far out of range, without a hope of us getting into an attacking position. Sadly, the much valued convoy never got through to Malta, being turned back after serious losses and in the face of further overwhelming threats from sea and air. But our antics were not yet finished, for a further three days we circled round the Ionian Sea in conjunction with some of the Tenth Flotilla. But it was all to no purpose for the expected enemy ships never appeared, but it gave rise to a private little ditty passed between us of 'Here we go round the Ionian Sea, Cor ★ ★ ★ ★ Cor ★ ★ ★ ★' long to remain a signature tune for those involved.

Released from this fruitless operation on the 20th June *Thrasher* returned to her happy hunting grounds of the Gulf of Sirte and was promptly rewarded two days later by a successful moonlight attack on a small escorted convoy approaching Benghazi, in which one ship was sunk. On the 24th June, she received orders to return to Alexandria. The increasing gloom of BBC news bulletins, heard on subsequent nights while on the surface as we slowly headed homewards, worried me as to whether we would ever get there before Rommel did. Tobruk had fallen and the Eighth Army was retreating fast into Egypt. The future looked black indeed, and we checked on whether we had enough fuel on board to turn round and get to Gibraltar.

While still to the west of Tobruk a flurry of signals was received on the 27th and 28th June, reporting enemy ships and a convoy heading towards that port. Whilst searching at night for the convoy, in bright moonlight in the very early hours of the 29th, *Thrasher* was attacked by an aircraft silently gliding down-moon; unseen and unheard, the first indication was the flashes from its bombs exploding as they struck the water, luckily not close enough to cause any damage, but it put paid to any further search for that convoy.

Fortunately there were other targets to receive our attention. We had spent the daylight hours of the 28th patrolling a certain spot about sixty miles north-west of Tobruk on receipt of information that a 3,000 ton ship would pass through that position at mid-day on a course of 180 degrees, at a speed of 20 knots. No ship, however, had appeared, but I was encouraged during the next night when a further signal was received, giving a new position through which the ship was expected to pass, at midday on the 29th, same course, same speed. It was further stated that it was, 'vitally, repeat vitally, important to sink this ship.'

My appetite was whetted by all these signals and I made doubly sure *Thrasher*'s navigation was accurate and that we would be in the right position to intercept. Weather conditions were almost ideal, excellent visibility and, but for a slight swell, a calm sea, almost too glassy. I prayed there would be no aircraft escorting the ship, though their presence last night was disturbing. The forenoon wore on with tension rising amongst those on watch in the control room, which I could sense from my adjoining cabin. An especially vigilant look-out through the periscope was being kept by the Officer of the Watch, my first lieutenant, Bill Elliott (Lieutenant J.N. Elliott).

Lying anxiously awake on my bunk shortly after eleven thirty I heard the periscope go up for the umpteenth time and then his call of 'Captain in the Control Room'. I was there in a flash and he reported he had sighted a mast showing just above the horizon bearing due north. A quick look confirmed it was there, sure enough, on the same bearing, but already much more to be seen, the bridge, funnel and upper works just beginning to show of a ship approaching fast. At the order 'Diving Stations' *Thrasher* sprang to life and seemingly within moments all torpedo tubes were reported at the 'ready'. By then I could see that we were very fine on the starboard bow of the target, too close to its track if it kept a steady course, as it seemed to be doing, to be able to fire torpedoes effectively. I adhered to the classic teaching of my 'perisher', 'in such circumstances go deep and run across the target's projected track at high speed on a 120 degree track; be back at periscope depth when an estimated 600 yards off track, make a retiring turn and be prepared to fire torpedoes on a broad track.' It worked like a dream; we just had time to settle on a firing course when the sights came on and *Thrasher* loosed a full salvo of six torpedoes, from a position on the port beam of the target at a range of seven hundred yards, using the periscope very carefully so that each could be aimed individually, spread along one and a half lengths of the target. There followed quickly the satisfying sharp taps and then loud explosions as three, if not four, torpedoes were heard to hit.

At the sound of the first explosion I raised the 'attack' periscope to see what was happening. As it went up there was an angry buzzing noise, clearly audible inside the submarine. Its origin was immediately visible as I put my eye to the eye-piece, an Italian MA/SB (motor anti-submarine boat) was passing close ahead at high speed. Before lowering the periscope I spotted three others in various positions astern of the target. To hear and see them

Diana – Mussolini's yacht carrying petrol for Rommel's Army was sunk by *Thrasher* on 29 June 1942.

was a surprise; in spite of many 'all round looks' during the attack I had not seen them, due no doubt to the minimum amount of periscope I was using – just sufficient to see the target – and their low profile hiding them in the prevailing swell. As soon as I saw them *Thrasher* went deep and took evasive action; they could be heard milling around, and in the next ten minutes they dropped seventeen depth-charges, vaguely in the vicinity, after which everything became very quiet. Twenty minutes later we were back at periscope depth and I could take stock. There was no sign of the target but all the MA/SBs were concentrated in one spot, picking up survivors. I left them to it and stole quietly away, once more heading back towards Alexandria.

I naturally wondered what was so important about this particular ship that on two successive nights signals had been received saying it was vitally important to sink it. I could guess that it was carrying something crucial to the battle then raging in the Western Desert, but it was not until long after the war that the facts became known. I was not then surprised to learn that the ship, the Italian *Diana*, was carrying hundreds of tons of cased petrol most urgently needed by Rommel's tanks and without which they could advance no further. It was also said that there was on board the Italian Flag Officer and his staff who were to administer the newly captured port of Tobruk. Stranger stories had circulated earlier. In January 1943, when on leave in Scotland, I was informed by my brother, who had heard it when on duty with the Clyde Auxiliary Patrol, that the important ship I had sunk in

June the previous year was carrying Mussolini's white horse to Libya so that he could ride it in triumph into Cairo when Rommel had captured Egypt. I never discovered the origin of this story, or even how it had reached the Clyde, but it remained a plausible, if fanciful, explanation until the truer facts became known. However explained, the episode remains for me a remarkable few hours of intense and exhilarating excitement – and satisfaction. When we eventually reached harbour some days later 'Shrimp' Simpson, on the jetty to greet us, told me that the news of the sinking, which had quickly reached British Headquarters, Middle East, on the 'Intelligence' network, had been the only bright spot in a very bleak week.

The night after that red-letter day *Thrasher* received a signal re-routing her to Haifa, but with no explanation. Why the change from Alexandria and was *Medway* all right? We could only speculate, but noted with increasing anxiety that Captain (S) One was 'off the air' and no longer sending signals to his submarines at sea. Captain (S) Ten, whom we knew had been lodging in *Medway* seemed to have taken his place and thus, we presumed, was still around somewhere in the eastern Mediterranean. It was a great relief when, on the second July, we again began to get signals from Captain (S) One and knew that he was again in control, but from where we were unaware.

One further excitement surprised *Thrasher* before she reached Haifa. At about nine o'clock on the morning of the 4th July she was proceeding slowly along at periscope depth with nothing likely to disturb the peace, except some orderly confusion in the fore part of the submarine. In accordance with normal practice it was 'topping-up' day when the main batteries were replenished with distilled water, which involved lifting the covers to the three battery tanks, i.e. the floor boards, the deck, on which we trod when passing through the submarine. The upheaval was considerable and it was awkward to move about. At the height of this comparative chaos I was urgently called to the control room by the Officer of the Watch who had sighted a U-boat on the surface. Topping-up was immediately suspended and Diving Stations ordered. My first look through the periscope revealed the U-boat, on a glassy calm sea, slowly zig-zagging past us at a range of three thousand yards. Using the periscope was not easy as the normal deck of the control room had temporarily vanished and I had to try to conduct the attack whilst gingerly tip-toeing around on the tops of the cells of No. 3 main battery. This fleeting chance of sinking a U-boat could not, however, be wasted and within minutes of first seeing it the last remaining three torpedoes in our internal tubes were fired (U-boats generally were accorded a full salvo of six but the three were all we had left). Unfortunately, their tracks were sighted and the U-boat turned away and increased speed. 'Gun Action' was ordered and *Thrasher* was quickly on the surface to engage it with her four-inch gun but by then the range was over four thousand yards and the target very small. Our shells began to fall close enough to make the U-boat dive without any direct hits being scored. There was nothing else to do but follow suit, lest we became, in turn, a target for the U-boat's torpedoes.

Apart from surfacing briefly a few hours after this encounter to pass a signal reporting the U-boat's position, nothing else occurred to disturb the rhythm of the last two days of the patrol. We were no longer in enemy-controlled waters and everyone was engaged in a general clean up of the submarine while thoughts were turning more and more to the relaxations and pleasures of being back in harbour. They were busy days for me personally, completing the detailed formal report of everything that had happened throughout the patrol, to have it all ready to hand in on arrival, as was the normal practice. On this occasion there was an odd current of anxiety running through the boat, of not knowing what we would find on reaching Haifa.

Soon after dawn on the 6th July *Thrasher* entered this hitherto unknown port. Present were some cruisers of Admiral Vian's 15th Cruiser Squadron and a few destroyers, remnants of the once great Mediterranean Fleet, and which had taken on so valiantly throughout the year the might of the Italian Navy and the German Luftwaffe. They gave the place some semblance of it being a naval base, but of *Medway* there was no sign. Standing on the wharf on which we berthed was 'Shrimp' Simpson, as ready as ever to give us a cheerful greeting whatever the circumstances. His immediate question was how we had got on; then came the news we were all dreading, *Medway* had been torpedoed and sunk on the 30th June, on the morning after she had left Alexandria. Fortunately casualties had been very few.

When, on the 8th June, we had cast off from her, securely moored in Alexandria as she had been for months and with no seriously threatening cloud on the horizon, everyone, as was customary, had taken with them on patrol the very minimum of clothing and necessities – in the heat of summer the former were not much. All else that we possessed had been left behind in the safe keeping of this best of all mother ships, whom we hoped would minister faithfully to our needs for all time. Now she was gone and we were without a home, we had lost virtually everything, our most treasured possessions, uniforms, books, photographs, the lot. It was a stunning blow, with enormous implications beyond all personal feelings, encompassing the First Flotilla's continuing operational effectiveness and the comfort and wellbeing of everyone concerned.

'Shrimp' wasted no time in explaining that matters were fully in hand to keep the Flotilla going as before, with only the slightest of interruptions to its operations at sea, of which he was temporarily in charge. Meanwhile, 'Ruckers' was in Beirut setting up a shore base with everything needed to replace *Medway*, an enormous task giving full scope to his unbounded energy, enthusiasm and powers of persuasion. He had already commandeered a French army barracks to provide the future living quarters for base staff and submarine crews, whilst work shops and machinery for them, store houses, berths in harbour for his submarines were all being requisitioned piecemeal from the existing port facilities and ex-French naval base.

For *Thrasher* at Haifa the Army would provide accommodation ashore, in a transit camp, and victuals, clothing and other essentials. The Palestine Police also co-operated, going out of their way to offer hospitality and recreation so we were well looked after. I seized the chance of a few days leave in Jerusalem, made all the happier by having the company of Mike St. John, recently arrived in the First Flotilla as captain of *Traveller* and cheerful as ever. There was not much of the city we did not enjoy, from visiting the Holy places to staying in the luxury of the King David Hotel.

Haifa did not see us for long. After ten days or so we moved to Port Said where the Suez Canal Company, backed by the expertise of a dedicated band of Admiralty Overseers, took *Thrasher* in hand for a routine docking and bottom-scrape. They were indefatigable in tackling and completing the myriad jobs that needed attention and, by the end of a week, thought was concentrated on the next patrol, for which we sailed on the evening of the 26th July.

It was a fateful evening. After the usual 'trim dive' when clear of the approaches to Port Said, by nine o'clock *Thrasher* was settled in patrol routine, on the surface on a clear night, zig-zagging along her allocated route and covered by bombing restrictions imposed on all our own forces. Satisfied that everything was in order I left the bridge and descended to the wardroom for supper, occupying my usual seat nearest the gangway to the control room. Scarcely had I sat down than a most urgent and absolutely impelling thought flashed through my mind – I must get to the bridge immediately. It was the clearest of calls, its origin unconnected with any human being, so giving no explanation to those around the wardroom table, I hurriedly got up to obey it. I had gone only a few feet and was passing through the doorway in the bulkhead between wardroom and control room when there was a most violent and shattering explosion. I was thrown about twenty feet through the air, landing with a crash on the deck at the after end of the control room. I retain a vivid recollection of the ship's galley in the passage abaft the control room leaving its normal position against the ship's side in a cloud of blue sparks, to finish up across the gangway more or less in the wireless office. The lights had gone out, everything was dark and some strange and unusual sounds added to my instant thought that we had been torpedoed. As I got to my feet, glad to find I was relatively unhurt, I heard with overwhelming relief the voice of the Officer of the Watch on the bridge giving the order to dive, to be followed immediately by the rattle of the Bren gun as it opened fire; at what, I did not care for the moment. To know that 'up top' they were alright was what mattered. The order to dive was obeyed without hesitation and *Thrasher* began to submerge, bringing down in a hurry those from the bridge. With no reports of water deluging into the submarine we gingerly increased depth, levelling off at eighty feet to take stock and give nerves a chance to steady. I was heard, according to stories circulating later, at one point to order loudly, 'Keep silence in the boat,' adding for the benefit of those around me in the control room, 'I can't *hear* myself *think*'. Certainly at one time the noise level was far above what I normally tolerated and I found that the almost catastrophic events of the past few minutes did not contribute towards clear thinking. I, and probably everyone else, was a bit dazed.

Bill Elliott, who had been the Officer of the Watch on the bridge, told me all he knew. A Swordfish aeroplane (Fleet Air Arm torpedo/bomber) had swooped in low from our port bow, dropping its load of depth charges as it passed over. The first had exploded under the hull about half-way between the bridge and the bows, and two more had then gone off close against the starboard side, abreast the engine room. He had clearly recognized it as a Swordfish and therefore 'friendly' but seeing it circling round possibly threatening another attack, he had opened fire at it with the Bren gun. In the event it took no further action and I later learnt that the stream of tracer from the Bren gun, of noticeably smaller calibre than what might be expected from a U-boat, was the first indication to the crew of the aircraft that their target was not a German submarine and might be one of ours.

It was soon clear from the reports of internal damage filtering through to the control room that there was no question of being able to continue the patrol. The most serious problem was the state of the main battery, all three sections of which were emitting smoke and fumes and in one a fierce fire had already started, soon to be extinguished by copiously dousing with distilled water. It was necessary to drop all main battery fuses to prevent more fires, but it left the submarine virtually bereft of electrical power and unable to remain submerged. To everyone's relief *Thrasher* was soon back on the surface but there were other problems still to be overcome; there was no option but to try to return to Port Said, but how to steer the right course to get there? The main Sperry gyro compass was a complete write-off, buzzing like a hive of angry bees in an untidy mess on the deck of the control room, and the magnetic diving compass and portable 'Faithful Freddy', fallen from its stowage in the conning tower, were both completely out of action. Fortunately, the stars were shining and knowing that Port Said was roughly due south of us I enlisted the help of the Pole star, conning the submarine from the bridge so as to keep it directly astern of us.

The last expiring vestiges of electrical power were summoned to get the Diesel engines started, which proved particularly difficult, and to pass a W/T signal informing all concerned of our plight and that we hoped to get back to Port Said. Its receipt lifted a load off the mind of Sam Woods (Commander W.J.W. Woods) the Staff Officer (Operations) on the C-in-C's staff. Earlier that night he had received the Swordfish's report of its successful attack on a U-boat (sic), and on plotting its position on his chart and seeing this was right on our safety route, he had, as he told me later, thrown down his pencil in despair, with the words, 'poor old Rufus'. He had feared he would not hear from us again.

In the grey light of dawn *Thrasher*, by now barely afloat because there was no longer sufficient compressed air on board to keep the sea out of her leaking main ballast tanks, joyfully made contact with an A/S trawler patrolling the outer approaches to Port Said. Our navigation had been good enough but I was very ready to let the trawler guide us the rest of the way to the entrance to the Suez Canal, where we anchored to await the arrival of tugs. They appeared quickly on the scene and soon had us back in the same dock that we had left so confidently a few days before. We were indeed in a parlous state, the pressure hull, the main ballast and some internal tanks all needed structural repair, the main battery had to be replaced and much essential equipment either replaced or restored, and everything then tested to ensure it was up to standard. The battery was a horrible mess; of the original 336 cells, each weighing nine hundredweight, only 32 could be lifted out whole, the rest were broken and shattered, their remains swilling about in a sea of acid at the bottom of each battery tank and only to be got rid of by portable pump and by shovel. The heat generated by this nauseous mixture was alarming, raising the temperature in the wardroom, right on top of No. 2 battery section, to well over 140 degrees (Fahrenheit). The energy and willingness with which the Suez Canal Company's work force tackled their unexpected and unpleasant tasks gained our respect and admiration.

Later that morning I received a summons to be at the offices of the NOIC (Naval Officer in Charge) Port Said at mid-day, when the pilot and observer of the Swordfish would be presented to me. There was little they could say except that they were sorry, and that I was still angry and shaken was no doubt obvious to them. They admitted that they had forgotten we might be passing through their area and it was only when they saw the tracer bullets that they began to have doubts, until then they had genuinely believed they had attacked a German U-boat. No one disputed the accuracy of their attack, nor how fortunate it was that it had not proved fatal, and all of us agreed that nothing would be gained by recriminations and that 'the fortunes of war' could best describe the incident. We parted on friendly terms and there the matter officially ended, though it was not long before we had them and others of 815 Squadron along for a drink, in the house-boat moored alongside the dock and serving as the wardroom whilst *Thrasher* was uninhabitable.

By superhuman efforts all the repairs were completed in under four weeks and we again doffed our hats to the way the Suez Canal Company and its men, largely inexperienced in submarine work, had overcome a multitude of problems. It was remarkable also, considering the state of the war at the time, the Axis armies almost in Alexandria, *Medway* and all her spares at the bottom of the sea, how items to replace irreparably damaged equipment appeared as if by magic. It says much for the organization set up in the Canal Zone to maintain and support the Fleet, and its back-up stretching all the way home.

On the 29th August *Thrasher* again left Port Said, with orders to patrol a large area between the north coast of Cyrenaica and the south-west corner of Crete. I had flown up to Beirut a few days beforehand to be 'briefed' on my patrol orders, and 'Ruckers' had emphasised a new technique he was developing with the RAF, whereby their aircraft on reconnaissance flights at night and in contact with enemy ships or convoys could direct or 'home' a submarine on to the target. The success of the system depended on good, direct communications between aircraft and submarine and, being before the days of R/T and 'voice', this was not always easy to achieve. It was an entirely new venture but 'Ruckers's enthusiasm was unbounded and he had won over the full co-operation and support of the RAF squadrons involved.

The scheme proved its worth in the early hours of the fourth September, when shortly after midnight *Thrasher* received an aircraft's report of an enemy ship escorted by two destroyers heading towards Tobruk. It was some distance away but she raced to intercept and was soon in direct touch with the shadowing Wellington bomber, itself armed with torpedoes. Acting on its constant flow of information it was easy to attain a favourable position ahead of the convoy and with the moon giving sufficient light for a submerged approach, *Thrasher* dived. It looked to be one of the simplest of attacks but at the last moment I was thwarted by one of the escorts and unable to fire a straightforward bow shot, and had to resort to the stern tubes; three torpedoes were fired from these, of which two hit the target. The Wellington bomber, about to reach the limit of its endurance, was at that moment coming in to drop its own torpedoes. In the words of the pilot, 'we were just lining up to drop when the target blew up in our faces.'

In the days and nights that followed there were many more reports of enemy shipping but none led to further successes and the patrol petered out rather dismally, made worse by missing a golden opportunity to sink a much prized ship, the German *Ankara*, the only Axis vessel in the Mediterranean capable of lifting and transporting the heaviest tanks. In poor visibility *Thrasher* unexpectedly met this ship with its escort of three destroyers and aircraft as it was returning, empty, from Tobruk to Greece. It was a snap attack and I was optimistic that we would bring it off, until the last crucial moments before firing when one of the escorting destroyers forced us to go deep. By the time periscope depth was regained the DA had been missed and the target was fast disappearing in the haze. It was a major disappointment.

Thrasher was recalled to Beirut, arriving at this new base of the First Flotilla on the 22nd September and finding it running smoothly after two months' existence, and well able to meet all our material needs. In other respects, such as opportunities for recreation and a change of scene, it was even better than *Medway* in Alexandria. 'Ruckers' insisted that during our time in harbour we make full use of all the facilities available and, most importantly, had adequate rest. The night life of Beirut hardly provided for the latter, but we had recourse to the use of a blissfully peaceful villa in the heart of the mountains behind Beirut where a few days stay achieved wonders in restoring jaded bodies and minds.

HMS *Thrasher* – Ship's Company 1942, Beirut.

Two weeks in harbour sped by all too quickly and on the 6th October *Thrasher* was at sea again, off on her thirteenth war patrol. As it turned out, this was to be her final one in the Mediterranean and, as she had begun, it was to be in the Aegean. A special operation to land some Greek agents was the first commitment, but the weather turned sour and with the agents expressing reluctance to go on, it had to be cancelled. In the days that followed our score of ships sunk by gun or torpedo mounted satisfactorily, but all did not always go smoothly. On the 25th October, after an abortive long range torpedo attack on an escorted convoy, *Thrasher* was detected two hours later by an Asdic fitted torpedo-boat, which then subjected her to prolonged and very accurate depth-charging, only losing Asdic contact when we got below a density layer at a depth of 270 feet. Shortly afterwards it retired from the scene at high speed, no doubt to get a fresh load of depth-charges from the neighbouring port of Candia, and in a few hours it was back again, its unwelcome Asdic transmissions clearly audible throughout the submarine as it searched around for us. We retired again below 270 feet, this time we were able to remain undetected and make our get-away. It was with some relief that we received orders that night to return to Beirut, where we arrived on the 28th October.

Greeting me on arrival and hearing my story of the patrol, 'Ruckers' promptly told me that I had had enough, I was worn out and that *Thrasher* would do no more patrols, her safe return to England being all that would

HMS *Thrasher* – Ship's Company 1942, Beirut.

next be required of us. He was right, we were all tired, and I have always been thankful for his perception. As good as his word, we left Beirut for the last time on the 14th November bound for Malta, Gibraltar and England, with strict orders not to get embroiled with any enemy forces whilst on passage through the Mediterranean. As an insurance towards this we left our full outfit of torpedoes in Beirut, where they provided a valued addition to the Flotilla's stocks. In their place we embarked certain reinforcements for Malta, including eight of the smaller eighteen-inch aircraft torpedoes, three tons of Spitfire ammunition and, to fill all available space, a motley collection of sundry stores.

Malta, which we reached on the 22nd November, was a hive of activity. It had come alive again after the Allied landings in Morocco and Algeria at the beginning of the month and it was fully on the offensive, with the Tenth Flotilla, reinforced and re-vitalized right in the thick of it. It was heartening to see. The torpedoes, ammunition and stores we had brought were eagerly received but having landed them there was no temptation to linger; carefully instructed by 'Shrimp' on how to negotiate the minefields in the Sicilian Channel and told to keep out of trouble thereafter, we were soon on our way again, with Gibraltar the next stop.

As dawn was breaking on the 2nd December, the day we were due to arrive at Gibraltar, there was a momentary flutter of excitement as a U-boat on the surface was sighted to the westward. It soon dived and there was nothing we could do but report its position and avoid being torpedoed by it. On arrival at Gibraltar we berthed alongside *Maidstone*, depot ship of the Eighth Flotilla, and were happily surprised to be welcomed by our late captain, Joe Cowell, now the Flotilla's Staff Officer (Operations). He made sure that the days and nights of our brief stay were fully occupied and that there would be no lack of fun ashore for everyone. The Rock Hotel and other haunts favoured by our visits may not have viewed things in the same light as we did.

Loaded up with crates of oranges and cases of sherry, and with two torpedo tubes stuffed with carcases of turkeys, as the coolest place for them in the hopes they would keep for Christmas, *Thrasher* said goodbye to the delights of Gibraltar and set course for Falmouth. To remind us that there was still a war on, four torpedoes had been re-embarked in case we met a U-boat, a distinct possibility while crossing the Bay of Biscay. A tempestuous gale halted progress off Ushant, when we were hove-to on the surface for twenty-four hours. The waves were gigantic, sweeping over the bridge endlessly, and at some time a particularly heavy one knocked off the solid, sturdy D/F (direction finding) frame aerial from its seating at the after end of the bridge. But the gale blew itself out and on the evening of the 14th December we were safely and securely berthed alongside a jetty in Falmouth. The telephones nearby must have had their busiest time for ages as everyone who could get ashore to ring up their nearest and dearest did so. I know my quick call home to Inverness brought much delight.

Pausing briefly at Blockhouse, *Thrasher* finally came to rest in Chatham Dockyard, in good time for everyone, except a skeleton crew left on board, to be home for Christmas. I found my journey to Inverness little changed from that of almost exactly two years before. The 'Royal Highlander' still left Euston from platform 13 at 7.30 in the evening, sleepers were still available and though meals were reduced in quality and quantity the train was as comfortable as ever. Its punctual arrival in Inverness, with parents waiting to wave as it went slowly by the outer end of the platform before reversing into its final resting place, was as it always had been. Austerity had a slightly tighter grip on the Highlands than I last remembered, but all I really craved was peace and quiet, and of that there was no lack. Physically I was very unfit after months of being cooped up in a submarine, of which I had ample proof on a day's rough shooting with Lord Lovat at Beaufort Castle; confronted towards the end with a steep, wooded hillside, covered with fallen trees, I was almost brought to a halt, completely physically exhausted, while he and the other guns, with all their Commando training, marched steadily on barely noticing any obstructions. It was shaming and I was glad we were about to call a halt and go into the castle for tea. After tea I was taken upstairs to see Maurice Baring, who had made such an impression on our gun-room lives ten years earlier. Though in bed, and soon to die, he was unchanged in spirit with his mind as alert and darting as ever. The minutes I spent with him were absolutely effervescent, immensely

HMS *Thrasher* in Chatham Dockyard, January 1943.

helpful in countering my incipient gloomy feelings following a day on which I had shot badly and discovered how unfit I was.

Before I finally said goodbye to *Thrasher* in February 1943, there was a last major function to be attended. As a consequence of the Government's schemes to raise money for building warships, the Borough of Shoreditch in London had, some time before, formally adopted her. On her safe return from the Mediterranean and to mark her successes there the Mayor and Borough Council had invited the ship's company to be their guests for a day. The programme began with an official luncheon in the Town Hall, which was followed by a tour of the much bomb-damaged borough and concluded with a visit in the evening to a West End theatre, for which they had reserved the front three rows of the stalls. At the luncheon the Mayor was to present me with the Freedom of the Borough, a totally unexpected personal honour very greatly appreciated by me, as was everything else they were doing for the ship's company.

I dreaded the publicity and speech-making that would be required, but in the event I need not have worried. The Mayor (Councillor Thos. J. Sillitoe) was kindness itself and, with the members of his Council, ensured that the day would be a very special one for everyone, marked by informality and their generous hospitality. On our way to the Cambridge Theatre to see Jack Hulbert and Cicely Courtneidge, then at the very height of their careers and popularity, we were driven non-stop through the heart of a blacked-out

London in a procession of luxurious limousines with a police motor cycle escort, regardless of traffic lights and whatever might be on the road. It was a unique experience for forty-five or so submariners, but fully in line with the Mayor's and Council's determination that the whole day should finish on a high note that none of us would ever forget. And we never have.

Soon after, it was time to say farewell to *Thrasher* and her ship's company. We had been through a lot together, times of success, times of trauma, and it had moulded us tightly together. It was sad to be leaving but we were all dispersing to other jobs, and the war, still at its height, was beckoning us to new ventures.

Chapter Eleven

Filling in Time, 1943

In the two months after leaving *Thrasher* some diverse jobs came my way. I was sent on a tour of the country to publicise to a variety of audiences the part submarines were playing in the country's war effort and what life was like on patrol. Speaking to large crowds of unknown people and unavoidably drawing on one's own adventures was not a role I enjoyed – too much blowing one's own trumpet; but it was a total change from any previous experience and I was given an insight into how a section of industry was coping with the war. After a 'warming-up' talk to the cadets of the Royal Naval College, now evacuated from Dartmouth to Eaton Hall in Cheshire, my itinerary took in a number of factories and engineering works in the north-west of England and around Glasgow, all largely engaged in work directly connected with submarines. I then returned to my home ground of the Highlands to address the townspeople of Inverness and of Kingussie in support of their 'Warship Weeks', with a visit to the British Aluminium Company's factory at Fort William sandwiched in between, to emphasise to its workforce the vital nature of their work.

The most memorable was a munitions factory in the depths of the Ayrshire countryside, in no way connected with submarines. Specially built for the purpose, its sole task was the filling of small incendiary bombs for use by the RAF, in an endless production of thousands and thousands daily. Manned almost entirely by women, the factory worked around the clock twenty-four hours a day, in three shifts, each shift one thousand strong. My talk coincided with the change-over of shifts, so that my audience numbered two thousand, amongst them some of the most virile and toughest women and girls that Glasgow could produce. They never ceased to bay like wolves at the sight of a young naval lieutenant. It was a nerve-wracking experience and I felt lucky to emerge unscathed at the end, avoiding a stream of invitations to go home, and more, with some of those going off work.

A less arduous assignment was to take part in the making, at a studio west of London, of a documentary film about British submarines on patrol in war-time, its title, if memory is correct, 'We dive at dawn'. David Gregory (Lieutenant G.D.A. Gregory), who had distinguished himself in command of *Sturgeon* in the North Sea, was the captain of the imaginary submarine featured in the film, whilst I filled the more humble part of spare CO, greeting him in the pseudo wardroom of the depot ship on his return from patrol and picking his brains on how he had got on. This particular scene had to be shot thirteen times before the producer was satisfied, which meant me having to drink, one after the other on a cold March morning, thirteen glasses of cold tea, simulating whisky. Suggestions that with a little of the real stuff we would get on better were set aside on the somewhat bogus grounds that being in the middle of a war none was available. I have never forgotten that inexhaustible supply of horrible cold tea, but, apart from that, it was an enjoyable interlude of a few days in an atmosphere strangely remote from the realities of war. There was the added bonus of having a few nights in London and also an opportunity to see my sister in the ATS and her work at some enormous MT (Mechanical Transport) depot near Burnham Beeches.

After these excursions it was back to *Dolphin* at Blockhouse, temporarily to relieve Teddy Woodward (Lieutenant E.A. Woodward) as 'teacher' to his class of 'perishers'. By this time in the war, the spring of 1943, such was the demand for qualified submarine captains, to meet the number of submarines coming into service from a vast expansion of the building programme, now producing two or more a week, that two 'perisher' courses were being run concurrently. Whilst one was at Blockhouse, engaged on the attack teacher ashore for the more elementary stages, the other was completing the advanced work at sea, based at Rothesay on the Clyde. To take over his course and substitute for Teddy Woodward, who had lately returned from the Mediterranean with an outstanding record and reputation as captain of *Unbeaten* in the Tenth Flotilla, quite apart from his being a mathematical genius, was a challenge which taxed me to the full.

When Teddy re-appeared to take his pupils to the Clyde I was faced with an even more difficult problem. A Russian submarine, of post World War One vintage and design based on the British 'L' class, had arrived at Blockhouse, en route to North Russia from Vladivostok in the Pacific. Three of them had set out originally, but she was the sole survivor, and it was thought advisable that whilst resting and recuperating at Blockhouse, her captain and his attack team should be offered the opportunity to practise submerged attacks on *Dolphin*'s shore attack teacher.

The task of supervising this fell on my shoulders. The Russian spoke no English, the attack teacher team and I knew no Russian so there was scope for any amount of misunderstanding, but we quickly established means of communication and a happy working relationship which overcame the language difficulties, in which the Wren crew of the attack teacher played no mean part; they were a notable attraction to our visitors. It was apparent at once that the Russian methods of carrying out a submerged attack were, to our eyes and to put it mildly, basically and hopelessly flawed. They had to be disabused of their idea that the periscope was permanently raised throughout an attack, but they became willing pupils and we got on famously, cemented by many after-dinner visits to the wardroom of the submarine to sample with the captain and his officers their stock of excellent

Californian port. He had had the foresight to buy dozens of bottles, he said it was the only drink he could obtain, when stopping off at a West Coast port in the United States on his long voyage home. He was enormously persuasive in his hospitality and it was always difficult to escape before the night was far advanced and the second or third bottle opened.

In a fortnight we said goodbye on their setting sail for Russia. Communists they may have been but they gave no sign of it, although hovering in the background was always the political commissar. Everyone in Blockhouse regarded them simply as fellow submariners whom we could but wish well on their journey home and in future operations against the common enemy.

I never heard any more of them, until after the war was over when, meeting a deputation of senior Russian officers including submariners on a visit to this country to decide the allocation of surrendered German U-boats, I asked after the captain, whose name was still fresh in my memory. I was told shortly that he was 'no more', but whether he had met his end on operations or because he had collaborated too closely with us, I never discovered; from the tone of the reply and the obvious unwillingness to disclose more I suspected the latter.

In April 1943, I was appointed to the command of *Tantalus*, a recently launched 'T' class submarine now in the throes of final fitting out at Vickers' yard at Barrow-in-Furness. She was due for completion in May, one of the steady stream of 'T' boats which Vickers were now turning out at a rate of about one a month. They were also building, at an even higher rate, a succession of the smaller 'U' and 'V' class submarines, so there was always a strong but ever changing colony of submariners present in Barrow, accommodated in lodgings throughout the town. The bachelor element amongst the officers had virtually turned the Victoria Park Hotel (VPH as commonly known) into a lively wardroom mess, but wholly subject to strict rules of behaviour, laid down by its formidable proprietress.

I did not lack for good company. *Tally-Ho, Tantalus*'s immediate predecessor in the building programme and now about to commission, had my old friend Bennington as her captain, with Peter Scott-Maxwell as his 'Chief' (Engineer Officer). The latter had been with me in *Osiris* in the early days of the war as a young 'makee-learn' engineer, a sub-lieutenant (E), RNVR, the only one of his breed in the Navy at that time. In *Tantalus* herself I found as first Lieutenant 'Bill' Elliott, who had been with me for most of my time in *Thrasher*, finishing up as her No. 1, and as Engineer Officer Tono Kidd (Lieutenant H.A. Kidd) who had added much lustre to his name, including a DSO, when 'Chief' of *Torbay* under Tony Miers, during their distinguished time in the First Submarine Flotilla in the Mediterranean in 1941/2. Two sub-lieutenants almost straight from training class completed the complement of officers.

As the ship's company steadily built up I was glad to find amongst it some familiar ex-*Thrasher* faces. There was Danny Conroy, three badge stoker and one of the oldest ratings still serving in submarines, a cheerful 'rogue' who knew all the answers about life in general, and rum in particular, as experienced in the after-ends of a submarine, but above all else, the most loyal of men; 'Comrade' Beale, Leading Steward and wardroom 'flunkey', who had decorated his pantry in *Thrasher* with large photographs of his three great heroes, Churchill, Stalin and Rommel; a genuine devotee of depth-charging, he would have us believe, his normal reaction to it had been that the more intense it was the greater the clatter of crockery and the flow of cups of tea from his glory-hole. On hearing that *Tantalus* was bound in due course for the Far East his comment to me, made with the usual inward drawing of breath and with a glow of anticipation in his eyes, was "bigger and better depth-charges the Japs have, haven't they, Sir?" With proven morale boosters around such as these I had no qualms about any difficulties or dangers the future might bring.

Tantalus duly commissioned and left Barrow in mid-May 1943, a commission that lasted more than two years and was to take her half-way round the world and back, before I finally parted company with her, when re-fitting in Dundee in July 1945. Now allocated to the Third Submarine Flotilla and based on the depot ship *Forth* in Holy Loch on the Clyde, she immediately became totally immersed in the Flotilla's strenuous programme of working-up newly commissioned submarines, converting their crews from a raw, disparate bunch of submariners into a trained body, fit and ready for any eventuality that might confront them on operational patrol.

It was a rigorous three months, remote from the hurried weeks, or even days, that had had to suffice earlier in the war, but essential now where a high proportion of the crew in every new submarine came straight from initial training with little sea experience. Firstly came a period of elementary practices, diving, surfacing and simple drills, followed by a week or more at the RN Torpedo Depot at Arrochar at the head of Loch Long to adjust and calibrate the firing mechanism on each and every torpedo tube. Thus it could be ensured that not a bubble from the blast of high pressure air released to drive the torpedo out of the tube would escape and, rising to the surface of the sea, betray the submarine's position. It was a protracted and tedious daily procedure of constantly diving, firing torpedoes down the range, surfacing and returning to the depot to take on more torpedoes, and so on until light failed as the long Scottish evenings came to an end. Once all eleven torpedo tubes were adjudged satisfactory, it was back to the more open waters of the Clyde to continue the round of progressively more advanced exercises.

Little time was spent alongside *Forth* but, as with all the other submarines working up, *Tantalus*'s progress came under the eagle eye of Commander (S), second in command of the Flotilla, the redoubtable Ben Bryant. I found it immensely reassuring to have the guidance and encouragement of one who had had such a wealth of experience in command and who had so distinguished himself in his 'S' boats in the North Sea and in the Mediterranean.

HMS *Tantalus* – simulating damaged U-boat for the benefit of our own A/S forces, 1943.

Towards the end of the programme we paid a few days visit to Scapa Flow, the base of the Home Fleet, mainly to give its destroyers some rare practice in finding and hunting a live submarine. Returning to the Flow late one afternoon from one such day's exercises at sea, *Tantalus* was ordered to berth on the *Duke of York*, flagship of the Commander-in-Chief, Admiral Sir Bruce Fraser. A frantic flurry of activity ensued as everyone tidied up and squared off compartments and living quarters in anticipation of the C-in-C coming on board in person. Sure enough, as soon as we had berthed alongside, he braved the slender plank connecting us to the massive bulk of this great battleship and, nimbly descending the ladder from the fore-hatch, he made a very thorough tour of the submarine. It was obvious at once that there was not much on the material side of submarines that he did not know about, nor was this altogether surprising in view of his previous appointment as Third Sea Lord and Controller of the Navy. What was even more impressive to us however was his close interest in the welfare of all on board, not only their living conditions but also a genuine concern for the wellbeing of each and every individual.

Sitting in the wardroom after he had been through the boat, he unexpectedly invited No. 1, the 'Chief' and myself to dine with him and his personal staff that evening on board *Duke of York*. It was a daunting prospect for such comparatively junior officers, even to the point of

HMS *Tantalus* full power trial.

worrying whether we had with us on board decent enough uniform to be properly dressed for such an august occasion. Fortunately, we were able to make ourselves presentable. It was far from a 'sticky' evening, in fact it was the best dinner, in both diversity of conversation and quality of food and drink, that I ever experienced throughout the long years of the war. It was rounded off by his offering me the luxury of sleeping that night in his cabin in the bridge structure of the ship, which he only used when at sea with the fleet. It was in every way a most memorable evening.

At the end of our work up, to add a final polish, we spent a week with *Philante* based at Larne in Northern Ireland. In peace time she had been a luxurious yacht belonging to Tom Sopwith, ardent pursuer of that keenly sought yachting trophy, the America's Cup. She now served as headquarters ship for the advanced tactical training of the destroyers and frigates in the Escort Groups of Western Approaches Command and the aircraft of Coastal Command, which were playing a vital, and increasingly winning,

HMS *Tantalus* full power trial.

role in the battle against the U-boats in the Atlantic. There were exhilarating moments by day and night as we tested our skill in making attacks, submerged or on the surface, against such sophisticated opposition. They provided a supreme test of our prowess. Thankfully, it was all a game and I took heart that we were unlikely to be pitted against such experts in the grim realities of war, but I hope we gave them good value for money and contributed towards their successful waging of the Battle of the Atlantic.

By the end of August *Tantalus* was judged to be fit and ready for operations and early in September she sailed from Holy Loch for a patrol in the far distant north, well inside the Arctic Circle, in an area to the west of Bear Island where the odd U-boat might be met. The patrol was uneventful until one morning, shortly after diving for the day, a garbled signal was received indicating that heavy units of the German Navy, including the *Tirpitz* and *Scharnhorst*, were destroying the coal mines at Icefjord on the west coast of Spitzbergen (now Svalbard), more than a hundred miles to the north of our position. It was to be the last 'fling' of the *Tirpitz*, before she was permanently crippled by our X-craft. *Tantalus* surfaced and headed north at speed, hoping to catch the German ships in the extensive waters of the fjord, or intercept them on their way back towards their base in Norway. The weather was not helpful, with rough seas, low clouds and poor visibility of under three miles. By evening *Tantalus* was a few miles off the entrance to

Icefjord, nothing had been seen of the enemy and she dived to enter the fjord and explore its inner waters on the chance, by now rather forlorn, of finding some 'sitting duck' targets. As she was passing through the narrow entrance a signal was received from Flag Officer Submarines forbidding her to enter the fjord as it was thought the Germans might have mined it. I decided to continue. The signal had been received too late, the die had been cast, and there was still hope that there might be some German ships inside. But it was not to be, all that the periscope revealed as we cautiously explored the inner recesses were the smoking, smouldering ruins of the Norwegian/Russian settlement and its coal mines. There was nothing a submarine could do for the survivors and disappointedly we withdrew. As we passed once more through the entrance we sighted a lone Catalina flying-boat of Coastal Command creeping past into the fjord, flying low close to the land. There was nothing they could do either, except corroborate our report that we had drawn a blank. A few hours later when on the surface charging batteries, in the half-light of a September Arctic night, we had a brief encounter with a German U-boat heading for Icefjord, but there was no chance to fire torpedoes at it. It was an unsatisfactory end to a disappointing day; to have caught the *Tirpitz* and company at rest in an undefended harbour would indeed have fulfilled any submariner's wildest dreams.

For the next few days *Tantalus* patrolled the approaches to Icefjord, dived for most of the day's twenty-four hours, surfacing only to charge batteries. There were no further signs of any enemy activity, but the hours were enlivened by the antics of numerous whales, cavorting about and leaping from the surface of the sea, and by the enormous number and variety of sea birds, which all seemed constantly to be attracted by our presence; and always in the background were the spectacular snow clad spires and bastions of the jagged mountains of Spitzbergen. Intermittent ice-floes demanded a keen periscope watch lest it be damaged by those in our path. By the end of September the weather, though mainly fine, was becoming increasingly colder and a penetrating chill dampness permeated the inside of the submarine. We were in the vicinity of 82° north, under five hundred miles from the North Pole, and it was not surprising that it was cold. It was, I believe, the farthest north that, by then, any British submarine had ever been.

By early October *Tantalus* was on her way back to Holy Loch, calling for twenty-four hours at Lerwick in the Shetlands to re-fuel. This visit is memorable for giving me one of the worst hangovers I have ever suffered. After over three weeks of total abstinence from alcohol, my usual practice while at sea, the volume of whisky forced down my throat by a welcoming and very hospitable Senior Officer Submarines, Lerwick, in the person of 'Hairy' Browne (Commander H.C. Browne) whom I had not seen since Staff Office days in *Medway* two years before, was almost catastrophic. I have little recollection of anything other than 'Hairy' placing a full bottle of whisky on the table after a copious and well lubricated dinner in his quarters ashore and his then forcibly telling his three guests that none could leave until they, and they alone, had finished it. As we all knew he, a very hefty ex-Irish rugger international forward, was not a man with whom it was wise to quarrel.

Amongst the news awaiting *Tantalus* on arrival alongside *Forth* in Holy Loch was the not unexpected decision that she was to undergo structural modification by having two of her main ballast tanks adapted to carry oil fuel, to give her the increased range and endurance needed for her future deployment to the Far East. Work to effect this had long been on the cards, indeed it had been mooted before leaving Barrow in May, when Vickers had stated they could accomplish it in a few weeks – as no doubt, with all the resources available to them, they could have done. The decision, however, was that Portsmouth Dockyard would undertake this comparatively simple task, and there we arrived within a few days.

Finding ourselves in Portsmouth may have had advantages for some, but for me it heralded the most frustrating three months that I have ever had to endure. *Tantalus* had just completed nearly four months of highly intensive training, including a full scale operational patrol, and now we discovered we were to be stuck in the bottom of a dry-dock seemingly forever, the very least of the yard's priorities which were concentrated on Mulberry Harbours and other preparations for the invasion of Europe. Day after day we lay there with little being done to put in place the few pipes and valves required for the modification; dockyard maties sat around all day whilst our own highly qualified people on board, capable of undertaking much of the actual work involved, were not allowed to lift a finger to get on with it. I saw the efficiency and the spirit of the crew, at a peak by the end of the work-up, steadily draining away and deteriorating as the weeks went by. Appeals to higher authority, Captain (S) at Blockhouse and Flag Officer Submarines in London, the Admiral Superintendent in the Dockyard and the C-in-C Portsmouth, were all unavailing. I rued the day we left Barrow without having had this modification completed before commissioning, and as time went by I had the nagging thought that if and when we eventually got to the Far East, any potential targets would no longer exist, making the whole effort pointless.

At last, after three months, the work was finished and by mid-January 1944, we were free of the Dockyard and at sea again, on our way back to the Clyde for an abbreviated work-up, concentrated largely with *Philante* and her Escort Groups at Larne. They certainly got us on our toes after all the sloth of the recent past.

It was fun to be back in Northern Ireland and, on the few occasions when *Tantalus* was not at sea and could berth in Larne, to seize the chance to re-visit Belfast, where the Guinness was apparently unlimited and quaint ways overcame shortages in other fields. Emerging from the Officers' Club late one evening and getting into a waiting taxi to take me to the station for a train back to Larne, I was astonished to see the driver climb on to the bonnet and sit down on the roof. I then perceived that a horse was harnessed in front of the taxi, and taking up the reins the driver encouraged it to set off at a steady trot, with the taxi in tow behind it; quite how it was steered I never discovered, but it was a novel, practical, if somewhat unhandy, way of overcoming petrol rationing.

Crammed full with every imaginable kind of spare gear, stores and personal baggage *Tantalus* finally left the Clyde at the end of January 1944 bound for the Fourth Submarine Flotilla at Trincomalee in Ceylon, with a first stop at Gibraltar. While on passage to the latter she was unexpectedly diverted to carry out a nine day dived patrol off the coast of neutral Portugal, to investigate suspected activity by ships of the Axis powers of Germany and Italy. Because of the very congested and crowded conditions on board, which amongst other things prevented the routine maintenance and servicing of torpedoes, the unwelcome prolongation of our voyage led to an unexpected repercussion, the strict rationing of fresh water. The reason could be traced to the re-ballasting of the submarine during the recent modifications. It had been apparent before sailing that a satisfactory 'trim' could only be obtained by reducing by half the amount of fresh water carried, this would have been enough for a straightforward passage to Gibraltar but was insufficient if our time at sea was extended. In the event our distilling plant, a new and still largely untried piece of equipment not previously fitted in 'T' boats, received a thorough trial for twenty-four hours a day and nobly proved its worth. Without its steady daily output of eighty gallons of fresh water the patrol could not have been sustained, its performance was an encouraging augury for the future.

Our call at Gibraltar was brief, and then on through the Mediterranean in very changed circumstances since I had last seen it, some fourteen months before. The war had retreated and with the whole length of North Africa in Allied hands shipping could move comparatively freely between Gibraltar and Port Said, though it was still restricted to sailing in convoy: rarely were these molested by the enemy. Submarines on passage were attached to such convoys and *Tantalus*, tagging along on the surface at the tail-end of one, had an uneventful trip to Port Said. There was no contact with the still existing submarine operational bases, the Tenth Flotilla at Maddalena in Sardinia and the First Flotilla at Beirut, the former concentrating their offensive operations in the Tyrrhenian Sea and waters off the South of France, and the latter in the Aegean Sea. We had, however, first hand news of how the First Flotilla was faring when we met up with *Sportsman* (Lieutenant R. Gatehouse) in Port Said for a happy respite of a few days, much enlivened by her presence.

Compared to 1941/42 when transit of the Suez Canal had sometimes been hazardous and subject to interference from aircraft-laid magnetic mines, such dangers no longer existed and the only delays likely to arise came from a shortage of Suez Canal Company pilots, obligatory for every ship, no matter its size, shape or nationality. Having embarked a pilot and sailed southbound from Port Said, *Tantalus* had a long wait in the Bitter Lakes to exchange pilots. Impatient to get on I could not help wondering why, in the urgency of war, the risk could not be taken of bending the rules so as to allow captains, if suitably experienced in handling their ships, to take them through the Canal on their own. Navigation was so straightforwardly simple but, perhaps, when meeting ships going in the opposite direction, with all the consequent underwater forces throwing a ship off course, it was helpful to have a pilot's advice.

Once clear of Suez at the southern end of the Canal we were off down the Red Sea, sailing independently on our own, on the surface, something I had not experienced for many a long year. We had to remind ourselves we were still at war and precautions such as readiness to dive, constant zig-zagging and keeping a needle sharp look-out could not be neglected.

The steady stream of ships proceeding through the Red Sea, on largely parallel tracks to *Tantalus*, provided excellent training for the look-outs, and at night, with them all darkened, they served as an excellent check on the night vision of officers of the watch and look-outs. Unfortunately, but perhaps fortunately for the future safety of all, one officer was discovered to be virtually blind at night. He could not distinguish even with the aid of night glasses, on a clear night, the dim shape of a large darkened tanker, broadside on, at about a mile's range. It was a shock to find that he had, somehow or other, slipped through the net of tests designed to bowl out those whose night vision was below standard, and sadly he had to be reverted to General Service on arrival at our destination in Ceylon.

When approaching Aden we were told to act as a target, on the surface, in an exercise to give practice in searching for submarines to the locally based RAF squadron of A/S aircraft. It demanded nothing more from us but to continue on our way, but when a Wellington bomber flew over the bridge at a height of 100 feet with its bomb doors wide open, displaying serried rows of depth-charges looking all ready to be dropped from its capacious bomb bay; I took exception to such a degree of realism, making an immediate request that in future exercises, if only for peace of mind in the submarine involved, the bomb doors be kept shut, or at least not fully opened. I like to think my rather 'windy' reaction had some effect. We had suffered much in the past from 'friendly' forces and here was a clear case where an 'accident' could so easily have happened.

The rest of our passage to Trincomalee, stopping briefly at Aden and Colombo, was uneventful, a succession of peaceful days and nights zig-zagging our way across the Arabian Sea in idyllic weather. We had a rude shock on arrival at Colombo, dismayed to find in dry-dock a scarred and battered *Tally Ho*, looking as though her port main ballast tanks had been filleted, ripped open by a Japanese escort vessel's propeller as it tried to ram her in a night encounter in the Straits of Malacca. It was salutary to be reminded that patrols in future would be dangerous.

By early April *Tantalus* was safely berthed alongside *Adamant*, depot ship of the Fourth Submarine Flotilla in Trincomalee, under the command of Captain H.M.C. Ionides, fondly known to us all as 'Tinsides'. 'Trinco', a most beautiful land locked harbour, was the base of the Eastern Fleet, whose battleships, aircraft carriers, cruisers, destroyers, and all supporting ships, were easily accommodated in its spacious waters. *Adamant*, and an ex-river steamer from China used as overflow accommodation ship, were tucked away in one corner, barely visible to the rest of the fleet.

It did not take long after arrival to get rid of all the additional 'cargo' which we had brought out from home and which had so cluttered up the interior of the submarine. It was a joy to have this once more in its proper state. Everyone then concentrated on preparing for our first patrol, in waters in which we would be complete novices and in which patrol conditions would be very different from the Mediterranean and Home Waters. We were back at war, and ready to meet it despite the changes in the crew I had had to accept. A new Coxswain (CPO Jordan) early on in the commission when his predecessor (CPO Potter) had to leave to take a course for promotion to Warrant Officer; 'Bill' Elliott (No. 1) had left for his 'perisher' before the end of 1943, his place taken by Hugh Oliphant (Lieut. L.H. Oliphant, RN 'The Wite') who had joined at Barrow as one of our two sub-lieutenants whilst the other sub-lieutenant had been relieved before our working-up patrol by Michael Tibbs (Lieut. G.M.G. Tibbs, RNVR, 'Wewak') who had taken a sudden pier-head jump, and the acquisition of a strange nickname, in his stride. Our full complement of officers, which now included a 'fifth hand', was brought up to strength by 'Canada' (Lieut. W.M. Gilmour, RCNVR) and 'Willy' (Sub-Lieut. J.M. Williams, RNR). They, with the 'Chief', Tono Kidd, formed an inimitable team known happily by their nicknames, never allowing me to see that anything whatsoever got them down.

Chapter Twelve

Tantalus on patrol, 1944–45

Patrol areas for the submarines of the Fourth Flotilla, then composed of 'T' and 'S' class, were situated in the Andaman Sea and in the Straits of Malacca. The latter was more usually occupied, between the west coast of Malaya and the north coast of Sumatra and extending as far south as the very constricted and shallow waters of 'One Fathom Bank', the limit beyond which submarine operations were not practical. It was a long haul to get to the areas and it was the normal practice for much of the passage to be made on the surface, there being no threat from Japanese A/S forces. Therefore 'dived by day and on the surface at night' became the routine only when to the east of the north-western extremity of Sumatra on passing through what was known as the 'Ten Degree Channel' between the Nicobar and Andaman Islands.

All on board had to adapt to conditions unlike anything experienced in the Mediterranean or in Northern waters. The climate, the sea itself and navigation, in fact the whole environment, was very different. It was invariably horribly hot and sticky, with sea and air temperatures almost matching, the former around the eighties and the latter the nineties, Fahrenheit. By the end of a long day's diving everyone in the submarine, clad in the very scantiest of clothing, was sweating profusely. There was not much relief or respite even when on the surface at night, except for those lucky enough to be on the bridge as look-outs, they at least had some chance to cool off. For myself, I abandoned my previous habit at night of getting what sleep I could in my cabin below and spent the nights on the hard, steel deck of the bridge, curled up in an out-of-the-way corner. It was not exactly comfortable but at least I stopped sweating, and if we ran into a rainstorm of torrential tropical ferocity, as we frequently did, I could send for a bar of soap, strip off and have a good shower, a luxury not permitted for anyone else.

In the prevailing heat and humidity the amount of fresh water carried on board was never enough to allow unlimited use and it had to be strictly rationed, to about a gallon a day per person, a ration which could, however, be increased significantly, almost doubled, by running the distilling plant. Another innovation with which *Tantalus* and later 'T' boats were blessed, was rather primitive air-conditioning, which helped to alleviate humidity and make things cooler. The amount of moisture it managed to extract from the atmosphere on board always amazed me and though it was considered not fit for drinking it was adequate for washing and was a measurable bonus to the daily ration.

These additions to a 'T' boat's equipment made a dived patrol tolerable and helped to ward off heat stroke and prostration, and to reduce the incidence of 'prickly heat', though we all suffered to a varying extent from this vilely irritating complaint. There were limitations, however, in that they were too noisy to use if enemy A/S forces were in the vicinity, which often meant long hours without their benefit. Japanese patrol craft, especially those belonging to what we came to call 'the first eleven', had a habit of hanging around tenaciously if they suspected the presence of a submarine.

The coasts of Malaya and Sumatra were largely low lying mangrove swamps and provided few distinctive landmarks to aid navigation close inshore, which was hazardous enough from such factors as extensive shallow water, sandbanks, strong tides and currents. There were, however, a sufficient number of small jungle-clad off-lying islands, easily identifiable and whose sharp outlines provided all that was needed for a reasonably accurate check on the submarine's position. Despite them there were occasions when we got into trouble. Once off the Sumatran coast one day when *Tantalus* had surfaced and was in impetuous pursuit of a small tug very close inshore, whilst firing at it with the gun, we were soon in water too shallow to dive in; even worse, I suddenly saw that the myriad tall wooden stakes of the fish traps, which cluttered the waters out to a considerable distance from the shore line, were no longer going past us or, more correctly, we past them. We had, in fact, come to a complete halt, aground on the muddy bottom. Fortunately, we were not at full buoyancy so it was comparatively easy to extricate ourselves by blowing main ballast tanks fully and then going astern until in deep enough water to dive. The target was left on fire, and it was lucky for us that no enemy warships or aircraft came on the scene to take advantage of our temporary plight. I was also glad that we had practised before the manoeuvre of diving whilst going astern.

No longer were we operating in pristine clear seas. The confined waters of the Straits of Malacca were filthy, a dirty greenish colour, with much floating debris and rubbish, palm trees, branches, coconuts, leaves, and when on the surface at night we could smell the rotting vegetation. Fish abounded and at times when surfacing they were found trapped within the bridge – they made a welcome addition to our diet. There were certain advantages from these otherwise unpleasant conditions, the submarine's hull underwater would not be visible to aircraft flying overhead and the periscope when raised would not be the only object disturbing or breaking the surface of the water. There were occasions however when a fish hawk, some were usually to be seen hunting the surrounding waters, decided that the periscope would be a suitable perch on which to rest awhile, thereby drawing unwelcome attention to it. It was comical to see their bewilderment when their 'perch' was suddenly rotated or withdrawn below the surface.

In the inner reaches of the Straits, and elsewhere close to the coasts, a large number of junks and smaller sampans were usually scattered over the surface of the sea, some moving slowly under sail, others lying idle; most, if not all, were innocently engaged in fishing and I did not view them as suitable targets for offensive action. Only on one occasion did one give grounds for thinking it might be acting in collusion with a nearby Japanese patrol craft. They had to be treated with suspicion, whether aiding and abetting the enemy or not, and were a distraction and hindrance to our movements. Later in the war when Japanese shipping had become very scarce it was thought that the larger junks were being used by the enemy to carry their supplies. They then came to be regarded as legitimate targets for attack, by gun or demolition charge, not being large enough to warrant expenditure of a torpedo. It was a policy I did not like and I am glad that *Tantalus* never included 'junks' in her tally of victims.

The three patrols we carried out between April and early August 1944, each far into the Straits of Malacca and lasting between three and four weeks, were all marked by a scarcity of sizeable targets worthy of attack by torpedo; not that there was any lack of excitement. Several small coasters were sunk by gunfire, others were chased but got away in shallow water, mines were laid close off the Malayan coast, and special operations – landing or picking up agents – featured in every patrol. In July there was a fleeting glimpse of a large Japanese submarine passing at extreme range as it headed for Singapore, half an hour later to be successfully torpedoed by *Telemachus* (Lieut. Cmdr. W.D.A. King) in the next door billet to us. I envied him greatly. The opposition, the 'first eleven' of A/S patrol craft, were frequently in evidence but we were not much troubled by aircraft.

I especially admired those we carried on board for the 'special operations'. They were the bravest of the brave to be working in the dangerous business of gathering intelligence in the hinterland of Malaya and I was saddened also by our failure to retrieve anyone in each of the 'picking-up' operations we carried out. The people we expected just never appeared at the rendezvous, adding force to the rumour that, such were their methods of extracting information from those they had captured, there was little the Japanese did not know about this clandestine business thus keeping them a step ahead, which made us all the more wary of being caught in a trap. *Tantalus* was never actually taken by surprise when engaged in this hazardous game, but the presence, more often than not, of A/S craft in the general vicinity of an operation gave cause to think that these were frequently 'blown'.

During one patrol the persistence of Japanese A/S vessels nearly brought about a catastrophe. We had been harried one afternoon, not seriously, but enough to take steps to ensure that when we surfaced after nightfall to charge batteries we should be safe from further attention. It was not to be so. Soon after surfacing a stream of red tracer bullets from out of the darkness indicated they had caught up with us again; we dived, again successfully evaded them and when all seemed quiet surfaced once more, only, almost immediately, to receive the same treatment, forcing us again to dive and take evasive action. By now it was nearly midnight and I was getting very anxious as to whether we would get the battery re-charged before daybreak. So, thinking that the enemy were enabled to regain contact every time we surfaced because they heard the very noisy blowing of main ballast tanks, I told No. 1 that next time we surfaced he was just to put a puff of air into the tanks, thus keeping noise to a minimum, and we would plane up to the surface. This was directly contrary to the age-old basic submarine rule, well ingrained in me, that 'When surfacing always blow main ballast tanks with full air pressure until full buoyancy has been obtained.' This rule was designed to ensure that a surfacing submarine would not succumb to the nasty, inherent habit of falling back below the surface should insufficient buoyancy have been achieved by the critical moments immediately following the opening of the conning tower hatch. In the present circumstances it seemed that disregarding the rule would be the lesser of two evils. I was shortly to regret the decision.

When once again there was no sound or sign of the enemy we surfaced for the third time, in the manner I had ordered. On opening the upper hatch to the conning tower and climbing out onto the bridge, followed by the signalman (Leading Signalman J. Maslin), I saw at once why we could not hear the enemy, nor they us. We were in the midst of the most violent tropical storm, lashing rain, a howling wind and very rough seas, and glancing ahead as I opened the valve on the voice pipe to the control room I saw to my horror that *Tantalus* was rapidly diving, the fore-casing already well below water and the gun about to go under. There was no time for me or the signalman to get down the conning tower so I ordered him to get up the periscope standards whilst I jumped on the hatch to shut it and keep it down until the weight of water over it would hold it so. I then scrambled up the standards to join the signalman at their top, telling him to hold on like grim death and praying that those in the control room below were not too engrossed by the euphoria of surfacing and lighting up their cigarettes to note what was happening and act promptly to correct matters.

As my head went underwater I had the reassuring thought that I *had* opened the valve on the voice pipe so a flood of water down it would surely alert those below. I do not know how long the signalman and I were under water, desperately clinging to the standards, but it seemed about the limit when, thankfully, our heads broke surface and we could breathe again. This time *Tantalus* fairly bounced up to full buoyancy, the conning tower hatch opened and we were in communication again with those in the control room, who were immensely relieved to find us still on the bridge; had we let go we would never have been found in the storm then raging. I was told that thirty-three feet was showing on the depth gauge in the control room before this involuntary plunge, the inevitable consequence of surfacing with insufficient buoyancy, could be checked. That we had escaped scot free from a frightening situation was made all the better by there being no further signs of our troublesome pursuers.

A distant puff of dense black smoke beyond the horizon led to the only occasion when, whilst serving in the Fourth Flotilla, a worthwhile torpedo target came our way. It happened at the end of our first patrol when *Tantalus* had left her area and was heading for the Ten Degree Channel and thence back to Trincomalee. On the surface just before dawn this sudden eruption of smoke was sighted, far ahead of us to the north-west. We altered course towards it, increasing speed and nothing was seen for some time, but then it appeared again, a cloud of smoke and so it continued regularly at intervals of half an hour. Gradually the source became visible, a supply ship zig-zagging steadily on a north-westerly course with one escorting vessel in attendance, the latter soon to be christened 'Smokey Joe', for from it and not the supply ship came these welcome advertisements of their position. There then ensued a prolonged and exciting chase with many vicissitudes, including one unsuccessful daylight submerged attack, and culminating on the second night in a submerged attack by moonlight which stopped the 3,000 ton ship, with finally its despatch four hours later by a single torpedo from No. 11 stern tube. It was a lucky ending, due very much to 'Smokey Joe' without whose regular emissions we would never have made contact in the first place nor been able to keep in touch, or re-gain it when lost, throughout the long drawn-out pursuit. Neither he nor the other escort which had joined him in the later stages bothered us greatly with their depth charges. By the time we had finally evaded their hunt after the sinking I had been on my feet, on the bridge or in the control room, for forty-three hours without a break. When, at last, I could stretch out on my bunk I was so tired and exhausted mentally that sleep refused to come for hours.

Great changes were afoot when *Tantalus* returned to Trincomalee in August. Allied grand strategy had accepted that Britain should take a larger part in the war at sea against Japan and that in addition to the formation of a British Pacific Fleet (BPF) a submarine flotilla should be deployed to operate in the South West Pacific theatre under overall American command. Accordingly, *Maidstone* (Captain L.M. Shadwell) was already temporarily at 'Trinco', to become depot ship for a re-formed Eighth Flotilla consisting of 'T' and 'S' boats. Their growing number east of Suez were now surplus to the needs of the Ceylon based Eastern Fleet, because of the paucity of targets and the restricted waters available for submarine operations in that Command. Joining this new Flotilla, *Tantalus* berthed on *Maidstone* on arrival back from patrol and learnt that after her next patrol she would return to Fremantle in Western Australia, where the Flotilla and its depot ship would by then be based. It was a very pleasant prospect.

Two days before sailing for this patrol an entirely fortuitous and unavoidable accident, in which I sustained three cracked ribs, forced me to admit, after a day at sea had shown how inhibited I was by the pain and nature of the injury, that I was not in a fit state to take *Tantalus* on patrol. Jeremy Nash (Lieut. J. Nash), spare CO in *Maidstone*, was hurriedly told to take my place. Therefore on the 25th August, with very mixed feelings and praying that all would go well until I next saw her in Fremantle in about a month's time, I watched from the deck of *Maidstone* as he, with great competence, took *Tantalus* to sea and headed for patrol off the coast of Sumatra.

Maidstone left 'Trinco' for Fremantle a few days later and I enjoyed a peaceful and restful voyage, except for the extreme discomfort while in the heat of the tropics of having my midriff wrapped in swathes and swathes of sticking plaster. A tremendous welcome greeted us on arrival at our destination, the White Ensign had not been much in evidence there throughout the war and Fremantle, Perth and the whole of Western Australia seemed determined to make up for lost time and demonstrate in every way possible how glad they were to see us. The hospitality was unbounded and as the Flotilla built up with the arrival of each and every submarine it seemed to be re-doubled; the goodwill, kindness and proffered entertainment which we all experienced was almost overwhelming. Truly, as we came to say as the months went by, 'the battle of Perth was more exhausting than the battle of the Pacific.'

The Eighth Flotilla was now under the operational command of Rear Admiral J. Fyfe, USN, Commander Submarines South West Pacific, short title COMSUBSOUWESPAC; he was nothing like as alarming as his title. In 1941, well before the United States came into the war he, then a commander, had done a patrol in the Mediterranean with Sam Woods in *Triumph*, to gain first hand experience of war-time submarine operations. For this he never ceased to be grateful and he showed it by doing all in his power to encourage friendly relations between us and the two squadrons of United States submarines already based at Fremantle, who would be sharing operations in the South China Sea, but further afield than we could reach. We needed this encouragement, for we felt we were very much the poor relations. In so many respects the US submarines were vastly superior, in their range and endurance, habitability, speed on the surface, torpedo control and radar equipment, all factors in which they quite outclassed us and which had so decisively determined the continuing great successes they were achieving in clearing the Pacific of Japanese warships and merchant shipping. We could but admire what they were doing and hope to emulate them in a modest way. On their part they respected what British submarines had achieved in the Mediterranean and Northern waters at home and in no way looked down on us. We were all submariners together. Friendly relations were cemented by Tony Miers, now Commander (S) in the Eighth Flotilla and recently returned from two years at Pearl Harbour as British Liaison Officer on the staff of Vice Admiral Lockwood USN, commanding US submarines in the whole Pacific theatre of war. Tony was well known to many American COs and did much to ensure that *Maidstone* and her Flotilla were happily absorbed into the SOUWESTPAC command.

To my relief *Tantalus* and her crew returned to schedule on the 27th September from a taxing but successful patrol, to find me ready and eager to resume command and also show them the ropes around Perth and Fremantle. Life ashore was a world apart from anything we had met for years, no black-out and apparently unlimited supplies of food and drink, though the odd licensing hours, with pubs and bars shutting at six pm, were the cause of much over-hasty consumption, in which some followed the lead of local inhabitants who knew how to get a skinful between coming off work and closing time. It did not suit those accustomed to a more leisurely evening's quiet tippling. Petrol rationing seemed to be the only restriction in an otherwise peaceful existence.

It was an effort to return to the war but by mid-October *Tantalus* was ready again and we sailed on the sixteenth for a patrol in, to us, a totally new environment, the wide open spaces of the South China Sea, where we had freedom of action in a huge area stretching from the east coast of Malaya on the west to Borneo on the east. It began with a tranquil six days northbound on the surface, diverting briefly to re-fuel from a United States oil barge stationed in Exmouth Gulf, an uninhabited and remote spot on the north-west corner of Australia surrounded by desert and sand, as bleak a place as could ever be imagined. The six days got Perth out of our system and brought us to Lombok Strait. This narrow stretch of sea, between Bali and the island of Lombok, was the only feasible way of gaining entry to the Java Sea and beyond, into waters still under enemy control. In regular use by all submarines based on Perth its passage presented problems, for it was guarded by Japanese shore batteries on Lombok island and by patrolling A/S craft. Transit northwards had to be made on the surface at night because the constant southerly current flowing through it from the Java Sea was too strong for a submerged submarine to make headway against. Homeward bound, with the current to help, there was no problem in making a surface or submerged passage, but, either way, it was always a relief to get through undetected and unscathed.

Once Lombok had been successfully negotiated, patrol(s) could be conducted mainly on the surface, only submerging to attack or evade enemy forces or when engaged in some particular operation close to known or suspected enemy defences. For everyone on board it was a new and pleasant experience; for those on the bridge to enjoy the sun and a cool breeze, for those below a constant stream of fresh air and a sense of relaxation. This was always subject to the over-riding necessity of an extremely vigilant look-out and an immediate readiness to dive so as to ensure that should the enemy appear, whether potential target or A/S patrol, in the sky or on the sea, we would see them before they saw us and could take appropriate action. As the days went by the only things lacking in an otherwise halcyon life were targets to attack.

For the first time in the war out torpedoes, the by now trustworthy Mark VIII with its gyro trouble long past, had their warheads fitted with CCR magnetic pistols, replacing the reliable 3F contact pistols which had required the torpedo to register a direct hit on the target and which had served us very well. The theory behind this recently developed innovation was that torpedoes could be set to run at a greater depth, making their tracks less visible, and on passing under the target its magnetic field would detonate the pistol, with the full force of the explosion of the warhead under the soft belly of the ship causing more damage than a hit on its side. This theory was all well and good but in practice the pistols were unreliable, as we found out on the only two occasions during the patrol when torpedoes were fired.

On the first, in a submerged daylight attack at very close range, in visibility of only a few hundred yards, two 'hits' were obtained on a 3,000 ton merchant ship. My impression, from a fleeting look through the periscope, was that the warheads exploded as 'near misses' before the torpedoes had actually reached the target, a supposition given weight by the fact that it took several hours for the target to sink, whereas two direct hits on a ship of that size should have sent it to the bottom at once. On the second occasion, later in the patrol, the attack was spoilt by one, if not two, torpedoes exploding shortly after being fired, as soon as the safety range had been run off, which alerted the target.

There were some very anxious moments in shallow waters off the east coast of Malaya when attempting a submerged daylight attack on a 5,000 ton merchant ship, with escorts weaving ahead and on its port bow and both transmitting on Asdics; the target steaming south on a steady course along the ten fathom line. Finding a spot where the chart showed a depth of twelve fathoms we had dived and were in the final stages of the attack, on the starboard bow of the target, when the nearest escort was seen to hoist a string of flags and turn directly towards *Tantalus*, at the same time seeming to gain firm contact on its Asdics. It approached steadily and we had to go deep but got no farther than sixty feet on the depth-gauge when we hit bottom; nervously and uncomfortably shuffling away along the sea bed towards deeper water we heard the escort, now joined in the hunt by its consort, pass overhead four times in all. On the third occasion it let loose a string of nine depth-charges, the first two of which were close enough to cause some damage, the remainder, fortunately, progressively more distant. Metaphorically cowering with our heads down, we heard with dismay the steady beat of its propellers as for the fourth time it passed directly overhead, only feet away. Was it all lined up for the final kill? How I longed for the deep waters which had always helped to hide us in the Mediterranean. The seconds crept past and, scarcely able to believe it, nothing happened, tension eased with a sense of anti-climax as our tormentor appeared to lose interest and was heard making off to re-join the other escort and their charge as they frantically cleared the area. Looking back on the episode perhaps I took an unjustifiable risk in attacking such a well protected target in such shallow water, but at the time, with ships worthy of a torpedo so very rarely encountered, it was altogether too tempting.

As the date of the 7th/8th November approached the secondary objective of the patrol, as laid down in our patrol orders, gave me increasing concern, especially its relative importance vis-a-vis the primary aim, the destruction of enemy shipping. This second task said that between the above date and the 8th December, depending on day-to-day circumstances and her safety, *Tantalus* was to close the island of Merapas on the southern fringe of the archipelago stretching south from Singapore. At night a reconnaissance party of two men was to be landed to make contact with members, if any were on the island, of a British/Australian expedition which had been in the area since the last week of September, engaged on an extremely brave and daring operation against shipping at Singapore. Then, on the following night we were again to be close off the island at an agreed position to pick up the whole party, or such members as might have been found, and transport them all back to Fremantle.

Quite rightly and properly I had not been made privy to the details of RIMAU (Malay for TIGER), as the operation was called, only being informed of the requirement to be off Merapas on the night of 7th/8th November, or any night thereafter until the 8th December, and retrieve anyone found there. The orders on that were quite clear, the actual date of pick-up being left open within the given limits. As the first date arrived *Tantalus*, temporarily engaged on 'Air guard' duty to the east of Singapore, had plenty of fuel and nearly a full outfit of torpedoes on board, and therefore still had scope for much offensive action against enemy ships, if only they could be found. There was no indication of any urgency for the pick-up and to confirm this I signalled operational headquarters in Australia saying that I intended to remain on patrol for about another week before carrying out the special operation. This received immediate approval.

A fruitless search for targets, except for a small coaster sunk by gunfire, was abandoned on 20th November and *Tantalus* left her patrol area for Merapas Island. The reconnaissance party was landed on the night of the 21st/22nd November and retrieved the following night. Their report was disturbing and distressing in that no members of RIMAU were found on the island, but there were indications that some, at some time previously, had occupied the base camp originally established in September and there were also signs of hasty evacuation. After discussing the situation with Major Chapman, RIMAU's representative who knew the whole plan and who had been on board throughout the patrol, and hearing in detail all that he and Corporal Croton, his 'winger', had discovered and deduced from their search of the island; it was reluctantly concluded that there was nothing further *Tantalus* could achieve. No one, nor any message indicating what had happened or what might be the present situation, had been found and we could only withdraw and set course for Fremantle. The pick-up, the second aim of the patrol, had failed to find anyone, despite a thorough search of the island and our presence off it on two successive nights.

For years I have worried that deferring the pick-up may have brought about the deaths of a very gallant band of men, my apprehensions not alleviated by an 'anti-Pom' lobby in Australia. This has been made much of in a recent book of the fact that *Tantalus* was not off the island on the 7th/8th November, blaming me and Major Chapman for the death of survivors from the operation and for not pursuing the possibility that these, such as there were, might still have been in hiding on neighbouring islands at the time we eventually arrived off Merapas. The truth as now known, after years of the most painstaking investigation, is that all evidence shows that the remnants of the expedition, those survivors who had made it back to Merapas to await our arrival, were discovered by the Japanese some days prior to the earliest pick-up date and had immediately evacuated it in accordance with the overall plan, or been killed. Thus, even if we had kept to that date we would have found no one. A random search of, and night-time visits to, islands in the vicinity, without any pre-arranged plan but in the vague hope of finding some survivors, would have been suicidal for any submarine, particularly in the light of the unusual A/S activity we had experienced off Merapas, indicating that Japanese suspicions had been aroused and that they were actively hunting down those who had taken part in RIMAU.

For the last month of the patrol *Tantalus* carried two additional passengers, one a Japanese soldier, the other a Chinaman. The former we had rescued very much against his will, requiring prolonged manoeuvring of the submarine as he continued to swim away to avoid capture, after we had sunk by gunfire a small coaster on which he was the sole armed guard. The remainder of the crew, Malays, and the Chinaman, had willingly accepted our efforts at rescuing them. The latter revealed on his arrival on the bridge that he was the only one who spoke English, which he did perfectly, by announcing to all and sundry, 'My name is Leslie Bracken'! He elected to remain on board and chance his luck in Australia when we eventually got there, whilst all the Malays, grateful for their rescue from the sea and for some 'rations' given them, were transferred to the first convenient junk we happened on.

'Tojo', as the Jap prisoner quickly came to be known, was ill, miserable and suffering burns to his face when first picked out of the sea. We gave what treatment we could, including a massive dose of 'No. 9' pills to cure his constipation, and he soon recovered and showed a willingness to work in order to occupy his time. Kept under armed guard in the fore-ends except for a regular evening visit to the control room for a breath of fresh air and token exercise, he was issued with a daily quota of dull, metal valve wheels (standard issue by the builders at that stage of the war instead of brass) to be cleaned and burnished unitl they shone like mirrors. Under 'Leslie Bracken's' care and tuition he soon became acclimatised to the submarine way of life, with some special additions devised by his tutor. On his daily 'rounds' of the submarine the first lieutenant was surprised to find 'Tojo' kneeling with his forehead on the deck. Asked for an explanation, 'Leslie Bracken' replied, 'Every day on board ship he made me kowtow to him, now I make him kowtow to you.' It seemed fair enough. Docile and subdued, he never displayed any signs of enmity or hostility and in time came to be regarded as something of a mascot. No one on board was happy to see the handling he received on our arrival at Fremantle when being marched off by a squad of tough Australian soldiers, armed to the teeth with bayonets fixed. Poor little 'Tojo' we all thought.

No sooner had our 'passengers' left the submarine than we were told to be ready to receive Admiral Sir Bruce Fraser, who had just flown into Perth on his long journey from Britain to take command of the British Pacific Fleet. I was delighted to welcome him on board once again and proud to show him a submarine internally more spick and span than on his last visit in Scapa Flow some sixteen months previously, despite having just returned from fifty-two days at sea. Thanks largely to 'Tojo's' efforts every valve wheel was gleaming brightly and the whole boat looked as if it had been preparing for months for an admiral's inspection. Sir Bruce flew on to Sydney that evening and he had, at his own personal invitation, an extra passenger in his aeroplane, a New Zealand member of our crew who had relations there whom he had not seen since the beginning of the war. Leading Stoker Berwick had been with me since *Thrasher* days and I could not have been more pleased that he should be rewarded with a few days leave in this special way.

Tantalus's first patrol in the South West Pacific had lasted fifty-two days in which she had covered 11,500 miles, with very meagre results. Her next patrol, for which she sailed early in January 1945, lasted even longer – 55 days – with slightly greater mileage and it was even more disappointing, in that there was never an opportunity to expend any torpedoes or ammunition. Day after day scouring the waters of the South China Sea between Malaya and Borneo revealed no suitable targets; except, and it was a marked exception, for a few thrilling hours one morning when, acting on intelligence reports, the pagoda-like masts and the funnels of two Japanese battleships were in sight over the horizon. They were racing home to Japan from Singapore accompanied by a cruiser, a number of escorting destroyers and all around a cloud of aircraft. They were the sort of target one had dreamed of for years, but *Tantalus* was badly placed to complete an attack, broad on their beam and far outside torpedo range. With engines pounding at more than full speed, with every extra fraction of a knot being squeezed out of them, we slowly gained bearing, desperately trying to attain a position ahead from which to make an attack. If all went well it seemed possible that by nightfall this might be achieved, but our hopes were dashed when, like an avenging bee, one of the aircraft detached itself from the swarm and darted towards us. As it approached we had to accept that we had been spotted and could not remain on the surface. As soon as we had dived it gave vent to its hostile intent by dropping, to judge from the sound of the explosion, a single very large bomb or depth-charge, fortunately not very close. But all hope of getting to a position from which to attack such a marvellous target had gone for good. How I wished that we had had a few more knots of surface speed, which would have made all the difference in our race to gain bearing whilst trying to keep out of sight. As soon as safe to do so we surfaced to send a signal reporting contact with the enemy force and its course and speed. It was some compensation to learn later that the major units never got back to Japan, US submarines and aircraft seeing to that.

At last, with fuel running short and both engines on their last legs, one or other always being under repair, it was time to head for home, intending to call at Exmouth Gulf to top up with sufficient fuel to see us safely back to Fremantle. However, all was not smooth sailing for on clearing Lombok Strait we were informed that a recent hurricane of exceptional violence had hit Exmouth Gulf and deposited the oil barge some way inland, far out of reach, and that we should proceed direct to Fremantle. It was a nasty blow, and it was only by proceeding at the most economical of speeds, and by most valiant work by the 'Chief' and his engine-room staff in nursing the engines, that we ever got there without outside assistance, with less than two tons of fuel remaining when we finally berthed alongside *Maidstone*.

By March 1945 we had been nearly two years in commission, the submarine was showing signs of needing major maintenance and, in particular, both diesel engines could no longer give reliable service. The war in the Pacific was moving farther and farther away from our base and the only sensible future for *Tantalus* was to return to the United Kingdom for a major re-fit. So, with many mixed feelings we said good-bye to Western Australia, that most hospitable of places, and set sail for home on the 25th March 1945. All further warlike activities were over and our way would now be through peaceful waters. However until past Suez we could not discount an encounter with the odd enemy submarine.

Trincomalee saw us again for a few days, longer than expected because of engine troubles. We chafed at the delay. Jackie Slaughter (Captain J.E. Slaughter), Captain (S) of the submarine flotilla still based there, exacted a fine of a bottle of Australian gin for every day's postponement: we had an abundance on board, while stocks of any liquor in 'Trinco' were like liquid gold.

When south-west of Ceylon, peaceably heading for Suez, the quiet of the afternoon was broken by the officer of the watch suddenly reporting he was altering course to avoid a whale; seconds later a slight tremor shook the submarine, bringing me swiftly to the bridge. A sixty-foot whale had crossed ahead, being seen too late for any avoiding action to be effective, and our knife-edged bows had sliced half way through its massive body, about a third of its length from its tail. Its back broken, it was making desperate efforts to dive as it wallowed in our wake, with the sea around it slowly turning red. It was a gruesome and horrid sight, made worse by sharks already beginning to gather round, and we turned back at once to get close enough to put it out of its misery by a few well directed rounds from the 20mm Oerlikon.

HMS *Tantalus* leaving Fremantle to return to UK, 1945.

Transit northwards of the Suez Canal caused no delay, but when we met a line of three or four southbound 'Liberty' ships I was surprised that the Canal Pilot, enjoying his breakfast in the wardroom, never appeared on the bridge, leaving it to me to get safely past them; and with 'resolute use of helm and screw' we did so.

We were at Port Said on VE Day, with orders to sail for Malta before dark. I told the Coxswain to find out from the crew whether they would like to remain for an extra day, so that they could get ashore that evening to celebrate the great occasion, and if so I would try to arrange matters accordingly. As I had hoped, the answer was a very positive 'no', their minds being firmly fixed on getting home as soon as possible and the well known night-time activities of Port Said were no attraction.

It was strange to be sailing the seas again in comparative freedom, without constant zig-zagging, with navigation lights and aids all showing and with no fear of attack, and it took time to adjust to the changed circumstances. Relief from all the stresses of the last few years over-rode everything else, but deep in my heart and mind I knew also that though life might be safer, less dangerous, in the years ahead it would not necessarily be easier, and that there would be many new and strange problems and difficulties to be overcome. For over five years almost everyone in the country had lived with the one, single, dominant objective of 'win the war'. Now it had been achieved and in its place would rise a multitude of differing priorities, conflicting with each other in many cases, and it would be more difficult to know and decide where one should be

HMS *Tantalus* leaving Fremantle after successful patrols, 1945.

going, let alone keep a steady course. Such were my thoughts as we left the lights of Port Said behind us.

With brief calls at Malta and Gibraltar the rest of the voyage was enjoyable but uneventful and by June *Tantalus* was securely in dry-dock with the Caledon Shipbuilding Company at Dundee. Everything slowly settled down for a long re-fit under peace-time conditions, with the crew being gradually reduced to a 'care and maintenance' basis. Inevitable though this was, I could not help feeling sad when it came to saying goodbye to members of a crew who had, from the earliest days of the commission, welded themselves into a closely-knit and happy team, and had successfully survived the throes of more than two years of war. Some had been with me even longer, nearly four years. Finally came the emotionally moving time for me to leave; on the day of the General Election in July I said farewell to those still remaining and flew over to Londonderry to my new job. It was the end of an era, and a different type of life lay ahead.

Chapter Thirteen

Peace – at last! 1945–50

In mid-1945 Londonderry was in the throes of change, relaxing from the demanding and vitally important role it had played in the Battle of the Atlantic, as a major operational base and as the headquarters of Commodore Western Approaches. Now, nearly three months after VE day, the Commodore himself ('Shrimp' Simpson), many of his staff and most of the surface ships and aircraft (Fleet Air Arm and RAF) had gone, with the whole organization being run down as rapidly as practicable. In its place, on a much smaller scale, was the newly born and still burgeoning Joint Anti-Submarine School (JASS), centred on the former Army barracks at Ebrington, on the other side of the river Foyle from the now largely empty Commodore's headquarters.

Superimposed on this changing pattern was a crucial, but temporary, organization in charge of nearly fifty surrendered German U-boats, a mixed bag of Types VII, IX and XXI, the latter the very latest that Germany had produced, hardly in time to be tested in war. They were tied up in serried rows, in trots of half-a-dozen or so, moored securely to the recently built long concrete jetty at Lisahally, several miles downstream from the city of Derry itself. A skeleton staff of British submariners had been set up under Captain (S) Lisahally (Captain P.Q. Roberts) with responsibility for the safe-keeping of this motley collection and I now found myself as his Commander (S) with an acting 'brass hat'. It was a peculiar job, bearing little resemblance to the normal duties of a Commander (S) in a regular British submarine flotilla.

Day-to-day maintenance of the U-boats was entrusted to their German crews, reduced in strength to one third for each boat. As prisoners of war they were guarded by the Army, who marched them daily down to the jetty from nearby warehouses which had been hastily converted into a heavily fenced prisoner-of-war camp and provided adequately secure accommodation for them. Their daily work on board the submarines was supervised by British staff, with a qualified submarine CO in charge of each group of six to eight boats, responsible for seeing that at the end of each day the boats were inspected and then locked up, when their German crews returned to their quarters. Pending a decision on final disposal, as yet to be taken at high level by the three major Allies, the U-boats had to be maintained as fit for sea-going and in no way could be allowed to rot. 'Security' was the order of the day and all duties revolved around this.

These were the major concerns of 'P.Q.' and those under him, but once established they were not an onerous burden, and with all the attractions of Londonderry and Donegal, across the border in Eire with free and easy access, life was indeed full of fun; as I quickly found.

The evening after my arrival at Lisahally its wardroom mess gave a farewell party for my predecessor (Lt. Cdr. T.B. Butler, who had been a prisoner of war almost all the war, as First Lieutenant of *Seal*). In the way of all parties at that time it was a thoroughly lively and happy gathering, but though I found myself amongst many old friends I had eyes only for one of the guests, a slim, fair-haired Third Officer in the Wrens, one of the few of 'Shrimp' Simpson's staff remaining in Derry. Deeply attracted, it was for me as close as one can get, I believe, to what the romantics call 'love at first sight', and to my lasting good fortune from then on romance blossomed. Maureen Bradish-Ellames – her tongue-twisting name required a bit of mastering – brought a new factor into my life; a new interest, not novel but one that rapidly cemented into something much more permanent than anything I had ever before experienced. My time in Northern Ireland became a dream, to be fulfilled on our marriage in August 1946. Through succeeding years, in good times and bad, nothing but the fondest memories remain for us both of the joyous times we had together at Londonderry.

By the autumn a decision had been reached on the fate of the U-boats and a high powered Allied delegation, headed by admirals from Russia, the United States and Britain, spent several days at Lisahally inspecting the assembled U-boats. Their task was to select the six which it had been agreed should be allocated to each of the Powers as 'spoils of war'. All other surrendered U-boats were to be towed out to sea and scuttled in deep water.

There was much argument and discussion before the allocations were finally made, with the Russians being particularly difficult and accusing us at Lisahally of 'dirty tricks' in shuffling the boats around each night from trot to trot, or within trots, so that they would not know from day to day which submarines they had inspected and which they had not. With the manpower and facilities available at Lisahally to have swapped any of the boats around would have been quite impossible. The imagination boggles at the depth of suspicion that must have been permeating their minds to even suggest that such manoeuvres had taken place, let alone to demand, as they did, that every boat's identity, already simply shown, be marked in some new, complicated and inviolate way. It was lucky that we had someone of 'P.Q.'s' calibre to deal with such cantankerous problems. I have never seen an admiral given such short shrift as when, on the second morning, 'P.Q.' and I were kept waiting, needless to say in the rain, for over an hour for the Russian delegation to arrive from Londonderry, all because their Admiral, reportedly, had overslept heavily. 'P.Q.' was famous for his incisive remarks and when he was roused it was better not to be at the receiving end. I would like to know how the interpreter translated the icy strip he tore off on this

Our wedding day, 10 August 1946.

occasion, but I could see the Russian admiral visibly wilting as it was delivered. We had no more trouble.

Eventually it was decided which U-boats would go where and the pattern of work at Lisahally changed accordingly. Those boats allocated to the major Allies had to be brought forward for service, with British crews trained to take them to sea for trials and ultimately to deliver the Russian allocation to their final destinations. The remainder had to be prepared for towing out to sea and scuttling. The expertise of the German crews became of less importance, allowing them to be moved elsewhere and join in the general repatriation of prisoners-of-war. They were happy to go, being relieved of their over-riding fear that they would be handed over to the Russians.

While these developments were still in progress I received a new appointment, to relieve Cdr. Lennox Napier as 'teacher' to the submarine Commanding Officers' Qualifying Course (COQC) in January 1946. In a haze of farewell parties I left Lisahally in mid-December. After a superlative leave in which I met Maureen's family and spent Christmas at her mother's home, surviving the ordeal of carving a turkey for the first time in my life, I duly reported at Blockhouse in the New Year. I was back again in the rank of Lieutenant Commander, but not worried by the loss of my acting 'brass hat'. To be 'teacher' was a plum appointment and I hoped it would bring the reward of promotion in due course. Of far greater concern to me as I prepared to meet my first class of aspiring COs was the question of my ability to instil in them the qualities and 'tricks of the trade' essential to their successful completion of the course as competent and confident submarine captains.

In keeping with a return to peace-time conditions, the COQC followed a more leisurely pattern than in war-time. Each lasted about three months, of which the first few weeks were as before, on the attack teacher ashore at Blockhouse (Gosport), with the remaining time on the Clyde, to begin with based on the depot ship at Rothesay, later moving to Holy Loch. This easier tempo could not, however, be allowed to infiltrate the actual content of the courses, which had to be expanded to incorporate all the accumulated knowledge and experience from the war. There was no departure from the strict standards the war had demanded in the conduct of submarine operations. It was a continuing challenge to put all this across in the most effective way I could devise, to a varied intake of pupils over the next two years, mainly British but also including submariners from the Netherlands and Norwegian Navies. So great grew the demand from the latter that at one time a special 'foreign' 'perisher' to meet their requirements had to be sandwiched in between the normal run of courses.

I found the task most rewarding, but it was also exhausting, particularly the long hours at sea closely supervising an endless succession of dummy torpedo attacks, where every latitude had to be given to the embryo CO before possibly having to intervene at the every latest moment and 'pull the plug', to prevent the submarine being endangered. It was nerve-wracking work, concentrated tensely on whichever periscope was not in use by the pupil, and by the end of each day I was very conscious of the strain on my eyes. Johnny Bull (Lieut. J.R.H. Bull, DSC+) the captain of *Spiteful*, the 'S' boat permanently allocated for the 'perishers's' sea time, gave unstinting help in taking some of the load off my shoulders. Between us we succeeded in avoiding any heart-stopping moments of crisis throughout the many days, and nights, we were at sea together.

There was a welcome break in the summer of 1946 for my marriage to Maureen on the tenth of August. I had been able to defer the 'end of war' leave owing to me and by taking it now in conjunction with the usual routine summer leave we enjoyed six weeks' honeymoon, mostly spent in Ireland and then at Dougarie on the west coast of the Isle of Arran. Happy times, though my attempts to persuade my wife that fishing was a pleasant sport were a dismal failure, not surprising since her initiation on an Irish lough meant sitting in a boat in pouring rain for hours on end, the dose repeated daily. Fortunately, I could lay some of the blame on her father who had more or less organized this particular episode, but there is no denying it was not a very sensible venture!

The winter of 1946/7 was severe, which added to troubles in the country's electricity supply industry. In order to deal with a mounting crisis in the power stations the Government ordered 'Operation Black Current', requiring the Submarine Command to deploy all available submarines to various ports around the country, where they would be used as generating stations supplying what electricity they could produce to the National Grid. The normal routine of the Third Flotilla, our home when the 'perishers' were on the Clyde, was completely disrupted, submarines and depot ship all disappearing for duties elsewhere, and we had to make-do with ad hoc arrangements, including accommodation ashore at Rothesay. Trudging through snow and ice in the early hours of a morning down to the pier from the little cottage lent to Maureen and me by Sam Woods (Captain (S) Three) and his wife remain a vivid memory of the spring of 1947. Our pet submarine and the destroyers and frigates on which we relied for targets were not affected in any way by 'Black Current' so the daily round of dummy attacks at sea continued unabated.

A minor casualty of the severity of that winter was my beloved old 3-litre Bentley; rescued on my return from the Far East from the garden shed where it had spent the war, it had required no more than a new battery and some petrol in its tank to be on the road again in running order. It served me faithfully during the times I was at Blockhouse and when on leave, and Maureen and I drove away in it trimphantly from our wedding in London. But it was vintage 1923, a year younger than she, and with its open body and other specialities of its breed, fun for a bachelor and acceptable, maybe, in fine weather for the fairer sex, but barely so in the cold, the rain and finally the snow of that winter. With reluctance we agreed a more comfortable closed car was now needed. Being loyal to the marque, a 4½ litre close-coupled saloon took its place. (The 3-litre Bentley was created by W.O. Bentley and formed in his mind prior to 1914. His idea was to produce a very fast motor car, on the principle of a racing car, but de-tuned. He built into it enough strength and weight to ensure reliability and durability in the hands of private owners. Later he produced 4½ litre and 6½ litre engines). Buying this was one of the most stupid decisions I have ever made. It looked marvellous and was a true Bentley; but it was seldom seen on the road, for with strict petrol rationing still in force, there was nothing like sufficient available to meet its consumption of a gallon for around twelve miles. It remained in the garage whilst I pedalled to and from work on an ancient bicycle and Maureen shopped by bus or on foot.

There was more to do in the appointment of 'teacher' than just teaching the 'perishers'. The Flag Officer Submarines, returned to his traditional headquarters at Blockhouse from his war-time base at Northways in London, used the incumbent as a kind of 'think-tank' for forward looking ideas in the development of submarine tactics and for the solution of associated problems. It was not sufficient just to look back at the recently ended war and rest content with the lessons it had taught, a very natural inclination in the immediate post-war years, for great changes were on the way. By far the most significant being the ideas beginning to emerge around the advent at some time in the future of a nuclear powered submarine, the true submarine as opposed to existing 'submersibles'. Flag Officer Submarines (Rear Admiral G.E. Creasy), with a very distinguished career behind him and the first non-submariner to hold the post, brought me directly into contact with such a far reaching development, by asking me to write a paper on the potential use and value of such a submarine. I had no real scientific facts to go on and I could only give rein to my imagination. My scribblings, tidied up into a formal submission, envisaged an under water future on the lines of how air power had developed, with 'fighter' and 'bomber' submarines of unlimited endurance, freed of the handicap of charging batteries, ranging the oceans far and wide permanently submerged. Perhaps it was far fetched at the time, or so some thought, but not when, thirty or forty years later, we see the corresponding nuclear powered hunter-killer and missile-carrier submarines of the major naval powers. I became an enthusiastic supporter of the concept of a nuclear powered submarine.

After more than two years looking after the 'perishers', I was ready for a change, but when it came about it did not take me out of the submarine world, as I had rather expected, and it landed me very firmly in a desk job. I had long dreaded such an eventuality but recognized its inevitability with the passage of time, and the pill was now sweetened by being appointed to the staff of Flag Officer Submarines (Vice Admiral Mansfield) as his Staff Officer, Operations (SOO) in January 1948. Not having taken the staff course I had qualms about being able to cope with the job, but was reassured by Joe Cowell when I came to relieve him, for the third time since the original occasion in 1939. Joe had worked miracles in clearing his desk of its usual load of piles of paper and documents, to ease the turnover between us and make it surprisingly simple. His most important message to me was that a bottle of gin and a bottle of whisky easily fitted within the capacious bulk of the standard Admiralty brief-case, without in any way outwardly revealing their presence, and that they were as essential as the more usual contents on occasions that took one beyond the normal sources of supply.

It did not take long for my desk to revert to its state of being submerged by paper. FOS, or FOS/M as he was about to become, was the professional adviser to the Board of Admiralty on all matters connected with submarines and his office was therefore included within the circulation of every Admiralty paper (docket) in any way concerned with them. There was a constant flow of dockets between the Admiralty, London and Bath, and Blockhouse and though many dealt with subjects other than 'Operations', nearly all had connotations thereto. On top of those of direct interest there were more than enough to keep me heavily engaged. Added to that was the routine work, the general oversight of FOS/M's far-flung empire of submarines, in Australia, Canada, the Far East, the Mediterranean and, not least, in Home Waters, with direct responsibility for the programme for their refits and relief. Overall, I found there was little spare time and Maureen rarely saw me at home before seven or eight of an evening.

There were many material changes taking place or being planned, much derived basically from what we had learnt from the Germans at the end of the war, particularly their Type XXI U-boat; all of which had an impact on the 'Operations desk'. 'Snort', copied from the German 'Schnorkel', was being fitted to all British operational submarines, 'A', 'T' and 'S' classes, and it was totally changing the pattern of submarine operations with much having to be learnt and new drills introduced to make the best and safest use of the new technique. 'The Snort' was a tube which could be raised whilst the submarine was submerged to allow it to 'breathe' fresh air for diesel engine propulsion. In theory it did away with having to charge the batteries on the surface. An 'S' class boat, *Scotsman*, was also being converted and streamlined to give exceptionally high under-water speed and endurance, followed by a long period of trials to assess manoeuvrability and tactics. Other 'S' boats were streamlined to provide high speed targets for the training of surface A/S forces. Two experimental submarines – *Excalibur* and *Explorer* – powered by High Test Peroxide (HTP) engines based on a German design (the Walther engine) were under construction by Vickers at Barrow. So there was much going on.

It was an immensely exciting period when everyone was consumed with new thoughts, new ideas, on how submarines, their weapons and operations would develop in the future. This ferment was fuelled by a directive issued by the Admiralty in the latter half of 1947 which stated that in any future war the primary aim of our submarines was to be the destruction of enemy submarines. The sinking of surface ships was to be secondary. The immediate consequence was a concentration of effort on the difficult problem of how to bring to successful fruition a torpedo attack on a submerged target, one that could not be seen but could only be heard. The periscope became of less importance, tracking the target by sound alone was the vital factor in any attack. It had been done once towards the end of the war, when *Venturer* (Lieut. J.S. Launders) sank the German U-boat U864 in February 1945 when both were dived. The theory and tactics of how best to achieve success needed much investigation and then all future training had to be adapted accordingly. There was corresponding need for material developments. Asdic sets must be produced to give more accurate information and submarines must be streamlined to give improved and more silent under-water performance; new, sophisticated, target-seeking torpedoes must also be designed and brought into service. A continuing programme of design and development, and training to suit the new role, occupied the minds of all on FOS/M's staff.

FOS/M's annual 'Summer War' was a diversion from the unending stream of paper that flooded my desk, though the planning for it and its subsequent analysis, SOO's responsibility, only added to its volume. The occasion provided a welcome break from office routine as I accompanied FOS/M, his Chief of Staff and Communications Officer (his Flag Lieutenant) to a temporary operational headquarters in one of the submarine depot ships located somewhere in the North-West Approaches or West coast of Scotland, for two weeks of large-scale tactical exercises. A large number of surface and air A/S forces were involved, and also as many of the operational submarines from the home based squadrons as could be made available; (the new nomenclature referring to squadrons instead of flotillas had recently come into force). Designed as much for the benefit of the A/S element as for the submariners, the exercises revolved around giving as many opportunities as possible to the submarines to attack escorted convoys and, conversely, the A/S forces to search for and hunt the submarines. The emphasis remained on the lines of the tactics in use at the end of the war, training in the new role of submarine versus submarine was not yet sufficiently advanced for this to be included. It was to come in future 'Summer Wars', before they finally faded out on being superseded in later years by major NATO exercises.

After nearly two years as SOO I began to think of my next job, by 1950 I would have had fifteen years of continuous submarine appointments and it was time for a change. I needed to see something of the rest of the Navy, certainly if I wished to advance in rank. I was very keen to do the Naval Staff Course, capitalizing on the experience and knowledge acquired in my present job, and thereafter chance my arm in General Service. Although the course was reputedly hard work, I would be under less pressure at Greenwich compared to my recent past and I could liken it to a 'sabbatical'. Furthermore, it would allow me to see more of my growing family on a more regular basis.

I pressed my claim with the Chief of Staff, Jackie Slaughter (Captain J.E. Slaughter). In his own inimitable way, and language, he turned it down flat, saying in no way would he recommend me for a year's idleness on the Staff Course. I persisted, demanding to see FOS/M himself (Rear Admiral G. Grantham) in the hope that he would agree that all I had learnt while his SOO should be consolidated properly by my taking the Staff Course and qualifying for the magic 'p.s.c.' (pass staff course) after my name in the

Navy List. Jackie could not refuse me this, but first he would have a word with the Admiral. The outcome was foregone. In the nicest possible way, as only to be expected from 'Granny' Grantham, he told me I was already quite adequately experienced in staff duties and that I was long overdue for a spell in General Service. Thus came about my appointment, in the summer of 1950, to the cruiser *Liverpool* as her Executive Officer.

Chapter Fourteen

General Service, 1950–54

My return to General Service after such a length of time in submarines was not a simple, straightforward change of appointments. Professionally I had to bring myself up-to-date with all the developments in surface ships and surface warfare since my midshipman's days, and learn from scratch the mastery of everything involved in running a 'big ship'. On the domestic front there was a harder problem, a difficult choice as to whether Maureen and our family, by now two small children, could accompany me to Malta, following the practice usually adopted by those appointed to ships abroad and able to take advantage of the special allowances provided by the Admiralty for 'accompanied service'.

Our eldest, born in 1947, had been found, to our dismay, to be profoundly deaf, a fact that had a major influence on our lives in the future, and especially so if any appointements would divorce me from normal family life. She was now already well established at a boarding school devoted entirely to the education of deaf children, taking them from the very earliest age of two years. We were faced with either taking her away from school so that the whole family could come out to Malta, with no educational facilities there for deaf children, or whether she should stay on at school, in which case Maureen would remain in England and keep our family home going. We were now established in our own house in the village of Shedfield, half way between Portsmouth and Winchester. The special needs of a deaf child, still almost in infancy, were over-riding and so we reluctantly decided that we would have to be separate for my time in *Liverpool*. If things worked out well, Maureen would be able to get to Malta for a short visit at some convenient time.

In June 1950, I travelled out by train through France and Italy to Syracuse in Sicily and thence by the steamer *Knight of Malta* to the usual age-old berth by the Customs House in Grand Harbour. My mind was preoccupied, primarily with the thoughts of parting from my family and what the future might hold. I have little recollection of the journey other than it went smoothly and there were no visible signs in the countryside we passed through of the devastation the war must have caused. The *Knight of Malta* had survived in some miraculous way and was now back on the regular Malta–Sicily run, which she had been doing for as long as I could remember. It was comforting to be reminded that some of Malta's pre-war features continued as of old.

Perhaps it was as well that I was without the distractions of a family when I arrived at Malta. *Liverpool* was in the dockyard, in dry-dock, in the final stages of a refit and combined with this was the process of partially re-commissioning, with many of her officers and men newly arrived from England. To my eyes things were chaotic and every moment of my time was taken up trying to establish control of a situation beyond anything I had ever experienced, or imagined.

Meeting my newly joined fellow Commanders for the first time, I reflected on the problems facing us. The Engineer Commander (T.W.E. Dommett) had been for many years totally involved in Ordnance Engineering, guns, hydraulics and such like, and admitted he had little experience of boilers and steam turbines. The Paymaster Commander (A. Lade) known now as Commander (S), had been an Admiral's Secretary for years and years and so had no detailed knowledge of pay, victuals, stores and accounting for such matters. My own ignorance was obvious to all. Over a drink in the wardroom we quickly named ourselves 'The Three Blind Mice' and hoped that the Surgeon Commander (S. Miles) was more up-to-date in medical matters, on which he was able to reassure us. There was no 'Farmer's Wife' to inflict injury as in the children's rhyme, but we knew the ship was destined to become the flagship of the Commander-in-Chief of the Mediterranean Fleet, and woe betide us then if things were not one hundred per cent right. This meant, in the vernacular of the time, that we had to pull our fingers out and work closely together as a team. We made some mistakes initially, but soon we had a very happy ship in our hands.

We were helped towards this by the reputation lingering on from the last commission when *Liverpool* had been the flagship of Rear Admiral Earl Mountbatten when he commanded the First Cruiser Squadron, a post he had vacated just before the ship had to submit to the present upheaval of re-fit and re-commissioning. To capitalise on her past record was not difficult once the inevitable reaction of 'didn't do things like that in the last commission' had been overcome. The Captain (Captain J. Shaw-Hamilton) had not changed and was a constant reminder of the standards we should be aiming at. A gunnery officer by training, a tall, austere, solitary man, of more erudite turn of mind than most of the naval officers I have ever come across, he gave me never-ending encouragement. It was not his wont to angrily interfere or send for me when he saw or heard something not to his liking, so my confidence grew as he would invite me to join him on his daily walks up and down the quarterdeck, using the opportunity quietly to deliver advice or judgement. Invitations expanded later, to accompany him on his long walks ashore at week-ends through the Maltese countryside and along its cliffs, occasions to see and learn more and more of the island's unique way of life, its beauties and especially the wealth of its wild flowers.

Two stalwarts from the Lower Deck, the Master-at-Arms (MAA Atkins) and the Chief Boatswain's Mate (CPO Bowden), loyally did all they could to make sure I never put a foot wrong within their respective spheres; the

HMS *Liverpool* (Captain J.D. Shaw-Hamilton) and officers, author on his right, 1950.

Chief Bosun's Mate of HMS *Liverpool*, CPO Bowden with Boy Hoare on his right and author on his left, 1951.

former when the daily routine of 'Commander's Requestmen and Defaulters' brought these before me and, more generally, in all matters of discipline and welfare. The 'Chief Buffer' could be relied on utterly for seeing that the many daily tasks loosely termed 'seamanship' or 'seamanlike' were satisfactorily performed, and that the external appearance of the ship was faultless. Without their support I could not have begun to master the day-to-day intricacies of keeping in close touch with that most important factor of all, the sailor. Besides them, of course, were the Heads of Departments and individual Divisional Officers whose contributions to the aim of a happy and contented ship's company were as essential as anyone's.

When the refit was finished, with much relief all round, *Liverpool* was clear of the dockyard and a lengthy period of drills and exercises followed throughout the autumn of 1950. It was very reminiscent in many ways of those long hours spent at sea in dull routine training which I had experienced in the early thirties, but there was a difference now, in two respects; weaponry and technology had advanced enormously and account had to be taken of all that the war had taught – for instance, fire fighting and damage control were important innovations. Even more noticeable, the age bracket of the ship's company had altered significantly. Before the war, two badge and three badge ratings had been commonplace, indicating a predominantly long service structure but now the average age of the ship's company was almost twenty-one years and with National Service still contributing a proportion, the majority had had little time at sea previously. The task of moulding such inexperienced material into an efficient fighting unit was daunting, and it would never have succeeded but for the teaching and example of the 'old hands', the Senior Ratings, who on the seaman side almost invariably were ex-*Ganges* or ex-*St. Vincent* boys. They were the backbone of the Navy.

The months slipped by quickly for we were kept busy, but by the end of the year it was reckoned *Liverpool* had 'come of age', an event soon to be marked by the ship hoisting the flag of the Commander-in-Chief, Admiral Sir John Edelsten. It was a proud moment, to be elevated to this position of 'top dog', but it imposed added responsibilities. Henceforth we must be seen to excel in all the activities of the Fleet, setting an example to everyone.

Before the new burden landed on my shoulders and taking advantage of our working-up programme easing towards its end, Maureen was able to take a short break from home chores and join me in late November for two weeks. We were thrown into a dizzy social round of cocktail parties, dinners and dances, the pace of which we were barely able to meet. It was an exhausting but blissful fortnight which not even the rigours of the Tigne Court Hotel in Sliema and rising early so that I could be on board for 'hands fall in' at six o'clock every morning, could detract from; it was akin to a second honeymoon. But, alas, it all came to an end too quickly, Maureen returning to the children, I back to my 'bachelor' existence on board.

HMS *Liverpool* in Grand Harbour, Malta, 1950.

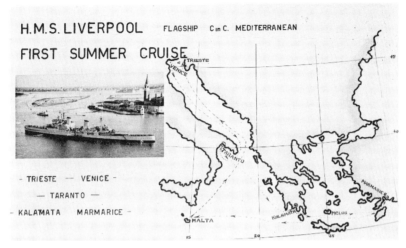

HMS *Liverpool* – First Summer Cruise, 1951.

In large measure the Fleet followed the pattern of the thirties in leaving Malta on regular cruises around the Mediterranean. As flagship, we ostensibly had first choice in selecting the most delectable ports of call but in effect the matter was usually dictated by other considerations. The Fleet was still a powerful force, with its Commander-in-Chief able to exert an influence on international politics and diplomacy. Our visits around the Mediterranean were tailored accordingly.

British relations with Yugoslavia were improving in 1951 following Marshal Tito's break with Stalin. With the aim of consolidating the process, it was arranged that the C-in-C should visit Split in Dalmatia in mid-summer of 1951 so that an official exchange of visits between him and Tito could take place. It would be the first occasion since the war that a ship flying the White Ensign had visited a country within the Communist bloc and great importance was attached to it being a success. It would be marked by a great deal of ceremonial comings and goings, between the British Ambassador and C-in-C on one side and Marshal Tito in person and some of his Ministers on the other. On board *Liverpool* we prepared accordingly.

The programme got off to a good start on the first morning of the visit, occupied by the C-in-C's official calls ashore. In the afternoon the day should have concluded with Marshal Tito arriving on board at four thirty, formally to return the C-in-C's call and then be conducted by him on a tour of the ship. This visit by a Head of State required the full pomp and circumstance of 21-gun salutes, guard and band paraded and the whole ship's company fallen in by Divisions on the upper deck, in all of which timing was a key element, as on any ceremonial occasion, but things did not work out quite as planned.

HMS *Liverpool* – Second Summer Cruise, 1951.

HMS *Liverpool* at Venice, 1951.

Twenty-five minutes before the Marshal was due to arrive, I was in my cabin changing into full dress white uniform, like everybody else on board at that moment, when my telephone rang. It was the yeoman of signals on watch on the flag deck, reporting that what appeared to be Marshal Tito's barge was heading towards the ship at high speed. A crisis obviously was on our hands, because we had about five minutes, at the most, to get everyone paraded before he reached the ship. I seized the microphone to the ship's broadcasting system, announcing to all that they would be ordered to fall in for Divisions in three minutes, a full ten minutes in advance of the previously planned time. The response was magnificent, and as Tito's barge drew alongside, for it was indeed him, at 4.15 pm instead of 4.30 pm, everyone was on deck, in place, correctly dressed including the last marine in the guard of honour on the quarterdeck still frantically trying to buckle his pipe-clayed belt. We subsequently heard that Tito never kept to a published time-table, always varying the times at his personal whim as a security precaution, and perhaps we should have made allowance for this. I breathed a mighty sigh of relief as he was received by the C-in-C at the top of the gangway, confident that the ship's company had risen to the occasion and that, outwardly, everything down to the last detail was as it should be.

After his inspection of the crew and his tour of the upper deck and bridges, the Marshal asked the C-in-C if his visit could be extended and he be taken round the ship below decks. I was aghast at the thought, imagining the state of the mess decks, discarded clothing scattered about as everyone had thrown off what they were wearing in haste to don their best uniforms in answer to my urgent call giving warning of Tito's early arrival. Also, no doubt, augmented by half empty cups of tea and other signs of disorder, reducing the ship's company's living quarters to a shambles of untidiness. I need not have worried; the C-in-C obviously had the same thoughts for he very firmly replied, 'I am sorry, Marshal, but that will *not* be possible.' I can only speculate on what the Marshal and his minions thought of this refusal, but from their reactions I suspect they believed we had a nuclear bomb or some sort of secret weapon concealed on board, somewhere below decks.

The visit, however, ended on an amicable note, with Tito full of smiles as he bade goodbye to the C-in-C and the British Ambassador, Sir Charles Peake; but I recollect that his entourage, the four or five close aides accompanying him, did not follow suit, remaining a grim and unpleasant looking bunch of thugs. *Liverpool* remained at anchor off Split for a further few days, with everyone having the opportunity for leave ashore. There was no great rush for this, the general consensus being that the place offered nothing, no life, no laughter, no music, nothing in the shops, everything (including the people and their clothes) universally gray, drab, dull and uninviting. Yugoslavia at that time was no advertisement for Communism.

Captain J.D. Luce (later, as Admiral Sir David Luce, to become First Sea Lord) was now in command of *Liverpool*. He was more enquiring than his predecessor and I had to adjust to being sent for frequently to answer his queries, but once satisfied he made no greater demands on my time and attention and, being a submariner, I found we had much in common. The routine of the ship continued to run smoothly and, when in Malta, we saw less of him on board as, like most senior officers, he had been able to arrange for his wife to join him.

There was trouble on the Suez Canal in the autumn of 1951 and *Liverpool* was suddenly sent from Malta to Tobruk to embark the 3rd Battalion of the Grenadier Guards and take them to Port Said. Hurried arrangements were

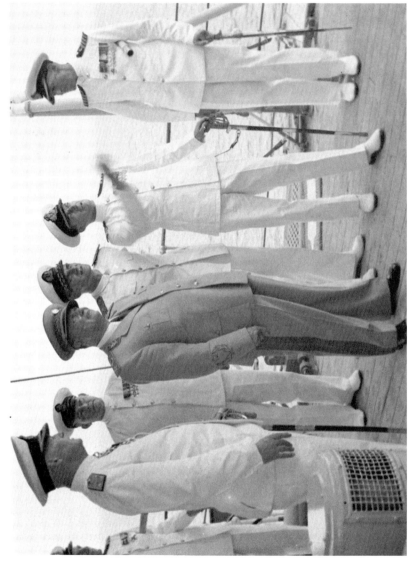

Tito visits HMS *Liverpool* – Commander-in-Chief Mediterranean, Admiral Sir John Edelsten on left, 1951.

made for their accommodation and feeding, their presence practically doubling the number of men on board, but fortunately this would not be for long as the trip to Port Said at high speed was brief. The guardsmen had been well prepared on what to expect, even to the extent of wearing gym shoes as they embarked, with their heavy boots slung round their necks. It was a wise precaution, saving them from sliding and slipping about on highly polished steel decks or scarring my precious teak quarterdeck, for which I blessed their Colonel and his foresight. The only trouble I encountered was that I could never develop any form of conversation with any of them, officers or other ranks. Whenever I opened my mouth the only response was a loud monosyllabic 'Sir' coupled with their smartly springing to attention. It was difficult to get beyond this.

Liverpool remained at Port Said for some weeks, acting as 'Guardship' and assisting the Canal Company in the daily routine of keeping ships moving through the Canal, which was almost brought to a halt by a prolonged strike by all their Egyptian employees. There were daily conferences on board with the British military authorities and representatives of the Canal Company to ensure that traffic was kept flowing, but there was virtually no contact with the local, Egyptian, authorities. Diplomatic relations with Eygpt were very strained at the time, over British occupation of the Canal Zone and the future of the Canal itself. Because of the tense situation, Port Said was out of bounds to everyone, and the only leave that could be granted was to a NAAFI canteen set up within the closely guarded compound around Navy House, of easy access as *Liverpool* was moored with her stern to its wharf. It was a trying situation for all on board, with very little to do but sit and wait for events to unfold, and was particularly irksome for those who had had the expectation of being with their wives and families in Malta throughout these weeks of now enforced isolation.

Relief came at last when *Liverpool* was ordered to return to Malta, to spend Christmas and New Year in dry-dock for routine maintenance and bottom cleaning. Everyone was happy to be back and to relax in familiar and more secure surroundings, with leave liberally given so that all could make the most of the season's festivities. We soon learnt, though, that as soon as we were out of dock, in early January 1952, we were to go back to Port Said, to resume the tedious round of duties there, with all its restrictions. This news spurred the urge to enjoy to the full our brief fortnight's break, with an added bonus for me personally when I heard on the thirty-first December 1951 that my name was included in the New Year's List for promotion to Captain. There were joyous celebrations that night, seeing in the New Year.

I was still on the crest of a wave when *Liverpool* left Malta in early January, feelings reinforced by a remarkable record of good behaviour by the ship's company. In our fortnight's stay there had been no offences at all of any serious nature and all I had had to deal with at my 'defaulter's table' were an insignificant number, barely in double figures, of very minor leave-breaking infringements, mere peccadilloes considering all the emotions and frustrations engendered by our previous weeks of inaction and restrictions at Port Said. I was proud indeed of how well behaved such a young ship's company had been, when subject to all the excitements and temptations ashore over Christmas and New Year.

By the time we were back in Port Said, moored in the same berth, I knew my successor had been appointed and could be expected within a few days, and that I was then to take passage home in the MV *Circassia*, a cargo liner of the Anchor Line. The situation ashore was worse than in December, with no abatement in the strike and its effects on the Canal's business; moreover, fighting, with sporadic rifle fire, had broken out between rival factions in the town of Port Said and its environs. *Liverpool* never appeared to be the direct target of the shooting, but when outbursts became particularly fierce the random bullet passed overhead, requiring caution in the use of the upper deck. One especially noisy morning, the guard and band could only be paraded for 'Colours', immobile and sheltering behind 'Y' turret on the quarterdeck. There was a risk attached to having them paraded, but it was immediately evident that it was worth taking. The playing of the National Anthems (British and Egyptian) brought an instant halt to all the shooting, a respite that endured for the rest of the day. The calming effect of this daily ceremonial routine was a hopeful sign that the fighting ashore was not too serious, and it seemed right that this procedure should continue unless conditions got much worse.

I had not long to wait before my relief arrived, time had gone swiftly, but then there was an agonising wait for the *Circassia*. Eventually, after an almost unendurable delay of a few hours, with farewell drinks extending far beyond what I had anticipated, I finally said goodbye around midnight to a ship that, in my eighteen months in her, had brought me many new experiences, mostly happy, but some anxious. As I was rowed away in a whaler, crewed by the senior officers from the wardroom, I could only reflect on how lucky I had been to have had such a loyal and wonderful ship's company behind me all the way through.

Safely home, and seeing our third child for the first time, it was a joy to have what I viewed as a well earned leave, clear of all professional commitments and responsibilities and where the family could come first. In February 1952, I had an appointment with the Naval Secretary to the First Lord of the Admiralty, the appointing authority for all Captains and those of higher rank and therefore the arbiter of my future.

Rear-Admiral R.G. Onslow was a very distinguished destroyer captain of the last war, the recipient of more DSOs (four) than almost anyone else in the Navy. As Maureen and I walked over from Waterloo Station to the Admiralty we noticed that an unusual hush seemed to have settled over London, then we saw the heavy black headlines on the news stands. The King had died during the night. The Naval Secretary consequently had much more on his hands that morning than the appointments of newly promoted Captains, but he found the time to welcome me to the new hierarchy and discuss what might lie ahead for me, starting with my next appointment, that of Captain of the Underwater Detection Establishment (UDE) at Portland in Dorset. It would be an entirely new field to me and I was very happy at the thought of being the first submariner to hold the post, hitherto always in the hands of the A/S specialist.

In the late spring of 1952, the family moved to Weymouth, to a comfortable rented house on its outskirts and handy to Portland, and I was soon in the throes of trying to find my feet in a job totally different from anything I had ever met before. UDE was a civilian establishment, staffed by scientists, technical laboratory assistants and a few naval 'application' officers, and I had to learn a new language and how to work with a new breed of people. UDE was the brains behind all research and development into means of detecting objects under water, from submarines to the much smaller and more difficult magnetic and acoustic mines lying on the sea bed. With its origins going back to the early days of Asdics at the end of the First World War, then the most promising means of finding submarines under water, it was now fully involved in designing and developing highly sophisticated equipment capable of meeting all the under-water threats, submarine and mine, posed by an expanding Soviety navy.

There was close co-operation in all its work with its kindred research and development establishment, the Underwater Weapons Establishment (UWE), then at Havant in Hampshire but about to occupy a monstrosity of a building, truly to become a 'white elephant', now being completed in the centre of Portland Bill. Both establishments came directly under the Director of Underwater Warfare (DUW) within the Admiralty, who kept a tight rein on all our activities, tried to keep the two establishments in step and, when in agreement with our ideas, fought our battles for the money and resources to develop these.

I doubt if I could have mastered the complexity of it all but for the skilful tutoring and helpful advice that I consistently received from the Chief Scientist (A.C. Law) professionally responsible for the technical content of UDE's work. A shrewd and pawky Aberdonian, Tony Law had 'got his feet wet' with the trials at sea of the very earliest Asdic sets, and throughout his career had insisted that such trials at sea were the essential and ultimate test before any equipment could be accepted by the Navy. He kept all eyes glued on this target. From my very first day he gave me every support, including my stipulation that no paper, document or treatise on any subject would be accepted on my desk unless it, or a covering explanation, was in plain English. As nothing reached me except via his desk, my aim was easily established.

Once I had got the hang of things and used to a regular 'nine to five' routine with undisturbed week-ends, only interrupted in exceptional circumstances, Maureen and I were able to enjoy the kind of settled life that

Maureen launching *Decibel* experimental trials ship 1953. A.C. Law, Chief Scientist, on right of author.

seldom came the way of a naval officer. Dorset was a beautiful county and we made the most of it. Kind neighbours invited us to watch the Coronation of HM The Queen on their newly acquired television set, a novelty in those days and I think the only set in the whole neighbourhood. We attended the Coronation Review of the Fleet at Spithead, on board HMS *Brocklesby*, a Hunt class destroyer attached to UDE for experimental work. Maureen launched, at a shipyard in Poole, the little vessel appropriately named *Decibel*, to become a tender to UDE for trials at sea of all mine-hunting equipment under development. There were many other functions and events bringing new facets into our lives, giving variety and ensuring things never became dull or monotonous.

This happy time could not, however, go on indefinitely and after two years I received my next appointment, one I could not but relish; it was to be Captain (D) of the First Destroyer Squadron, then part of the Mediterranean Fleet.

Chapter Fifteen

Afloat and Ashore, 1954–61

To be back at sea again in command of a crack destroyer squadron, and with Malta beckoning as a temporary home for the family, was a most pleasing and inviting prospect, for which we began to plan as soon as I had left UDE. All was going smoothly until the Admiralty suddenly changed the rules governing ships serving full two year commissions in the Mediterranean, qualifying them for all the related benefits of 'accompanied service', with its special terms enabling wives and families to live in Malta. This concession was now to be abolished but in recompense the time abroad was to be reduced, with ships rotating between the Mediterranean and Home Fleets, spending half the commission in each fleet.

The first such ship to be so affected was *Chevron* of the First Destroyer Squadron. She was now in Portsmouth Dockyard completing a refit, was

HMS *Chevron*'s re-commissioning 1954. Crew marching through HM Dockyard, Portsmouth. Author leading on the right.

due to re-commission in June and on return to the Mediterranean would become the 'Leader' of the 1st DS in place of *Chequers*, the Squadron's regular 'Leader', who would then return to the UK for major refit. My new appointment was 'to *Chevron* and as Captain (D)' and hence, like all on board for her new commission, I did not qualify for the now outdated 'accompanied service'. Maureen and I had to forgo, like many others, all plans for two years' family life in Malta and, once again, accept that she and the children would have to remain in England. It was a bitter blow and disappointment, but financially there was no alternative. It became even harder to accept when *Chevron* reached Malta, where the rest of the ships in the Fleet were still enjoying all the privileges and benefits of having their families with them.

On the voyage out to Malta, after a few days trials and elementary working-up at Portland, my seamanship and that of others on board was put to an acid test when *Chevron* was ordered to tow an unmanned ALGERINE class minesweeper from Gibraltar dockyard, where she had been refitted, to Malta, to join others of her class laid up in reserve. A 'dumb' tow, she was a fractious charge, riding high in the water and consequently horribly subject to windage, liable to career wildly off course if and when the wind blew strongly or changed direction, or, from time to time just as the whim took her. But once we learnt how to master these pernicious tricks all went smoothly, though with speed limited to seven or eight knots the passage took twice as long as usual. I was glad to hand her over to a tug off Grand Harbour before facing, as I recollected from my midshipman's destroyer time many years ago, the daunting task of driving *Chevron* at speed stern first up Sliema Creek to her moorings, threading her way past all the other destroyers of the Fleet, who were hardened veterans keen to see how the newcomer would fare. The manoeuvre had always been regarded as a foremost test of ship-handling ability, as indeed it was and I am glad to remember that Flag Officer, Destroyers (Rear Admiral R.D. Watson), watching from the balcony of his headquarters ashore on Manoel Island, signalled his approval when *Chevron* was safely and expeditiously secured to her buoys.

Over the next few days, between the usual official calls on Senior Officers from the C-in-C downwards, I formally took over as Captain (D) from my predecessor, Captain R.C.M. Duckworth, who then promptly sailed for home in *Chequers*. As soon as she had gone, *Chevron* painted the top of her funnel black, the sign for all to see and as tradition laid down, that she was now Leader of the Squadron. Outwardly the transformation may have appeared straightforward, but it was not all that simple. *Chequers* had been designed and built as a leader, somewhat larger than the rest of her class and capable of accommodating a full squadron staff, whereas *Chevron* was smaller and room could not be found on board for all. Therefore the surplus had to be lodged amongst the rest of the Squadron. This dispersion did not make for easy administration. At the time the Squadron was four-strong, up

Sliema Creek, Malta. Manoel Island in centre. Destroyers above and to left, 1954.

HMS *Chevron* re-fuelling from HMS *Newcastle*.

to its official strength with *Chevron, Chaplet, Charity* and *Comet.* They were lovely destroyers, built around the end of the war and almost the last of their type; a delight to handle, they were well armed with guns, torpedoes and the ahead-throwing A/S mortars, SQUID, more deadly weapons than depth charges which by now had virtually disappeared from the Fleet. I counted myself very lucky to have such a wonderful command.

In the early autumn when at sea on a large scale strategic exercise, the Squadron was escorting the aircraft carrier *Centaur* southbound through the Straits of Messina. It was shortly before daybreak but still dark, with the force gradually increasing speed as it gained more open waters. The destroyers were spread out about two miles apart as an A/S screen, about the same distance ahead of the carrier and all ships were darkened, showing no lights. By a series of inexcusable mishaps and mistakes *Chevron* failed to act on one of the signalled increases of speed, from six knots to nine knots, and dropped astern of her station until she was overtaken by *Centaur,* ending up virtually alongside this huge vessel whose overhanging flight deck started to wreak havoc on our upper works. The first intimation I had was a frightening noise which brought me to the bridge in a rush from my cabin one deck below; as my head emerged through the hatchway on the bridge, looking up the first thing I saw overhead was the wing of an AVENGER aeroplane which was parked on the edge of the carrier's flight deck. It was a terrible sight as I realized the full horror of our situation, but I was able to extricate *Chevron* without her suffering more damage than had already been done.

The director, that vital bit of equipment for controlling the guns, had been hit a savage blow and was spinning like a top when I reached the bridge, it was a major casualty with all its electrical cables in a tangled mess. The Bofors gun in the starboard wing of the bridge structure was another casualty, the top of the funnel had been bashed in and some radio aerials had been lost. We were lucky that things were not worse, and, above all, that no one had been hurt. *Centaur* appeared to be undamaged.

It was an appalling example of a failure to keep an alert look-out on the part of both ships. Neither the Officers of the Watch and Duty Staff Officers on their respective bridges, nor the look-outs where posted, in *Chevron's* case on either wing of the bridge and right aft on the quarterdeck, had seen or reported that they had sighted the other ship, when the two, over a long period, had been drawing closer and closer together. I was shaken to the core that such a thing could have happened.

There followed, naturally, a host of post mortems, and on arrival back in Malta the formal Board of Inquiry. I never saw its findings, but in their light the C-in-C, Admiral Earl Mountbatten, decided, contrary to all expectations, that there would be no Courts Martial and that he would deal with the matter himself, with which the Admiralty agreed. In my subsequent unhappy interview with him in which he delivered his formal severe admonishment, officially recorded on paper, I could not but wholly agree with him that it was 'the stupidest collision ever.' It really was. The war, and all my experience through it, had taught me the absolutely vital importance to the safety of the ship of maintaining at all times the most vigilant visual look-out, which the advent of radar had not changed. That I had failed to impress all of this on those on watch in *my* ship, so that nobody actually *saw* and reported anything during the many crucial minutes prior to the collision, was a self-inflicted wound that I felt deeply and which has left a lasting scar.

Fortunately *Chevron's* seaworthiness had not been affected in any way, so she continued to lead the Squadron until, two months later, Gibraltar dockyard could accept her for repairs. My spirits were lifted by Maureen coming out from England to join me for a few days when the Squadron was at Villefranche in the south of France, and then coming on to Malta for some happy weeks, staying with Sam Woods and his wife Murray, he now being Chief of Staff to the C-in-C. On my taking *Chevron* to Gibraltar Maureen was able to hitch a lift there in the RFA (Royal Fleet Auxiliary) *Fort Duquesne*, before returning to England a few days later when I went back to Malta. To have had her with me at that particular time, soon after an event in which I had so obviously 'blotted my copy-book', gave my morale a tremendous boost.

Returning to Malta I had to accept that I was largely confined to an office ashore on Manoel Island, from which I continued to run the Squadron,

Ship's Company, HMS *Chevron* 1955, Gibralter.

HMS *Chevron* full power trial, 1955.

whilst living comfortably with Sam and Murray Woods. But it was not the same thing as having one's own ship to live in and command. I was very glad when, eventually, *Chevron* was fully repaired and I was able to fly to Gibraltar to bring her back to Malta to resume leadership of the Squadron. The difficult and frustrating days were over and in a few months' time, by the summer of 1955, we were back in England, as part of the Home Fleet, for the second leg of the commission.

In late September *Chevron* had the best of all the 'foreign' visits she paid during her commission, nearly a week in Copenhagen. This visit was classed as 'informal', thus benefiting from the very minimum of ceremonies and formalities, and its enjoyment for me was more than doubled by Maureen being able to join me. Passing through the Kiel Canal on *Chevron*'s way there, I had found that the memories of the war were still too close for me to be friendly with the Germans; but with the Danes, who could not but enjoy all that Copenhagen had to offer? The days went all too swiftly and then, in October, *Chevron* joined up with a number of other ships from the Home Fleet, led by the C-in-C, Admiral Sir Michael Denny, flying his flag in the minelayer *Apollo*. We steamed through the Baltic and up the river Neva to moor right in the centre of Leningrad (as it then was), on an official, formal visit to the USSR. It was the first occasion that ships of the Royal Navy had formally visited a Russian port since the end of the war and it was viewed as

H.M.S. *Chevron* full power trial, 1955.

of some diplomatic importance, as had been the case with *Liverpool*'s visit to Yugoslavia four years before.

I was reminded immediately of that earlier occasion when I became aware of the drabness and dreariness of life for the masses under Communist rule. Throughout this visit, for every hour of the day and the night, the pavements along the banks of the Neva were lined by crowds three or four deep, and dressed in the universal rough, dark-coloured cloth, silently staring at the visiting ships. On passing through their ranks when going ashore or returning on board, they stretched out their hands to finger our clothes, to feel the texture; it was a strange and eerie experience, as though we were men from some different planet. Beyond the serried ranks there was the same lack of laughter, gaiety and music; it was a depressing picture, reinforced by the uniform dirty grey of the houses, their paint peeling off, and all bearing a tired, uncared-for-look. In most striking contrast were the performances of Ballet and Opera, many of which we were invited to attend; performances unsurpassed, I believe, anywhere in the world for their total lavishness. Their audiences, all clad in the same dull, drab clothing, came alive in a most extraordinary way on being transported into another world where brilliance predominated; light, colour, décor, beautiful dresses, stirring action, music. The difference from life outside was altogether astonishing. A visit to the former Winter Palace of the Tzars produced a similar reaction, nothing had been spared in turning it into the most wonderful and beautiful art gallery and museum.

I do not believe there were any converts to Communism on board when we came to leave. Apart from organized tours, visits and football matches, there was little to attract the sailors when ashore, and any social mixing with the citizens was frowned upon by the Russian authorities, who made it plain that there could be unpleasant repercussions for people caught inviting any of us to private entertainment in their homes. To the visitor Leningrad remained a grim and forbidding place, except for the élite with special privileges.

While we were in Leningrad there took place a reciprocal visit by a Russian cruiser to Portsmouth, which had brought the Russian leaders Bulganin and Kruschev for meetings with the British Government in London. When the time came for us to depart there was an exasperating delay, the Russians refusing to sanction our sailing by the simple expedient of not opening the bridges over the Neva immediately below us. For hours those on *Chevron*'s bridge stood exposed to a strong and bitterly cold northerly wind, blowing directly upstream and bringing with it flurries of snow and all the fumes from our own funnel; facing upstream as we were, with the back of the bridge totally open to all that the wind was bearing, the hours we had to endure being virtually gassed was the most unpleasant time I have ever spent on a ship's bridge, not excepting even the most violent storms at sea. When, at last, the bridges opened we were off like the proverbial scalded cat, stern first down the river as fast as we could go, regardless of the Liaison Officer's still repeated 'Niets'. Later we attributed the delay to the Russian authorities waiting to hear that B. and K. in their cruiser were safely out of Portsmouth on their way home.

November saw *Chevron* back in Portsmouth to pay off at the end of her commission, and sadly with that the demise of the First Destroyer Squadron as many had known it. The structure and pattern of the Navy was changing fast, frigates were displacing the old type of destroyer and what were now referred to as 'destroyers' had grown to ships the size of cruisers. Coincidental but more fundamental, Captains were now classed as either 'Wet' or 'Dry', the former eligible for service and command at sea, the latter consigned to chairborne staff appointments and command of shore establishments. This division of the Captain's List was a cause of much anxiety and distress, particularly to those designated 'Dry'. When the fearfully anticipated letter from the Naval Secretary arrived, I hardly dared open it but with relief I read that I was 'Wet'. The word had a very different meaning from that attributed to it years later in the time of Thatcherism.

Chevron and the First Destroyer Squadron had been a wonderful command and had fulfilled all my wishes; I now turned my thoughts to the future. I had another four or five years to serve as a Captain before reaching the top of the list and facing either retirement or promotion to Flag rank. Whether I would get another sea-going job was in the lap of the gods, but I was hopeful. To find out how the land lay I went to see the Naval Secretary, now Rear Admiral David Luce, my late Captain in *Liverpool*. I was still hankering after a break from standard naval routine and hoping for a 'sabbatical' of some description. I suggested I might do the next course at the Imperial Defence College (IDC – now known as the Royal College of Defence Studies), lasting a year and starting in January 1956. The proposal was not received well and I was told very decisively that it was the last thing likely to happen to me and that I was to wait and see, there being no appointment yet firmly in line for me. In the event I had not long to wait, and when it arrived the new appointment was exactly as I had wished, to the IDC as a student, for the year's course starting the next January. Thus were the ways of appointing authorities! Surprised and delighted, Maureen and I were able to look forward to a year when we could reasonably expect not to be separated by 'the exigencies of the Service', that term providing, justifiably in most cases, the reason for a multitude of unexpected and usually hurried partings of husband and wife.

The IDC was indeed a break from normal service life; housed in the magnificence of Seaford House in Belgrave Square in London, the year's intake of students was mostly made up from the Armed, Civil and Foreign Services of Britain, with smaller contingents or individuals from all the major countries of the Commonwealth and from the United States. In his welcoming address the Commandant, Admiral Sir Guy Russell, quoting from the Bible he said, 'In order to acquire wisdom a man must have leisure'. He then went on to say that throughout the course he would ensure the leisure and it was up to us to acquire the wisdom. It was a happy beginning to a fascinating year of study and learning, with plenty of time and opportunity for the 'leisure'. The Commandant, whom I had last met in 1933 when he was Commander of the *Queen Elizabeth* and trained our Gunroom gig's crew for the Regatta, had grown no less in stature and kept rigidly to his word.

The even tenor of this enjoyable year was rudely disturbed in the summer by the eruption of 'The Suez Crisis', which affected a few of the students far more dramatically than the majority. The unlucky ones were recalled by their respective services to assist in the operational planning for eventual military action. For those of us remaining at the College, as we analysed rumour following rumour and the information slowly percolating through from more reliable sources, we became privy to a great deal, but by no means all, of what was going on behind the scenes in the corridors of power in Whitehall. As the crisis developed and military action looked more certain, I doubt if any viewed the invasion of the Canal Zone as a wise or sensible operation.

Refreshed and re-invigorated by my 'sabbatical' year my next appointment came as no surprise – back to the submarine world in January 1957 as Chief Staff Officer (CSO) to Flag Officer Submarines (Rear Admiral W.J.W. Woods). I was delighted to serve under Sam Woods, whom

I had known and admired for years and who was Godfather to our elder daughter. There were many changes since I had last been at Blockhouse, nearly seven years before; most of the old war-time 'T' class submarines had gone, though the stream-lined conversions were still serving and with the 'A' and PORPOISE classes were the backbone of the under-water fleet, with the latest design, the 'O' class, yet to come into service. All were highly trained and equipped for the A/S role. Looking to the future all thought was devoted to the development of the nuclear powered submarine. The United States Navy led the field with *Nautilus* newly at sea, we at Blockhouse were fighting to get approval to build *Dreadnought*, and nobody knew quite what the Russians were doing. It was surmised they would not be far behind and it seemed obvious that their huge capacity for building submarines would inevitably lead to a very serious threat to NATO and the West. The ballistic missile launched from a submarine had not yet evolved, but things on a smaller scale were moving that way, with the US 'cruise' missile REGULUS undergoing sea trials in a submarine.

That first summer as CSO I accompanied Sam Woods on a month's trip round the world. FOS/M's remit included responsibility for the wellbeing of submarines in Singapore, Australia, New Zealand (with boats borrowed from the Division based in Sydney) and in Nova Scotia on the East coast of Canada; to visit them all was the object of the tour. The Admiralty were not enthusiastic about the costs of such an extended journey and stingily decreed that, as he was only a Rear Admiral, FOS/M was not entitled to anything but 'Economy' class when travelling by air. Sam Woods was a large man, well over six feet tall and broad in proportion, and he overflowed on all sides of the narrow 'Economy' seats, knees hard up against the seat in front and no room to stretch his legs. This was before the days of jet aircraft and the trans-ocean and inter-continental flights were long and bumpy; sitting next to Sam it was disturbing to see the degree of discomfort he had to endure for twelve hours or more at a time. It was ill preparation for the inspections, conferences and discussions awaiting us at our destinations. At one stage we were ironically confronted with the situation where the Commander S/M of the Fourth Division of submarines based at Sydney had a First Class ticket to accompany us on our flight to New Zealand, thanks to a more generous Australian Government who held the purse-strings for the Division's expenses. John Bromage tactfully surrendered his seat to his Admiral.

The tribulations of long distance flights were totally obliterated by the warmth of the receptions we invariably received from these small and independent units of FOS/M's far-flung empire. It was tremendously heartening to see how happily and satisfactorily they had carved out a niche for themselves with their host nations and navies, and how well they were fulfilling the task of providing submarine services for their temporary masters, under all sorts of conditions and, on occasion, over vast distances.

There was another important and worthwhile aspect to the tour. Since the end of the war there had grown up a unique and special relationship between the British and United States submarine services, something that went far beyond mere co-ordination of planning to meet the role which each would play under NATO in the 'Cold War', or worse if it became 'Hot'. This long-standing association was cemented by Sam Woods including, after his visits to Australia and New Zealand, a comprehensive round of calls on United States submarine authorities in both the Pacific and Atlantic commands, with consultations thrown in at US Navy headquarters in Washington and a visit to the 'alma mater' of their submarine service at New London in Connecticut. Wherever we went we were presented with a fascinating picture of future developments as seen by the leading submariners in the world, a picture given freely and apparently untainted by dictates of security. In every way we were made to feel we were their equals, in spite of the overwhelming difference in the strengths of our respective submarine fleets and the incomparable resources they had access to for research and development.

The highlight of our whole journey came at New London, when we were treated to twenty-four hours at sea in *Nautilus*, that exciting first-ever nuclear powered submarine, still undergoing her extensive series of trials. It was a wonderful experience and a veritable eye-opener to Sam Woods and myself. We were the first 'foreign' officers ever to be allowed on board and we were further privileged and honoured to be taken to sea and allowed to witness the full range of her capabilities. Such favoured treatment spoke legions for the trust existing between the two services, so well sustained over the years by FOS/M's special representative on the British naval staff in Washington, in this case Johnnie Coote (Commander J.O. Coote).

I was to see *Nautilus* again before leaving FOS/M's staff, when she berthed at Portland in Dorset at the end of her epic voyage under the Arctic ice to the North Pole. It was proof of the immense capabilities of the nuclear powered submarine, shortly to be further confirmed when she came under FOS/M's operational control in a major NATO strategic exercise. On the 'opposition' side she wreaked absolute havoc amongst the main NATO striking forces of carriers and escorting vessels, and the attendant logistic ships; although her successes were never openly acknowledged, for submariners they were a triumphant demonstration of all that we believed in.

For my second year as CSO Sam Woods had been succeeded by Bertram Taylor (Rear Admiral B.W. Taylor). When it came to planning his visits to his submarines abroad the Admiralty conceded, in the light of his predecessor's experiences and representations, that air travel could be First Class, but on the other hand they declared that he should go unaccompanied, no Secretary or Staff Officer with him. Such niggardly action was almost unbelievable, but Bertram bravely set out on his journey, which, in spite of recurrent and painful 'back trouble' he successfully completed.

After two absolutely enthralling years professionally, but ones that kept me very hard at work so that I saw little of home and family, I had the good fortune to be relieved once again by Georgie Hunt (Captain G.E. Hunt), when for the third time since the war he stepped into my shoes.

He had taken over from me as 'teacher' captain, then as SOO on FOS/M's staff, and now here he was again. I could not have been more pleased to have his very capable hands taking over the reins. To my later regret, shared by many others, before completing his two years as CSO he elected to retire, not seeking promotion to Flag rank. It was a loss the submarine service could well have done without, but Australia beckoned and no one more deserved a happy retirement.

I had hoped I might get to sea again, perhaps even to complete my education by commanding an aircraft carrier; but it was decided otherwise and I was offered command of *Ganges*, the Boys' Training Establishment at Shotley in Suffolk, renowned as the cradle of those who in their later years of service came to be regarded by common consent as the backbone of the Navy. I hesitated, feeling ill-fitted for its responsibilities and doubting my ability to fill them, but I was quickly persuaded by an old and valued friend, Nick Rutherford (Commander (S) W.J.N. Rutherford), who had been both Rucker's and Shrimp's Secretary during the war and was now the Naval Secretary's right hand, that it was an absolutely plum job and I would be a fool to turn it down. How right he was. It was indeed a peach of a job, rewarded in full measure by seeing its complement at any one time of just under two thousand boys, recruited as volunteers from all walks and levels of civilian life, being transformed into disciplined young men ready and able to take their place in the Fleet. My family shared the benefits and we occupied a wonderful Elizabethan mansion, Erwarton Hall, which had been the Captain's official residence since *Ganges* had been established ashore at Shotley in the early years of the century. There were, inevitably, problems with its maintenance, heating, staffing and general upkeep, but they were small beer compared to the pleasure Maureen and I derived, for the first time, from living in such style in 'quarters' provided by the Admiralty. Also the enjoyment of the social life of Suffolk, that my many illustrious predecessors had ensured was there for the taking as part of the appointment, was another pleasurable aspect.

Ganges would be my last job as a Captain, perhaps the last in my naval career, and it was wonderful to have the prospect of ending it on such a high note. All seemed set for a blissful two years, but after a few months, when I returned in August from a glorious holiday in the Outer Hebrides, I was suffering from a mysterious illness which, day by day, was slowly affecting my eyesight and movement of my limbs. Its nature was eventually, after

Captain's House, HMS *Ganges* – Erwarton Hall.

weeks, diagnosed as hemiplegia and I can only describe its onset as seeming like a very slow-motion stroke. As my condition deteriorated the possible consequences for us all were ever more frightening. Jackie Gent (Surgeon Captain J.G. Gent, PMO at *Ganges*) was determined that I would recover fully and, enlisting the help of one of the Navy's eminent consultants in London, continued to fight valiantly on my behalf against those who said I should be invalided. After weeks in the Hospital for Nervous Diseases in Queen's Square, London, undergoing at the outset some horrific tests for a tumour on the brain, fortunately proving negative, I was judged fit enough to return to Erwarton Hall, where Jackie continued the recommended treatment.

By the end of January 1960, I had been passed as fit for further service by a Medical Board and was able to take up the reins of office again. In my absence these had been most ably held by my second-in-command, Tom Trick (Commander T.S. Trick), himself an ex-*Ganges* boy and one of its most outstanding products, who had shouldered all the additional responsibilities with complete confidence and equanimity. Knowing that throughout my illness *Ganges* was in such good hands, and continued to thrive, was an enormous boost to my morale and assistance towards full recovery. I was very conscious of the great debt I owed to a host of people for bringing this about.

BBC technician discusses with author the televising of the Mast Manning. Commander Trick in the background, 1960.

Once back at work 1960 flew past, but my tenure of the job was abruptly cut short in the autumn, when I was relieved prematurely in order that my successor could have a measurable time as Captain before he, in turn, reached the top of the Captain's list. It was an unwelcome blow to have our two years thus cut short and it was a sad moment when we had to say good-bye to *Ganges* and Erwarton Hall. I was initially left at a loose end for the next few months of uncertainty whilst awaiting the news of retirement or promotion. To be on leave was, as always, more than welcome, and, to fill in time, I was sent to the Senior Officer's War Course at Greenwich. Half way through its two months there was cause for much celebration when a letter from the Naval Secretary told me I was to be promoted to Rear-Admiral in July and was then to relieve 'Baldy' Hezlet (Rear Admiral A.R. Hezlet) as Flag Officer Submarines. 'Baldy' I had known since China days before the war, younger than me by a year, he was the most brilliant submariner of his generation.

To be back at Blockhouse as head of the submarine service more than fulfilled every wish or ambition that I may ever have had professionally, and the pleasure was increased, doubly so, by the provision of Dolphin House in Alverstoke as a happy family home. Inheriting the dynamism that my predecessors had inspired across the full range of matters coming

Manning the Mast. HMS *Ganges*, 1960.

Lightweight field gun drill, HMS *Ganges*, 1960.

Admiral of the Fleet Lord Fraser of North Cape inspecting boys at HMS *Ganges*, 1960.

Queen's Birthday Review. HMS *Ganges*, 1960.

Author congratulating Button Boy, 1960.

Lord Carrington tries out the bowling alley, HMS *Ganges*, 1960.

Author being towed away after relinquishing command of HMS *Ganges*, 1960.

FOS/M's way, pushing ahead with all the new ideas, new practices, new material, that had arisen in recent years, it was all a great challenge, with the opportunity for much to be brought to fruition if I could maintain the pressure.

It was familiar ground, thanks to my being CSO two years before, but things had progressed significantly. In the nuclear field it was encouraging to find that *Dreadnought*, with American help in providing the reactor and propulsion plant, was now under construction at Vicker's yard in Barrow-in-Furness, and that a wholly British successor, *Valiant*, had been ordered and was about to be laid down. But there was much prevarication about long-term plans for building up a significant fleet of nuclear-powered submarines, and such plans as were being considered were, I thought, woefully inadequate. Harking back to the early years of the century and the very first *Dreadnought*, I revived Jackie Fisher's (Admiral Lord Fisher's) great call that ran round the country, 'We want eight and we won't wait.' I doubt if, in the then current circumstances, it contributed much to the rate of new construction, but I believe it helped to make Their Lordships more aware that a new, and deadly, type of capital ship had entered the sphere of maritime warfare, bringing potentially very dangerous consequences for the Royal Navy, and indeed the country, should we ever again become involved in hostilities at sea. Much of my time as FOS/M was spent on this matter, trying to persuade the Admiralty that the nuclear-powered submarine had indeed utterly changed all previous concepts of war at sea, it *was* the new capital ship, and they must move with the times. This had already been amply illustrated by the United States Navy, whose submarine branch was, thankfully, only too ready to keep FOS/M up-to-date with all developments, a relationship I took pains to cement by personal trans-Atlantic visits.

Although there was no repetition of Sam Wood's exhausting trip round the world, I followed in 1962 the practice of visiting the squadrons and divisions of submarines abroad, as well as those at home. Malta and Halifax each had separate visits, Singapore, Sydney and Auckland were included in a more extended tour. I was briefed by the First Lord, Lord Carrington, to warn the Australian Government that Britain could no longer afford to keep a force of submarines in Australian waters, to provide their navy with submarine services; conveying this message I added the view that if they wanted such services they should build their own submarines, preferably nuclear. The idea went down like a lead balloon and received a very hostile reception from the Press, headlines proclaiming 'MACKENZIE GO HOME'. I was summoned to Canberra by the Minister of the Navy, Senator Gorton, to receive a 'rocket' for interfering in Australian affairs. De-briefing to Lord Carrington on my return, sympathetically he told me to discount their reaction. Despite their then attitude, within years there was no longer a Division of British submarines in Sydney and the RAN had built up their own submarine branch.

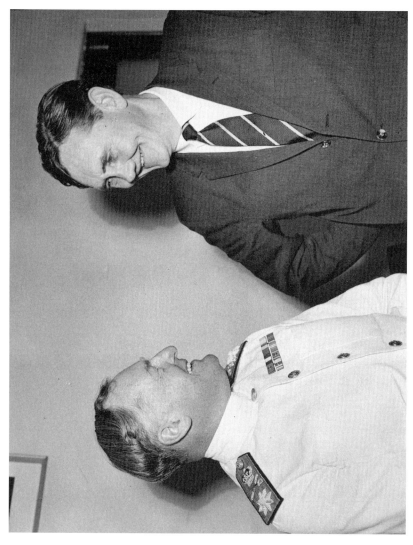

Author in happier mood with Senator Gorton of Australia, 1962.

The last months of 1962 saw dramatic developments that were to bring into being an entirely new role for the Royal Navy, much disputed both within and without, that of carrying responsibility for the country's strategic nuclear deterrent. As this was to be submarine-borne, FOS/M was fully implicated and I became heavily involved by the end of the year, as the next chapters will tell.

Chapter Sixteen

Polaris – Setting the Scene

I now began the most strenuous five years of my whole career, but also in the end the most satisfying, because of their direct contribution to the ultimate defence of this country.

The story begins for me in the mid-1950s, when the submarine commander on the staff of Commander, British Naval Staff (CBNS) Washington, began sending a series of reports to Flag Officer Submarines about the development in the United States of a new strategic weapon system and its associated missile – POLARIS. That he could do so freely and openly is again an example of the very close and friendly reltaionship existing between the submarine services of the Royal Navy and the United States Navy.

In consequence of these regular reports, Flag Officer Submarines (then Rear Admiral W.J.W. Woods) and myself, his Chief Staff Officer, on a visit to Washington in the summer of 1957, were given a full briefing on POLARIS and its future development by Rear Admiral Raborn, USN, then Director of the Special Projects Office (SPO) of the United States Navy. The ties for future close and friendly co-operation were consolidated.

FOS/M informed the Admiralty of all he had learnt and despite long-standing and deep-seated reservations about its relevance to the role of the Royal Navy, the Board decided to keep abreast of how POLARIS was faring. Accordingly, an additional commander was appointed, in 1958, to the staff of CBNS, charged specifically with maintaining close touch with SPO and reporting on progress and developments. The Board followed this up a year later by sending its Director General, Weapons, (then Rear Admiral M. Le Fanu) to the United States to investigate the organization within the United States Navy which had so successfully and speedily developed POLARIS, to bring it into operational service in the United States Navy's submarines. Based on this investigation he was to prepare an outline plan of what the Board might have to do should there be a change in the Government's nuclear deterrent policy, then entirely reliant on the Royal Air Force.

As time went by straws in the wind hinted at the possibility of such a change and further action ensued. A technical mission was sent to the United States in 1960/61 to gather more detailed information on the POLARIS programme, and particularly on its ramifications for the ship-building and related industries.

As the months passed in 1962 concern increased in Government circles about the future form of Britain's nuclear deterrent, to the general principles of which they remained wholly committed. It had been planned that the V-Bomber force of the Royal Air Force, hitherto carrying the responsibility of delivering nuclear bombs, would be kept in service equipped with a new weapon, SKYBOLT, a nuclear armed medium range missile designed to be launched from aircraft. It was still under development in the United States, but doubts were multiplying monthly as to whether it would ever meet the very high technical specifications required of it; its phenomenally mounting costs also caused alarm.

Enough was now known about POLARIS to make it an attractive alternative. As Government opinion hardened in its favour, so strife developed in Whitehall and a virulent air lobby furiously defended their right, as they saw it, to continue to carry the country's nuclear deterrent. The Admiralty were two-minded, and unwilling to enter the battle publicly. They accepted the view that POLARIS had over-riding advantages over any other contemporary form of strategic deterrent, either in service or under development, but were fearful of the effect its adoption would have on the Navy, particularly on its manpower and budget. They foresaw (correctly) that the Treasury would be reluctant to provide additional money to meet the increased costs.

SKYBOLT was formally abandoned by the United States in December 1962. Things moved dramatically thereafter. The Prime Minister, Harold Macmillan, met President Kennedy at Nassau in the Bahamas before Christmas, ostensibly to determine how best to bring up-to-date and continue Britain's contribution to the West's nuclear deterrence forces. The UK team concentrated their efforts on persuading the United States to agree to provide POLARIS. Success was achieved and the resulting 'Nassau Agreement' laid down, in very broad terms, the conditions governing such provision. In short, these were that the United States would provide, on a continuing basis, POLARIS missiles and their associated systems and equipment, plus spares, but *NOT* warheads; whilst the United Kingdom would provide the submarines and warheads. It was a simply stated communiqué, but its implementation heralded vast, unknown problems, only solved by the creation of new ventures in the management and control of production and procurement.

The Third Sea Lord and Controller of the Navy (Vice Admiral Michael Le Fanu) was part of the team supporting the Prime Minister; thus the Admiralty Board were fully alive to the discussions and to the final decision, which landed a new role, and additional responsibilities of awe-inspiring significance, on the Royal Navy. On the party's return from Nassau, just before Christmas 1962, the Board started the ball rolling, to meet the immense task of providing the country's future nuclear deterrent. Public announcements went no further than the bare terms of the Nassau Agreement, but behind the scenes much went on, though all wrapped in the veils of secrecy.

I received the surprise of my life on Friday, 28th December 1962. That morning I had attended a meeting in the Admiralty, not directly concerned with POLARIS; later, returning to Gosport on my way home, I was informed that the First Sea Lord (Admiral Sir Caspar John) wanted to speak to me on the telephone, on the 'scrambler'. I went to my office and was connected, and a conversation on the following lines took place:-

FSL: 'You're fully in the picture about POLARIS: well, I want you to head the organization we are setting up in the Admiralty to run the thing through.'

FOS/M: 'Yes, Sir.' (doubtfully)

FSL: 'Come and have lunch with me on Monday, at one o'clock, at White's in St. James's, and give me your answer then. You can have the weekend to think it over.'

FOS/M: 'Yes, thank you, Sir.'

FSL: 'I tell you here and now that if you say 'no', I'll twist your arm until you bloody well scream.'

FOS/M: (after a pause) 'Right, Sir, I'll see you Monday.'

End of conversation.

Come the Monday (31st December 1962) the answer given was 'Yes', but only after a weekend of much heart-searching. Acceptance would give rise to many personal and family problems and sacrifice, to which was added the disappointment of prematurely relinquishing the enjoyably inspiring and rewarding appointment of FOS/M. But the challenge, however daunting, proved over-riding and the die was cast. Thus came into being my appointment as Chief Polaris Executive (CPE). It was made plain that I could expect to be there until the submarines were operational.

The next day, New Year's day, 1963, I said goodbye to my staff at Blockhouse and on the following day I found myself in an empty room on the ground floor of North Block of the Admiralty building; empty, that is, except for a chair and a large desk, on which sat a telephone not yet connected and no staff, no paper-work. It was, to say the least, an unusual and perplexing situation. I attended a meeting with the First Lord of the Admiralty (Lord Carrington) that forenoon. At this meeting the First Lord emphasised the importance and urgency of getting POLARIS into service within five years, and the powers that would be given to whoever headed the special organization to be set up within the Admiralty, an essential factor to achieving the aim.

The provisional terms of the new job indicated that I was responsible to the Controller of the Navy for the POLARIS programme as a whole, but that I had direct and immediate access, at any time, to any member of the Board of Admiralty if I needed assistance in overcoming difficulties or problems arising in that particular member's field. Admiral Le Fanu's three year old report, with its proposals and recommendations for the organization required to bring POLARIS swiftly into service in the Royal Navy, was brought out of its pigeon-hole, at his instigation, dusted down, and promptly landed on my desk, to become my bible for the immediate future. It was also fortunate that I, as FOS/M, during a routine visit to Washington the previous summer, had been given a very comprehensive briefing by the Director, Special Projects, (Rear Admiral I.J. Galantin, USN – who had succeeded Admiral Raborn) on all the methods and procedures used in SPO to keep, so successfully, the strictest control, on a very tight timescale, of the United States Navy's POLARIS programme. Armed with all this background information, matters quickly clarified and the task began to take on a more definable shape. The Le Fanu report was invaluable as a starting point for a race against all the odds, a race in which it was already clear that many obstacles would arise in the years ahead. Not the least of these could be summed up by the phrase 'We don't know how much we don't know.' In fact, we were at the very bottom of a steep and formidably high learning curve.

Immediate action was needed to put flesh on the bare skeleton of the organization outlined in the Le Fanu report. The Admiralty Board accepted in principle that some special measures would be necessary if the programme was to be driven through on time, but it was largely left to me to devise its exact shape and size. I was told I would have a free choice in filling the key posts, naval and civilian. In a matter of days these were selected and appointed as I, having personally experienced the proverbial 'pier head jump' in taking up this new appointment, had no qualms about forcing the pace. The Secretary of the Admiralty (Clifford S. Jarrett) and the Controller gave full support, and much helpful advice, on how the team should be set up, and who should fill the top billets.

There was one area where things did not run so smoothly. The Admiralty had no responsibilities (or experience) for the design and production of nuclear weapons nor, POLARIS being a true ballistic missile, for the related Re-entry System (RES). These lay respectively with the Atomic Weapons Research Establishment and the Ministry of Aviation; indeed, this Ministry also claimed it had statutory responsibility for all 'missiles' and therefore it should have overall charge of the POLARIS programme. The Minister of Aviation was adamant that it was his Ministry's job and only much work and tactful handling by the First Lord prevented a damaging head-on clash. The all-important argument that the submarines, with their navigation, control and launching equipment, were an integral and inseparable part of the whole POLARIS weapon system, won the day. The issue was, after several weeks, resolved by setting up within the Ministry of Aviation the 'Polaris Project Office', headed by a naval officer (Rear Admiral F. Dossor) (PPO); he would have dual responsibility, to his Minister and to me, for the design and production of the Re-entry System and the warheads, to the timescale required. The Admiralty were to be responsible for the procurement, fitting and servicing of the actual missiles and associated control systems.

By the end of the first week, the main form of the Polaris Executive's organization within the Admiralty was agreed, and already some key members were in post. Much detail had still to be settled, and there were, mounting daily as the enormity of the project emerged from the fog of ignorance, innumerable problems of every kind and variety: security, liaison with SPO, co-ordination within Admiralty departments and between Government Ministries (e.g. Treasury, Foreign Office, Ministry of Public Buildings and Works), the actual location (Admiralty, London, or Admiralty, Bath), of the growing team, office space to accommodate it, funding of the programme, handling of contracts with industry in general and the ship-builders in particular and selection of the latter. All these, and many others, were of paramount importance; problems to be resolved quickly and correctly before a coherent programme could be drawn up.

Above all, more information from the American end was desperately needed. On 8th January a mission flew from London to Washington. It was headed by the Chief Scientific Adviser to the Ministry of Defence (Sir Solly Zuckerman) and the Vice Chief of the Naval Staff (then Vice Admiral Varyl Begg), and included a Deputy Secretary and myself from the Admiralty and the Chief Scientist and other representatives from the Ministry of Aviation. I was able to renew personal contact with Admiral Galantin (Director, Special Projects) and his Special Projects Office. Thus the foundations were laid for the closest of future co-operation, including the early setting up of a Joint Steering Task Group (JSTG), to ensure that the British POLARIS Programme was kept fully integrated with its US counterpart, and that it received adequate priority throughout. With Admiral Galantin's vigorous backing, a bond was struck between both organizations, which grew and strengthened as the years went by. *Without this support, the British programme would never have even got off the ground.*

Other issues discussed during the hectic three-day visit were the number of missiles to be carried by each British submarine (whose number was not yet resolved) and whether those supplied were to be the A2 or A3 version; these issues were absolutely critical to further consideration and planning of the UK programme. The Americans, within the terms of the Nassau Agreement, gave uninhibited information and strongly expressed their views, all immensely helpful to the urgent decisions yet to be taken at Government level.

Back in the Admiralty on 14th January, I found my own organization growing strongly according to plan. The most important step was the transfer to the Polaris Executive of the DREADNOUGHT Project Team under its immensely able, dynamic and forthright leader, Mr Rowland Baker, of the Royal Corps of Naval Constructors. This team had been set up, under the Director-General, Ships, (Sir Alfred Sims) to design and oversee the building, by Vickers of Barrow-in-Furness, of HMS *Dreadnought*, Britain's first nuclear powered submarine, albeit with a nuclear reactor provided by the United States. With first hand experience, in this sensitive field, of contractual relationships with American authorities, they were the leading source of knowledge in the United Kingdom on nuclear propulsion, and clearly would have a very great deal to contribute to the Polaris Executive. That Director-General, Ships, was prepared to release them to me was a tremendous step forward, and his readily given agreement paved the way for acceptance, in time, of the Polaris Executive by other Admiralty Departments, whose first response to the new organization tended to be grudging, if not plainly hostile.

Effective progress was, however, still stultified by lengthy arguments on the design of the submarine, whether it should carry eight or sixteen missiles and on whether these latter should be A2 or A3. American advice on the submarine design was wholly in favour of sixteen, they warned that any departure from this would require a complete re-design of the entire weapon system, at vast cost in time and money. As regards the missiles themselves, they stated unequivocally that the A2 production line was to be closed down, so confident were they that the A3, actually still under trial, would be a complete success. A prolonged and time-wasting distraction to these arguments was introduced by a proposal, emanating from Washington, that NATO should have its deterrent strength increased by equipping it with a multi-national force of surface vessels armed with POLARIS missiles (the MLF). I was drawn into the discussions of this wild scheme, totally irrelevant to the task of the POLARIS Executive, because, by now, Whitehall regarded me as the 'expert' whenever and wherever the word 'POLARIS' cropped up. The very idea of putting such a highly technical, nuclear armed, weapon system into the hands of multi-national mixed crews on board merchant-type ships just did not bear serious examination, but it took a long time before the MLF fantasy was finally killed off.

But before it had even arisen I had to deal with two other pressing problems; one, easy and pleasant to solve, the other more contentious. The first was Admiral Galantin's arrival in London on 17th January, a return visit to that of the high-powered team to Washington the previous week; loose ends between myself and SP were tied up, and the need confirmed for a further formal agreement between the two Governments, more explicit than the one produced at Nassau. It would have to include the exact terms governing the supply and maintenance of POLARIS missiles and all associated equipment, the provision in detail of all relevant technical information – essential to successful incorporation of the complete weapon system in the British design of submarine – measures for co-ordinating mutual progress and priorities with the US and UK programmes, and, finally, how and when it was all to be paid for. A broad outline plan was evolved of how these mammoth problems should be resolved.

The other, more worrying problem was closer to home. Since the very start I had been working under a strictly enforced cloak of secrecy and there had been no official release of my appointment. The submarine command only knew that FOS/M, in person, had suddenly vanished from his headquarters at Blockhouse, and that Captain S/M Five (Captain E.J.D. Turner), as he then was, was 'holding the fort' in his place; FOS/M's Rear Admiral's flag still flew in *Dolphin*. Within the Admiralty a similar obscure situation existed, with no formal promulgation of the decision to set up a new organization, with its aims and terms of reference; intense speculation in the Press fuelled the uncertainty and confusion which steadily gained ground afloat and ashore. I appealed directly to the First Lord and the Controller, stating my view that it was intolerable that both the Submarine Command and the Admiralty Departments were being kept in the dark in this way, and that it was utterly wrong that, to the outside world, I, personally, was apparently still head of the submarine command but not in a position to exercise any responsibility; to precipitate matters, I intended to order my flag to be struck. It transpired, as I had surmised, that continuing argument with the Minister of Aviation as to who should run the POLARIS programme was at the root of the delay. The First Lord then forced the issue and the Government gave its blessing to the Admiralty being in charge. Whereupon my appointment was publicly issued, Captain S/M was confirmed as Commodore S/Ms for all to know, and all concerned within Whitehall were informed of the existence, aims and broad terms of reference of the Polaris Executive. At last, in the third week of January, my position was publicly established and I had thereafter a clear, open target: POLARIS to be operational in 1968, five years ahead. It was a daunting task.

Meanwhile, what of family life? We had, prior to my becoming FOS/M, sold the house we had had in Shedfield for many years, and while in Dolphin House were relying on having plenty of time before the normal conclusion of the appointment to find a suitable replacement, depending on what my long-term future might be. My sudden translation to the Admiralty now left us nominally homeless, and the furious pace of events gave little opportunity for such mundane matters as house hunting. With no successor immediately ready to step into my shoes, and into Dolphin House, the latter remained our home until we found a haven in London, where we could be re-united and I could cease the unwelcome existence of 'week and week-ending', which the appalling conditions of snow, ice and cold that had hit the country that winter, made infinitely worse than normal.

Fortunately, Maureen's brother, then in an Army married quarter on Salisbury Plain, kindly lent us his flat in Hampstead and there we had moved by the end of January. It took time to find something more permanent, but in May we moved to a house we had bought in East Sheen, on the edge of Richmond Park, which remained our home over the next five years. These few words give scant recognition to the disruption that POLARIS caused to our family life. It was as though I had been sent off to war. Everything became subservient to the timely completion of the programme, and Maureen and the children suffered from my attention being predominantly focused elsewhere for too much of the time during these long years.

Chapter Seventeen

Polaris – The Beginning . . .

The Government required POLARIS to be operational in 1968 so the Admiralty laid responsibility for this firmly and squarely on me and my organization, the Polaris Executive.

Formal recognition of the Polaris Executive was a major step forward. No longer 'an unknown quantity working in a vacuum' it could now sensibly develop a long term plan directly related to the target date of 1968 for operational deployment of POLARIS. Although any detailed programme to meet this must still be in its infancy, with many vital factors yet to be resolved, the main structure of the organization needed to suit the task was now fully established within days and was ready for expansion.

I had set up my headquarters within the Admiralty in London. There, from the very beginning, I had superb support from my Chief Administrative Officer (Mr R.N.P. Lewin) and from my 'Assistant', or Chief of Staff as I preferred to regard him (Captain J.R. McKaig), later to be formally designated Deputy CPE. Bob Lewin, an Assistant Secretary from the Admiralty, had vast experience of the workings of Whitehall – of which I had virtually none, never before having served in the Admiralty. His unstinted loyalty and invaluable, wise advice did much to ensure that the new organization would be, to the greatest extent possible, autonomous, but yet fully integrated into existing Admiralty and Government machinery. In this he had an able assistant in Mr P. Nailor, who later succeeded him in 1966, and years afterwards, as Professor P. Nailor, wrote 'The Nassau Connection', published by HM Stationery Office in 1988, a highly authoritative and well-referenced account of the crucial years of bringing POLARIS into service.

Rae McKaig had been the Commander in HMS *Ganges*, the Boys Training Establishment in Suffolk, for my first few months in 1959 when I had been its Captain. On the 'dry list' he had, despite this, just been appointed, as a junior Captain, to take command of *Apollo*, a minelayer brought out of Reserve for a 'trooping trip' to Hong Kong. His qualities and record, however, were so outstanding and had made such an early impression on me that I insisted he be 'hi-jacked', at the briefest of notice, from this longed-for and attractive sea-going appointment, to take up yet another chairbound job. It says everything for his sense of duty and loyalty that, in spite of the very real disappointment of being suddenly wrenched from the quite exceptional chance of his getting to sea, he threw himself so whole-heartedly and energetically into this new, very onerous post, demanding all of his talents, and more. His input into planning the programme was the major factor in its eventual success.

I was also fortunate in being able to retain the services of my Secretary (Commander J.R. Grimwood) whom I had had when FOS/M at Blockhouse; and an immediate essential addition to the Team was a Security Officer (Commander P. Shaw), whose overall writ covered Admiralty, London, and Admiralty, Bath, together with, as the organization grew, all out-stations. Others were soon drawn in – Jimmy Launders, Ken Dunlop, Henry Ellis, et al. Backing them all was a small and efficient typing staff.

This initial tiny nucleus, so hurriedly assembled in London, expanded to become the corner-stone on which the whole project was built and ultimately depended: for supervision and direction, for ensuring financial support and, when or where necessary, for fighting the battles with higher authority and gaining political approval. In times of major difficulty or crisis – which were many in the early years and never finally disappeared – it was where 'the buck stopped'!

Simultaneously, a much larger, complicated, and more technically weighted organization was growing within Admiralty, Bath. As already described, the Dreadnought Project Team (DPT) under its charismatic and dynamic leader, Rowley Baker, had been made over, en bloc, to the Polaris Executive; *his title of DPT was retained, as Director Polaris, Technical.* Under him a Technical Directorate was rapidly established, consisting of Mr S.J. Palmer, RCNC, Captain C.W.H. Shepherd, Captain L.D. Dymoke and Mr H.C. Fitzer, respectively responsible for submarine design and construction, the procurement, installation and proving of the POLARIS weapon system, and the Marine Engineering and Electrical Engineering aspects of the submarine's nuclear propulsion plant. They were all strong personalities, experts in their own fields, and their closest co-operation and co-ordination as a team was vital to the immense task of designing, building, equipping, testing and tuning, and finally completing as 100 per cent ready for operational service, the largest, most technically advanced and complicated submarine and associated weapon system ever built in this country. Only someone of Rowley Baker's calibre could have pulled them all together so successfully.

A great load of responsibility rested on their shoulders, much of it in unknown or scarcely explored territory. Charles Shepherd had to master the intricacies of a weapon system new to him: submarine, missile, launching, control, navigation; and, in particular, all the requirements for training of personnel, naval and civilian, for installation and for testing and tuning of equipment. His was the most daunting task of all; only to be accomplished with the assistance of a very able and dedicated team, which he conjured up from the widest sources remarkably quickly.

Overall submarine design, how to incorporate an entire American weapon system, and the nuclear propulsion field, all three presented special problems on a scale not yet experienced. The widely acclaimed, newly launched, first British nuclear submarine *Dreadnought* was fitting out at Barrow-in-Furness; she had an American nuclear reactor, supplied under very special and strict terms, and so was not suitable as a prototype for Polaris design work. A British reactor was still under trial at Dounreay and had yet to be installed in *Valiant*, presently also building at Barrow, so no British nuclear propulsion plant had yet been tried at sea or proven. Further down the line, also in the hands of Vickers at Barrow, and of similar design to *Valiant*, was *Warspite*, on whom work had only just started.

As day followed day and the scope of the task became clearer, so grew the problems facing the Technical Directorate. These were not only professional problems, there were administrative ones as well: recruitment of suitably qualified staff, accommodation for these; requiring new buildings and drawing offices; security clearance of personnel and physical security of buildings; all pressing for early solution, all with their effect on any long-term plan for the overall programme, and therefore, involving, to varying degree, myself and my London staff.

I had recognized from the very start that modern management techniques would be essential to strict control of the programme. I had been well briefed by SPO on how these had contributed to the success of the American programme, and I was determined to introduce such methods as Critical Path Analysis, Programme Evaluation Review Technique (PERT) and Programme Management Plans (PMPs), suitably adapted for British use. The Secretary of the Admiralty gave his full backing, and CPE's staff was augmented accordingly. It was not an easy job to fulfil, for these new ideas were by no means readily or universally accepted. In the initial months of the programme much time and effort had to be devoted to persuading Admiralty Departments, and industry where directly concerned, of the necessity and of the purpose of the new methods. It was an uphill struggle, but we won through in the end.

Pressures and uncertainties were relieved momentarily when it was finally decided, around the end of January, that the submarines would each carry sixteen missiles. This enabled serious design work to start on an area which, it was already clearly seen, was absolutely critical to eventual success. Until design criteria for the submarine were established, no action could be taken to get the, as yet, potential shipbuilders properly committed, nor could 'long lead' items be ordered.

With the missiles per submarine now determined, it was comparatively easy to decide that, initially, the programme should cater for building four submarines. The Government decreed that they be completed at six-monthly intervals, and that the option for building a fifth be kept open. Much disputatious argument, and lobbying for custom, then took place on who should be the shipbuilders. Vickers at Barrow-in-Furness was the obvious front-runner, being the only yard with experience of building nuclear-powered submarines; naturally, they offered to take on all four, but it was abundantly clear that they had neither the resources nor capacity to meet the tight timescale to which the programme was tied. Another yard, or yards, had to be found. Cammell Lairds at Birkenhead and Scotts at Greenock, both with great experience of building conventional submarines, were the only contestants. The choice fell on Cammell Lairds, who were judged to be better able to modernise and enlarge their facilities, and especially slipways, essential work if the requirement was to be met. It thus emerged that Vickers and Cammell Lairds would each build two, respectively the first and third and second and fourth. Vickers was to be 'lead-yard' with responsibility for supplying Cammell Lairds with all necessary drawings and information, a difficult contract to fulfil, posing endless problems induced principally by shortages of suitably qualified staff, and leading to constant recriminations between the two rival firms. All this required never ending attention from DPT to smooth matters over.

With the major question of the number of missiles per submarine settled and the Polaris Executive thus able to devote more of its energies to devising a valid long-term plan for the overall programme, I – with an easier mind that I had had for some time – left for Washington on 19th February as part of a strong Admiralty team, plus Ministry of Aviation representation. Led by Deputy Secretary (G) of the Admiralty (Mr J.M. Mackay), its object was to negotiate in detail the terms – financial, material, security – governing the timely supply of POLARIS missiles and equipment as envisaged in the Nassau Agreement. After weeks of intense argument and discussion, for which the British delegation had well prepared itself in advance of going to Washington, there emerged a draft Polaris Sales Agreement, which it was hoped would be acceptable to both Governments. That it achieved remarkably favourable terms for the United Kingdom was due to Jim Mackay; a big man in every way, both mentally and physically, he was an extremely patient but forceful negotiator who, when he thought it justified, pursued matters inexorably and inflexibly until he had achieved a successful conclusion. The skill with which he tackled each issue, some highly technical and complicated, was an eye-opener, and earned great respect and admiration from both sides. In the event, without demur or further amendment, the Agreement was signed by both Governments on 6th April 1963. Its terms were clear (given in full in Appendix I to 'The Nassau Connection') and it formally opened the way to the closest co-operation, at all levels, between the Polaris Executive and the Special Projects Office. This co-operation was steadily, though not so easily, extended into wider fields, between the main British and American contractors, e.g. Vickers and Electric Boat. It was noteworthy that the Agreement specifically excluded the field of nuclear propulsion. Thus I was never drawn into direct contact with Admiral Rickover and the empire he dominated; if problems arose in this area they were pursued via separate channels.

I returned to London on 2nd March 1963, some weeks before the negotiations were concluded. I had sensed that these were going satisfactorily, and that I could better serve the needs of the British Polaris Programme by being back in my headquarters in London to progress the vital issues continually coming to a head. Getting the two shipbuilders, with Rolls Royce and Associates (RR & A), into the act; the latter were responsible for the nuclear reactors for the propulsion systems of all the submarines, projected or building; there were also 'long lead' items required by all three organizations and the time for ordering was already critical. Decision was needed on the A2 or A3 version of the missile. The Ministry of Aviation was dragging its feet, a better organization was required within it, and better relationships must be mutually established. The Polaris Executive, and particularly the Technical Directorate, needed to be expanded in recognition of the vast logistic effort required to design and build a POLARIS base with appropriate maintenance facilities for submarines and missiles. A 'public relations' exercise was paramount, to improve the public image of POLARIS, and counter much ill-informed propaganda that was still rife.

The problems never grew any less, they constantly expanded as knowledge of the task grew day by day.

Despite this apparent turmoil of never-ending new problems, there were, indeed, encouraging signs to greet me on my return. By superhuman efforts Bob Lewin and Rae McKaig, between them, had produced a 'LONGCAST' for the whole POLARIS programme, giving a date for the operational deployment of the first submarine in June 1968, with the remainder following at six-monthly intervals. It was a monumental work, showing all major critical dates as then known, and was backed by solid cost estimates, a sound basis for the inevitable further arguments with the Treasury; and it contained realistic target dates for the construction, fitting out and trials of four submarines, plus full base supporting facilities, as believed practical by Rowley Baker and his Technical Directorate in Bath.

Naturally, as time progressed, LONGCAST 63 was refined as knowledge was acquired, but in essence it became firmly established as the basis for all planning of the programme, and to it was geared all the management techniques in use, such as PERT and PMPs. The Admiralty Board accepted it, without any significant amendment, in April and thereafter it was promulgated to all directly involved in the programme, which eased, immeasurably, the task of the Polaris Executive. There was now an officially approved document showing projected expenditure and target dates. It proved to be, in great degree, a true forecast and *was an absolutely invaluable tool of management*, it set the parameters for keeping costs within the original estimates and for the timely completion of the programme.

Coincidental with Longcast 63, I introduced regular Progress Meetings and once established these became fortnightly reviews of how the Polaris Programme was faring, embracing its whole wide scope. The various members of the Polaris Executive reported in detail on whether satisfactory progress was, or was *not*, being made in this particular section or part of the programme, for which they were individually responsible. Attended by the Management Committee, consisting of CPE, PPO, DPT, CAO and Deputy CPE, they were designed to illuminate problems and difficulties, little time being spent on things that were going well. The Management Committee could thus concentrate their efforts on action to keep the programme on course. Preparation for the meetings undoubtedly consumed much time and effort from all concerned, but, provided reports were truthfully based and not over-optimistic, on which I insisted, they presented regular and frequently recurring opportunities for remedial measures to be quickly instituted, whenever and wherever it appeared that target dates, or costs, were in danger of slipping, or over-running. They also required that those reporting had a real knowledge, in depth, of all that was involved in meeting their own target dates: any light or superficial approach was unacceptable.

With the formation of Longcast 63, it became clear that 'full supporting facilities' for POLARIS when in service would require the design and construction of a completely new shore base for nuclear-powered submarines, including the provision of a floating dock large enough to take POLARIS submarines, SSBNs as they were now commonly referred to. Also needed was an appropriate armament depot for the storage of the Polaris missiles and their nuclear warheads, combined with storing conventional torpedoes and warheads. The new tasks of maintaining and servicing the missiles presented new technical problems, to which the existing Admiralty armament supply organization had to be adjusted. The nuclear warheads would have to be serviced by the Atomic Weapons Research Establishment (AWRE), which meant that special arrangements had to be made for their transport to and fro. Married quarters for sailors and housing for civilian staff, to meet an enormous increase of people at the base, all had to be included. This logistic part of the programme, on its own, was a vast undertaking spread across an enormously wide spectrum; not only Admiralty departments hitherto unaffected, but involving, inter alia, the Ministry of Public Buildings and Works (MPBW), Local Authorities, Health and Safety Executive, Scottish Department, Ministry of Transport, and a host of Civil Engineering interests. Special measures were urgently needed within the Polaris Executive to grapple with this many-headed monster, which could only be brought to successful fruition if its management was kept under strictest control and given the full treatment of the new techniques such as PERT and PMPs.

The Technical Directorate under DPT was accordingly expanded to include a new division responsible for all such logistic matters, headed by the Polaris Logistics Officer (PLO). It took some time to select the right man, with arguments on whether he should be a naval officer or a civilian, but by early May Captain L. Bomford, newly retired from the Navy, was in post, ready and willing to shoulder an immensely complicated and involved assignment. It is true that without his determination and ability to drive the right path through a tangled web of many diverse and self-centred interests, the programme would have fallen into complete disarray. Leslie Bomford was a remarkable man; a civilian electrical engineer brought into the wartime Navy late in life, he made a success of everything he touched, his background as both civilian and naval officer giving him unique understanding of the problem he faced. His selection as PLO was an inspired choice.

Although all the requirements for a special base were clear to me, the Government was slow to give its go-ahead. After examining the suitability of other ports, e.g. Devonport, the Admiralty accepted that Faslane on the Clyde, already approved as the base for 'hunter-killer' nuclear powered submarines, was the most suitable place. The Treasury and Ministries of Defence and of Transport disagreed, because of possible financial savings if the base was at Rosyth; they argued also that at Faslane there were potential dangers to an 'Emergency Oil Depot' located in the Gareloch. With the support of FOS/M, I fought the case on the grounds that, operationally, Rosyth was unacceptable and that Faslane should be developed to cater for both 'hunter-killer' and POLARIS submarines. Eventually, with the backing of the Admiralty Board, final approval was obtained for an entirely new shore base – jetties, maintenance and training facilities, accommodation, married quarters, etc. – to be built at Faslane on the Gareloch, supported by an Armament Depot at Coulport on the shores of the adjoining Loch Long. From the overall 'military' point of view it was the only sensible conclusion, but it gave rise to much opposition locally, from sincerely held views on potential nuclear threats to health and safety and because of general disturbance to the environment. The Base could never be 'a happy ship' if the local inhabitants were determinedly against it. I felt that every measure of publicity to circumvent any such opposition was fully justified, and accordingly the matter received full attention from the highest level; much time and effort was expended on persuading people in the area that their fears were groundless and on getting them and the Local Authorities on our side.

In April a proposal from the Secretary of State for Defence (Mr P. Thorneycroft) threw my very existence into the melting pot. It was suggested that I be replaced by Dr Beeching, who had recently acquired fame, or infamy, for his reorganization of British Rail. Fortunately, the First Lord, First Sea Lord and Controller all believed the Navy could 'run the show' and rose to my defence. The proposal, which could only have been totally disruptive of all the effort so far expended by the Navy on building up the Polaris Executive, was hurriedly dropped. It did, however, give rise to thoughts on the advisability of enlisting, from business or industry, such experience of modern 'project management' as was then available – (not very much!). In consequence, Sir Frederic Hooper, lately retired as a very distinguished Chairman of Schweppes Ltd., a then current 'market-leader' in successful business practices, was invited by the Controller to act as an 'Honorary Consultant'. It was a helpful and useful move, through which I gained much from informal meetings and discussions with Sir Frederic. These talks, entirely on a personal level, confirmed that planning and programme were generally on the right lines and that no fundamental changes were required; they also reinforced a compelling need for contracts with industry to include rigid terms, and penalty clauses, governing timely completion, and that negotiations over such contracts, which tended to be long drawn out, must be swiftly concluded. Sadly, the talks came to an end before the year (1963) was out, through Sir Frederic's unexpected and untimely death. But his input into the Polaris programme's successful conclusion should not go unrecorded.

As already referred to, at our first meeting in January, Admiral Galantin suggested to me that an essential factor in the smooth running of our joint enterprise would be the setting up of some manner of working party. This would meet regularly to review the British programme, to ensure that there was no clash of priorities with the American programme, to identify any possible causes of delay to the former arising from conflict with the latter, and, if necessary, to put in train remedial measures where necessary. This matter was then steadily developed in further discussions, until it was subsequently covered in the Polaris Sales Agreement. It was finally implemented with the first meeting of the Joint Steering Task Group (JSTG) held in June 1963, in Washington, under the Chairmanship of the Director, Special Projects. Henceforth the JSTG meetings were to become a regular feature of the Polaris programme, held alternatively in Washington and in either London or Bath, quarterly initially, and then at 4 monthly intervals.

Formal business of the JSTG was customarily confined to matters relating to and arising from implementation, including interpretation, of the Polaris Sales Agreement. Comprehensive though the latter was, it laid down only the main principles governing the supply of POLARIS to the UK: guidelines, extending in much greater depth, were plainly required to define in detail what, how, and when supply was to take place of material, technical information, documentation, drawings, training and instruction, even down to resolving differences in language. Thus there came into being the Technical Arrangements, ancillary to the Polaris Sales Agreement, but a very essential part of it. The formulation and execution of these Arrangements formed much of the work of the JSTG meetings, and involved those concerned in mastering detailed knowledge of POLARIS in regard to their respective spheres.

It is interesting to note that, in 1993, JSTG meetings, basically still in the same form, are part of the joint TRIDENT programme. There is no doubt in my mind that Admiral Galantin's original suggestion was a key factor in the success of the British Polaris programme.

The Polaris Sales Agreement, the JSTG, the Technical Arrangments, taken together, were all a logical outcome, and an acknowledgement, of the Nassau Agreement. They provided the formalities for bringing to fruition

Author visiting the US Naval Supply Centre as Chief Polaris Executive.

the vital issues contained in the latter, but yet more was required to ensure that things ran smoothly, especially to overcome the geographical separation of the two organizations directly responsible. Happily the two 'Project Officers', as established by the Polaris Sales Agreement, saw eye to eye over the need for closest co-operation, and were quick to appoint Liaison Officers to each other's headquarters. A Captain RN (SPRN), although under the titular authority of CBNS in Washington, served on Admiral Galantin's staff and provided a direct link between Special Projects and the Polaris Executive; similarly a Captain USN (SPUK) was on my staff in London. By April Captain P.G. La Niece was in post in Washington and Captain P. Rollings in London, ill-health unfortunately forced the latter's retirement within a few months. His temporary replacement was Captain Hamilton, to be finally succeeded by Captain W.P. Murphy. Peter La Niece and Pat Murphy were indeed the oil which kept the many intricate and closely inter-meshed wheels of the British and American organizations revolving smoothly. The burden of the work fell mostly in Washington, and hence on Peter La Niece's shoulders so his previous experience in Washington was a fortunate bonus. In essence, both officers were very vital cogs in the machinery of bringing POLARIS into Royal Naval service.

Whilst much time and effort was, properly, devoted in those early months to obtaining a sound foundation for the closest trans-Atlantic co-operation at all levels, it was also very clear that there was, simultaneously, an imperative need to make known, nearer at home, the full meaning of POLARIS and what would be entailed in the vast programme about to be embarked on. Neither its scope, nor urgency, had percolated through Whitehall beyond a few highly placed officials. A unique degree of collaboration between Ministries contributing to the Polaris programme, and co-ordination of effort within them, would be necessary if the required head of steam was to be raised, and maintained. Chaired by the Secretary of the Admiralty, the Polaris Interdepartmental Policy Steering Committee (PIPSC) was, in spite of its horrific title, a useful adjunct to spreading the gospel and, if problems arose with Ministries which I was unable to resolve by direct negotiation, it helped to find a solution in keeping with the importance and priorities of the programme. Similarly, within the Admiralty, the Polaris Committee (later known as the Polaris Policy Committee), chaired by the Assistant Chief of Naval Staff (ACNS), then Rear Admiral P. Hill-Norton, was a considerable help to me in keeping the Naval Staff Divisions, and the Second Sea Lord's departments dealing with (uniformed) manning requirements, alive to the ever-mounting needs of POLARIS. To advise on ways and means of countering ill-informed and adverse publicity still carried by sections of the media, a small Publicity Committee was formed under the chairmanship of the Civil Lord of the Admiralty (Mr Ian Orr-Ewing). It served its purpose effectively and by the late autumn of 1963 had overcome what had tended to be a running sore adversely affecting the cohesion and efficiency of the Polaris Executive.

By May 1963, as the full implications of the SSBN building programme became clearer, its dependence on the successful installation and proving of the first British designed nuclear propulsion plant in VALIANT (the first entirely British SSN), under construction at Vickers at Barrow-in-Furness, was seen to be absolutely crucial. It was thus an anomaly that, while I had overall responsibility for the SSBN programme and, under me, DPT and his team possessed virtually all the expertise in nuclear submarine design and building, Director General Ships (DGS), under the old-established Admiralty organization, retained all responsibility for the two SSNs *Valiant* and *Warspite*, then authorised. To avoid conflicts of interest it seemed logical they should come under the CPE's wing, and their building programmes receive our management treatment, and their priorities be judged in relation to LONGCAST 63. I proposed accordingly. But to deprive DGS of his professional responsibilities was a sensitive matter requiring delicate handling. Happily, Sir Alfred Sims accepted the arguments for such a change, which not only paved the way for Admiralty Board approval of the proposal, but avoided an open and destructive clash between DPT's Naval Constructors and those working for DGS.

Warspite at this time was still barely beyond the drawing board stage, with the contract for her construction only recently placed. Notwithstanding, the Treasury, when considering the contracts for building the SSBNs, re-opened the matter, with strong pressure that her construction be deferred until after the whole Polaris programme had been completed. I, actively briefed by DPT, argued otherwise. The inclusion of *Warspite* in Vickers' planned load of work, and the avoidance of a hiatus between *Valiant* and the first SSBN, was seen as an absolutely essential step in the firm's build-up to taking on the full weight of their SSBN building programme. Common sense prevailed, and so by August I had added to my responsibilities the timely completion of *Valiant* and *Warspite*.

By mid-summer of 1963, i.e. within six months of the Nassau Agreement, the 'sketch design' for the SSBNs had been completed, and it had received Board approval. Basically it took *Valiant*'s design, cut it in two and between the two halves inserted the complete Polaris weapon system of sixteen missile launching tubes and all related control equipment.

It was a stupendous, mammoth task, dependent on much close collaboration with SPO and their 'lead' shipyard, the Electric Boat Co., particularly on the receipt from them of much detailed technical information, all requiring the resolution of innumerable and complicated 'interfaces' between what was of British and what was of American origin. That it was accomplished in so short a time, throughout which there was the added local distraction of the imposition of special new measures for security, which demanded that DPT and all his staff be housed in a self-contained (and still under erection) complex of offices and drawing offices, separate from the rest of Admiralty, Bath, is a measure of Rowley Baker's forceful leadership. He had complete command of the situation, backed by determination that the programme, as agreed in LONGCAST 63, was capable of fulfilment, despite continued protestations from outside sources and occasionally from within, that it was 'crying for the moon'.

The design, having been approved, was 'frozen'. DPT, backed fully by me, was adamant that there be no alterations or additions at the whim of Tom, Dick or Harry, no changes other than those dictated by safety or from trials of *Valiant*, and that all four Polaris submarines be exactly the same. This was a vital factor in their timely completion, though the edict suffered one or two bruising attacks. The first of them came early on, from a strongly argued plea from the Director of the Compass Division, within the Admiralty, that a British designed Ships Inertial Navigation System (SINS) replace the American supplied equipment fulfilling this function, a very essential part of the Polaris weapon control outfit. The proposal was fiercely supported by Director-General Weapons (DGW); but to replace in this way one component of the whole carefully balanced system was anathema to me, as ably advised by Charles Shepherd. It took prolonged argument over many months before we won the battle, and much longer before friendly relations were restored with DGW.

The other case came much later in the programme, about late 1966 or early 1967, when it suddenly came to light that the length, between bulkheads, of the torpedo stowage compartment in *Renown* (the first of Cammell Lairds' two boats) differed by one inch from that of her prototype *Resolution* at Vickers. Consternation erupted all round, but fortunately there were no major consequences. Laxity in adherence to, or in interpretation of, documents and drawings, somewhere along the line between the lead yard and follow-up yard, was deemed the cause. It was a horrifying discovery at the time, but it gave little more than a ripple of disturbance to the overall programme.

Though occasions inevitably arose from time to time when Rowley Baker and I had differences, mainly over details of relative priorities, the initial and determined support which he gave to the whole conception of strict control of the Polaris programme never wavered. In particular his dedication to achieving dates and to detailed planning, with timely completion of contracts and, just as importantly, sub-contracts, was absolutely vital in dragging the ship builders, both Vickers and Cammell Lairds, out of the nineteenth into the twentieth century, by persuading them that they must adopt new measures and techniques of management; without these they could not hope to meet the targets set. Expert they may have been in basic steel working and the actual construction and fitting out of conventional ships' hulls, but in 1963 they had no conception of what they were taking on in the building, fitting out, and testing and tuning of a SSBN. It was something far more complicated than anything they had dealt with before, involving the assembly, installation and rigorous testing of thousands and thousands of items of equipment, many highly technical, to be supplied by several hundred sub-contractors, some in the United Kingdom, some in

America, all to be achieved to a strict time scale. It took months and months of argument and persuasion by DPT, and myself, before they committed the resources necessary for detailed planning, which was absolutely essential if the SSBNs were to be built on time.

Perhaps the argument was finally won at some point during the winter of 1964/65. There were weaknesses in the programme and an emergency meeting was arranged at Barrow, attended by myself with the strong support of DPT and the leaders of his team at Bath. Dates were slipping; Vickers, represented by the Managing Director (Mr L. Redshaw) of the shipyard and many more members of his staff than I could muster on my side, were being urged to mend their ways and devote more effort to planning the programme. Affairs grew heated, to the extent that the Managing Director furiously accused me across the table of 'being only a bloody amateur who knew nothing of shipbuilding'. It was, of course, true as far as the actual construction of ships went, but not so in regard to modern management techniques, which were the subject-immediatley under discussion and in the use of which Vickers were sorely lacking. However, despite the anger on both sides, the meeting continued and ended relatively peacefully, and I felt that some points had been gained. Next morning, in my office in London, I was rung up by Charles Shepherd from Bath, he having been at the previous day's stormy meeting. 'Had I seen in today's papers that a horse called 'Polaris Missile' had won the 4.30 (or some such) race at Newcastle yesterday, *owned, trained and ridden by an amateur?*' 'No, I had not seen it, but I took the point, and was very grateful for having my attention drawn to it in the light of yesterday's meeting.' I promptly sent the following telegram addressed to the Managing Director at Barrow: 'Please note that the 4.30 at Newcastle yesterday was won by 'Polaris Missile', owned, trained and ridden by a bloody amateur.' The message was received in the same spirit as it was sent, and from then on there never again arose rancour or enmity between myself and Len Redshaw. Friendly relations prevailed, without which the many problems that continued to arise would never have been successfully resolved. It was a happy outcome to what had threatened to become a critical row.

The pressure on myself and my staff continued throughout the summer of 1963. The initial essential elements of the overall programme had been defined – the design of the submarines, the locality of the base, the milestones to be achieved – but as knowledge expanded so did the problems. How, when and from where were the resources to be found to meet the new and ever-growing requirements, and how could their costs be contained within the budget? On all sides, particularly from the Polaris weapon sector, there were strident but well-founded cries for more highly qualified staff. Information should have been flooding in from America, but it wasn't. How could it be speeded up? Could it be digested usefully when it came? How were the submarines to be manned, one or two crews per boat, and how and where were these to be trained, what training facilities would be needed in the new base? Wherever one looked there was a new question to be answered.

I was also much concerned at the ignorance that existed on POLARIS generally within the Admiralty, and beyond; more specifically, on the lack of understanding of the organization that had been specifically set up to bring into operational use, *within a very pressing timescale*, the new national deterrent. This lack of knowledge, wherever it occurred, was a stumbling block to steady progress. Accordingly, a series of courses and lectures on 'Polaris and its Management' were given to audiences drawn from Admiralty Departments and other Government bodies involved with the programme. Additionally, formal 'Presentations' were prepared, to be given as necessary to the Admiralty Board, to the Ministry of Defence (as yet not the power in Whitehall or the land as it was to become in 1964), to Ministers, and to Members of Parliament. Time and effort spent on these informatary endeavours reaped a worthwhile reward by helping to speed up decisions and by removing much innate opposition.

Throughout the second half of 1963, my London staff and I became more and more involved with factors affecting the operational deployment of Polaris, particularly as it was to be the country's sole deterrent force from 1970 onwards. With four SSBNs as planned the minimum requirement of one submarine always at sea on deterrent patrol could just be met, whilst yet accommodating the obligatory periods in harbour for routine maintenance, long refits and nuclear re-fuelling. On paper if appeared feasible, but the plan made no allowance for possible accident or major breakdown in any of the submarines. Because of the over-riding importance of maintaining *at all times the absolute credibility of the deterrent* I was convinced that the plan was basically unsound. Equally importantly, I believed that it would impose, in peace time, an unnecessarily high degree of stress and strain on sea-going crews and base staff alike. I sensed a lack of appreciation of the fact that to ensure a submarine-borne deterrent remained *truly credible at all times*, it required that, for week upon week when at sea, the crew were in all respects equivalent to being on patrol under conditions of war. Likewise, to keep the submarines at sea on a schedule permitting not the slightest variation, required a similar approach from all those who worked ashore. For those reasons I maintained that the Polaris force should consist of *five* SSBNs instead of four; only in this way could *the constant credibility of the deterrent be totally guaranteed*, and the inevitable pressures on all concerned that this demanded be reduced to tolerable levels.

The argument continued for months and was not finally resolved until 1964. Meanwhile, on the assumption that a fifth SSBN would eventually be authorised, it was imperative to place orders for its 'long lead' items in order to avoid foreseeable delays to its construction. To circumvent inevitable objections from those holding the purse-strings, these were referred to as being a 'contingency reserve' or as essential 'spares'; in this guise they passed muster, and timely provision was made for building the additional submarine.

Two further important issues required resolution before the end of 1963. The first was *Training*, beginning with the scope and function of the Royal Naval Polaris School (RNPS), which was to be incorporated in the shore base at Faslane. Its early completion a year ahead of the operational deployment of the first SSBN, was a critical milestone as with no exact prototype in the United States to emulate, it had to be designed from scratch, with a decision taken on whether it was to be for training and instructional purposes only, or its use expanded to include 'Test Instrumentation'. After prolonged trans-Atlantic discussion, the latter was rejected as an unnecessary complication. Coincidental with this problem was that of the initial training of the Polaris weapon system crews who would be manning the RNPS and the first of the SSBNs, until the former was completed, facilities in the United Kingdom were non-existent. Accordingly, an instructional programme, covered by the Polaris Sales Agreement, was arranged with SPO, whereby the first of the officers and ratings selected for this highly specialised training would carry out an intensive course of six months or so at the U.S. Navy's Polaris School at Dam Neck in Virginia. To find suitable officers and ratings with the necessary high qualifications presented some difficulties; the submarine service on its own could not provide them, and there had to be a call on those in General Service. The response was satisfactory, but it was a drain on the rest of the Navy. I later had to join battle with the Treasury, over the payment of adequate allowances for the trainees at Dam Neck, to compensate for their increased 'cost of living' whilst on such extended courses. It was a protracted fight, but eventually it was won.

The second major issue concerned the design and construction of a floating dock capable of lifting an SSBN, to be in place at Faslane and ready for use by mid-1967, that is to say, in under four years. The skids had to be placed under all work on its design, and once this had been speedily completed its construction was given to Portsmouth Dockyard, who, to everyone's surprise, delivered satisfactorily without constant prodding. It was a major achievement.

Chapter Eighteen

Polaris . . . but the continuing of the same until it be thoroughly finished.

With a year gone by, the task of the Polaris Executive in January 1964, appeared manageable, though remaining immensely formidable. The Executive's strength had grown to twenty four in the London headquarters and to two hundred and sixty in Bath, all had acquired a realistic grasp of what was required of them and were imbued with the spirit of Drake's Prayer. None were unaware that the years ahead would never be an easy ride. But the management plans and regular fortnightly progress meetings were beginning to pay a dividend and I and my staff in London felt we had a firm grip on the situation and were in a position to meet the many difficulties and problems, foreseen and unforeseen, that daily arose.

Whitehall had accepted, generally, the existence of a unique organization in its midst and were prepared to co-operate in the achievement of its aims; though there remained a few pockets of obstruction or resistance which continued to require special action by me. Within the Admiralty the Departments of the Director-General, Weapons, responsible for Navigation and Communications, continued to aspire to run their own show, regardless of the 'interface' problems that would arise should changes be made to the overall design of the Polaris Weapon System. The introduction of regular DGW/CPE Liaison meetings ironed out the problems and ensured that everyone concerned with conventional weaponry and equipment had only one target in mind – the successful completion of the force of submarines and its supporting facilities, *to the timescale laid down by CPE and to the design parameters established by DPT.* Action in the shape of regular meetings was also needed to monitor progress at AWRE and the Royal Ordnance Factory, Burghfield, where shortages of staff, compounded by difficulties in deciding design criteria, threatened at times the ultimate aim of the whole programme by jeopardising production dates for the nuclear warheads and associated re-entry systems. These 'penetration aids', to help defeat Russian anti-ballistic missile defences, were a very critical issue.

Construction of the hulls of the first SSBNs by Vickers and by Cammell Lairds was well underway by the end of 1963, and both shipyards were steadily expanding the facilities needed to cope with such a demanding programme. The scale of the civil engineering work was colossal, all to be integrated with the actual construction and assembly of the huge hull units of the submarines themselves, and despite the appalling conditions of the winter's weather, there were no serious hold-ups, not even over costs, which fortunately had been largely agreed in the earlier discussions on the placing of the submarine building contracts.

There was, however, one critical threat to progress; the supply of the special steel, QT 35, needed for the pressure hulls of the submarines. Not only were there few suitably equipped and qualified manufacturers within the UK, but they themselves had little experience in producing, in quantity, such high quality material. This situation was further complicated by an acute shortage of molybdenum, an essential component in this particular brand of steel and, moreover, one that had to be imported from abroad. The United States, a normal source of supply, could not help because of their own overriding demands so the world had to be scoured for alternative sources. Some critical weeks passed before DPT informed me that the steel-makers were now happy, having secured a sufficient quantity of molybdenum to meet their needs for some time to come. *Its origin, Russia!* Despite this quirky solution, the building of the submarines continued to be threatened by shortages of QT 35 steel; as the ship-builders' requirements increased under the full weight of the programme, they had to fall back on supplies of American HY 80 steel, of comparable quality, and which fortunately became available as the US Navy's own SSBN building programme coincidentally eased.

To get a better grasp of these problems, in the first few months of 1964 I embarked on a comprehensive round of visits to the main steel manufacturers and to other heavy engineering firms engaged in the production of 'long lead' items critical to the nuclear propulsion plants of all the submarines building. These visits had a two-way purpose: on the one hand they allowed me to acquaint myself at first hand with major contractors and the difficulties they were experiencing, whilst on the other I used the opportunity to impress on them the urgency of the work they were engaged on, and the need for the most detailed planning and for strictest quality control. I stressed that only if these two matters received adequate attention could they hope to meet the country's vital requirement of a credible deterrent.

For over a year, the Press, and the media generally, had not lacked copious mention of POLARIS, with opinions pro- and anti-, and imaginative articles of every description. To try to 'keep the record straight' I had had interviews with the Defence Correspondents of the major newspapers, but this had little effect and it was still a matter of surprise to find, on my visits away from Whitehall, how little understood were the real issues lying behind the deterrent and all the clamour it aroused. People were largely ignorant of, or ignored or disputed, the fundamental purpose of deterrent forces, whether POLARIS, V-Bombers or whatever: namely, to preserve peace in the face of an aggressive USSR whose military might and stock of nuclear weapons were second to none, and whose occasional actions and constantly proclaimed intentions were the very antithesis of peaceful co-existence. *But the deterrent would only work if the potential aggressor was fully aware that any transgression on his part would bring on him, inevitably, an unacceptable level of damage. CREDIBILITY* was the key. The effectiveness of the deterrent all depended on the potential enemy not daring to believe that it would not be used or, if used, would not function properly: provided the deterrent, or the country wielding it, gave no grounds for such beliefs, it would continue to guarantee that the world's greatest military power would not embark on any aggressive adventure. A sideline to this vital factor of credibility was the remark made to me light-heartedly once when discussing the design of the nuclear warhead for the Polaris missile with Solly Zuckerman. 'If only we could be sure the Russians *never* knew, and *never* found out *or* suspected, we could then put a bag of sand instead in the front end – it would save a lot of money!' And so it would have, but the risk could not be taken.

POLARIS, as developed by the United States Navy, fulfilled all the essential criteria for a credible deterrent; tremendous efforts had been successfully expended to ensure the reliability of the whole system, from the front end of the missile to its 'launching pad', the SSBN. I was determined that the same standards be set and maintained in the British Naval Ballistic Missile System (BNBMS), as the British Polaris force came to be named. To emphasise this aspect it became necessary to include the basic arguments for Britain possessing the deterrent in all my 'pep' talks to industry and in my presentations and lectures on the make-up and functioning of the Polaris Executive, whenever and to whomever these were given. Inevitably this led to my direct involvement in the political arena – which, personally, went much against the grain – but without such an approach the misguided arguments of CND and kindred 'peace marchers', unchallenged, posed a constant source of disruption to the task of the Polaris Executive. The more active became CND, the more the case for Polaris had to be repeated, time and time again.

As 1964 advanced, the prospect of a Labour victory in the forthcoming autumn general election loomed larger and larger. Their widely proclaimed views on Defence generally and on POLARIS in particular, the latter varying from 're-negotiation of the Nassau Agreement' (whatever that meant – it was never made clear!) to cancellation of the whole programme, were no source of confidence or comfort for the Polaris Executive. But strong in the belief that our cause was worthwhile and in the genuine interests of the country, myself and my team, in the face of this mounting wave of political propaganda, re-doubled our efforts to keep the programme forging ahead. If enough progress could be achieved and sufficient money be firmly committed, by the time of the election, the future would be that much more assured. Notwithstanding our efforts towards this, there is no doubt that the wide publicity given to Labour's views in the run-up to the election gave rise to doubts and fears amongst many, in industry and elsewhere, nibbling away at the level of co-operation so critical to the Polaris programme. To counter such misgivings a yet heavier burden was now laid on the Polaris Executive in their never-ending fight against anything that could cause the programme to falter.

The first concrete evidence of progress was exposed to public view on a bleak, cold day at Vickers' shipyard in Barrow on 26th February 1964, when at a brief ceremony the keel of the first of the SSBNs was formally 'laid'. In contrast to what was normally involved on such an occasion, in this case a massive 250 ton section of the pressure hull had been moved from the welding bay in the huge construction shed where it had been built, to rest in its final position on the slipway where it would be joined in due course by other sections, and when all complete, finally launched. It was a momentous, even historical, moment as Director General, Ships, declared it in place. It had been achieved on time and was an encouraging augury for the future.

On the same day the Government finally approved the construction of the fifth SSBN I went happily to bed that night – only to succumb two days later to double pneumonia, which effectively removed me from all work for over a month. In my absence the fort was ably held by Rae McKaig in London and Rowley Baker in Bath, the latter having to lead the team attending the fourth meeting of the JSTG (Joint Steering Task Group) in Washington in March.

In April 1964, the Government's major reorganisation of the Ministry of Defence and the three hitherto separate Armed Services came into effect. The Admiralty as a distinct organization disappeared and its function was centralised within a greatly expanded Ministry of Defence. Admiralty Board members, Naval Staff Divisions and senior Civil Service officials and departments, along with the Polaris Executive, suffered the physical upheaval of having to move office into the vast, impersonal, but much newer, main building of the Ministry of Defence, just across Whitehall from their long-established quarters in the much older Admiralty building. Fortunately, there had been ample time to plan the move in advance, and it was superbly executed, with virtually no interruption to day-to-day business. Compared to our former conditions – hurriedly improvised, cramped, and where maintenance of proper security had been a nightmare – my London staff and I were now given a suite of offices, conference room, etc., adequate for our needs. Furthermore, these were equipped with their own self-contained and specially designed security measures and their own teleprinter network, over and above those provided in the main building. It was an enormously improved set-up. I also gained personally. I now found that I could have an 'official' car, from the general pool, to take me to and from work. Hitherto public transport had had to suffice for journeys to and

Laying the keel of HMS *Resolution* the first Polaris Submarine, 26th Feb 1964.

from home. This concession had not come easily, but was thanks to the persistent lobbying of my loyal Secretary, John Grimwood. The transfer to MOD, Main Building had, in certain ways, made life that much easier!

But despite these advantages the transition by no means led to the solution of all our problems; in fact, in some degree it made the path to success more difficult. Under the old Admiralty organisation members of the Board were a power unto themselves and I knew that an appeal to any one of them would produce immediate results. Now there was no longer a First Lord, and appeal to one of the 'Sea Lords' or to the Minister of the Navy could always be subject to scrutiny and ruling by the Secretary of State for Defence and/or the Defence Council. The path had become longer and more tortuous, leading the Polaris Executive increasingly to rely on their own efforts and carve their own way. Fortunately, there was no change in the objective they had been given.

The keel of the second SSBN was laid on 26th June, in Cammell Laird's shipyard at Birkenhead. It was another significant milestone achieved on time, but giving no grounds for any complacency with the submarine building programme, difficulties abounded for both the Polaris submarines and the hunter-killers (SSNs). A shortage of high grade welders, suitably qualified for the special QT 35 steel prescribed for their hulls, was chronic in both shipyards, requiring a nation-wide search to be instituted, which included Devonport and Rosyth Royal dockyards, to see if more could be recruited. This had limited success, and the problem remained lurking until the main construction work on the hulls had been completed.

Strikes, and threats of strikes, by various key sections of the skilled work force in each shipyard continued to have a generally unsettling effect on the programme by jeopardizing many critical dates. In particular a draughtsmen's strike at Barrow, lasting several months, caused serious disruption to the ordered flow of essential drawings from the drawing office, vital to both Vickers and Cammel Lairds, and also had a downstream, long term effect on the placing of orders with sub-contractors for the multitude of 'ship-builder supply' items of equipment required for each submarine.

Progress in *Valiant* was unsatisfactory. She had been launched in December 1963, and was at a critical stage of fitting out; but, in my view as briefed by DPT, insufficient manpower was allocated to the task if she was to be finished on time. Action had to be taken with Vickers, to urge them to provide more resources, but this had to be done without jeopardizing progress on their other contracts; in other words, it was no use robbing Peter to pay Paul. There was no easy solution; shortage of skilled work people was endemic to the whole Polaris programme, particularly because of its highly technical content and the demands of stringent quality control. This latter originated with the nuclear propulsion system, was equally essential to the Polaris Weapon System and had now cast its web throughout the whole submarine, introducing new and much higher standards of workmanship, attention to detail and, for everyone concerned, a vastly higher level of cleanliness in the work place, whether submarine or shop, than ever before expected, or achieved. Great efforts had to be expended in the way of recruitment, indoctrination and training of people in order that they master the new criteria.

There were persistent difficulties in satisfactorily completing the primary circuit of *Valiant*'s nuclear reactor. As mentioned earlier, this was the first British design of a submarine nuclear propulsion plant and a prototype tested at Dounreay had seemed satisfactory; but doubts now arose about the quality of some of the piping, stemming from a substance called Inconel, which was essential to the make up of the stainless steel obligatory for the piping system. These doubts were compounded by difficulties arising in the manufacture of some of the main circulating valves, which were failing to meet the rigorous tests demanded. The help of Admiral Rickover in Washington had to be sought. This was channelled through Solly Zuckerman and the Chief of Defence Staff, Admiral Mountbatten, the only people with whom Admiral Rickover would have any dealings; despite his well known antipathy to everything British, he was more than helpful and quickly provided a satisfactory solution to both problems.

Within eight days of the new Labour Government taking power following the General Election of 15th October 1964, my staff and I gave a full-scale illustrated presentation to all the newly appointed Ministers who were in any way connected with the Polaris programme, from the Secretary of State for Defence (Denis Healey) downwards. Much thought, time and effort went into the preparation of this, in full recognition of the view that the audience might be somewhat hostile. The theme concentrated on three straightforward and simple aspects; firstly, who were the Polaris Executive and what was their task, secondly, how were they setting about it, and thirdly, how far had they got. The opportunity was also used to emphasise the need for Government decisions, if any were to be taken, being either 'Go' or 'No Go'; wavering permutations would be anathema, saving neither money nor effort. In the event, reception was far from adverse. I was encouraged by a docile but interested reaction and I hoped that to both sides the presentation was illuminating – except, perhaps for one Minister in the front row who remained soundly asleep from within five minutes of the start of proceedings. Perhaps it had been a mistake to stage the occasion in the afternoon, so soon after lunch!

There were no immediate results from the presentation. The Government's intentions for Polaris became no clearer, and all the pre-election propaganda of re-negotiating Nassau or doing away with Polaris continued to dominate the scene. By mid-November both Vickers and Cammell Lairds were reporting that political uncertainty was causing key men to drift away from their Polaris organization. But within Whitehall the wheels were turning, however, and I was constantly called upon to give further briefings, to the Secretary of State for Defence, Chief of Defence Staff, First Sea Lord (now Admiral Luce) amongst others. With all the many question marks hanging over the Polaris programme, that autumn was a particularly busy time. In addition to the political uncertainties and the never-ending difficulties in the shipyards there were other pressing problems needing action. The build-up of the projected base at Faslane, particularly the married quarters for officers and men, some of which must be ready well within three years; also the terms of service for the staff of the new Armament Depot at Coulport, many of whom would be highly qualified technically, and for whom there was no precedent. This was a source of endless argument with the Civil Service, their unions and the Treasury. There would be men under training at the United States Navy's Polaris school at Dam Neck in Virginia from the next year and much had to be done to ensure their welfare and to establish appropriate allowances to meet the then high cost of living in the U.S. and the unfavourable dollar rate. Once again the Treasury resisted and the help of senior Ministers had to be sought before the matter was settled satisfactorily.

By the end of the year the situation looked brighter politically. A weekend at Chequers given over to Defence matters had at least established that the Government intended to keep Polaris as the national deterrent and that there would be no change in the priority accorded to bringing it into service, though there remained the vital question of how many submarines would be built. The immediate task of the Polaris Executive had been confirmed – the first submarine to be operational by mid-1968, the others to follow at six-monthly intervals, with supporting facilities at the shore base to conform. There was no deviation from the original challenge, which was reinforced by the Minister for the Navy early in 1965 when introducing the annual Naval Estimates in the House of Commons. He stated it in plain terms: . . . '*the toughest peace-time task the Navy has ever been given*'.

In mid-December 1964, at the seventh JSTG meeting in London it was time to say 'goodbye' to Admiral Galantin, who was moving on to become Chief of Naval Material of the United States Navy (CNM, corresponding to Controller and Third Sea Lord in the RN). He was to be succeeded by Rear Admiral Levering Smith, who had been Technical Director to Special Projects for many years and was, indeed, *the* architect and expert on all matters concerning POLARIS. There were no changes whatsoever in the special relationship between Special Projects and Polaris Executive, except that, if anything, the technical team in the latter gained from an input of personal expertise from Admiral Levering Smith himself. He was just as insistent as his predecessor that the British would get a fair deal in the timely provision of information and material so the log-jam of mountains of documentation began to clear.

The argument over the number of submarines to be built came to a head in January 1965. At a meeting of the full Defence Council considering this, with the Secretary of State in the chair, I was invited to open the batting with my views. I maintained, as I had done with the previous administration, that five were required to assure that in operational service one at least

would always be on patrol, this guaranteeing with as near 100 per cent
certainty as possible the all-time credibility of the deterrent, yet without risk
from too much 'overstretch' and too great stress on those manning and
supporting the force. I dwelt in some detail on these operational factors, and
laid particular emphasis on the morale angle, knowing full well the strain
that could fall on the submarine crews on patrol, and on those ashore on
whose support they relied. On conclusion I was thanked by the Secretary of
State for all I had said, but politely told that my arguments were 'irrelevant'.
Only Sir Solly Zuckerman (Chief Scientific Adviser to the MOD) gave any
indication of support – neither the Chief of Defence Staff's representative
nor First Sea Lord said anything – and there was no further discussion.
There soon followed a meeting of the Defence and Overseas Policy
Committee of the Cabinet at which the Treasury demanded the force be cut
to three submarines; but the Ministry of Defence won the day with a
compromise of four, which the Government accepted readily.

The consequences of this decision were not difficult and steps were
immediately taken to stop further expenditure on the fifth submarine.
Where contracts were irrevocable, with material already in the pipe-line, or
where huge cancellation charges would arise, the order would be completed
and the product would serve as 'spares' whereas other orders were
cancelled, with minimum cancellation charges. It was a relief to have a firm
decision at last. The programme was now back on what had originally been
planned in April 1963, and everyone could now concentrate on bringing it
to a successful conclusion. Any further action in connection with the fifth
boat was of secondary importance. 'No looking back, get on with the
authorized programme,' was my message to the Polaris Executive.

Nevertheless there remained personally with CPE a lingering doubt; by
accepting this reduction from five submarines to four, was I committing the
men who would man the force to a degree of stress over and above that
which was normally acceptable for service in submarines in peace time? The
pressure arising from the duty of keeping the nation's deterrent permanently
at virtually immediate readiness for action would undoubtedly be very
different from anything hitherto experienced in time of peace – the only
similarities were with conditions on patrol – in wartime – and with no fifth
boat there was no reserve to fall back on. Only time would tell whether the
load placed on those in the Polaris force by this decision would prove too
much. In the event perhaps it was not so, but in my heart I continue to
believe that keeping a fifth submarine in the programme would have been a
wiser decision. The additional cost would have been small, and the
advantage to all who had to operate and maintain the force would have been
immeasurable. I believe the true reason for its cancellation was political, not
financial; a sop to the left wing of the Labour party. All that their clamour
achieved was to lay an almost intolerable burden on the men, and women,
responsible for the efficiency of the deterrent.

With the major hurdle of Labour's apparent pre-election antagonism to the deterrent and corresponding doubts as to the size or continuance of the Polaris force finally surmounted, the Management Team and Polaris Executive could settle down to what became a largely routine task. The scope and detailed requirements of the overall programme were clearly defined, the major 'milestones' established, critical areas identified, lack of progress or unforeseen obstacles accurately and quickly reported, and the earlier opposition to the unusual organization and its methods had faded away. All that was needed now was to maintain, almost on a twenty-four hour, round the clock basis, the tightest of grips on an ever-changing situation. As construction progressed in shipyards and future base, whenever and wherever delays threatened, positive action had to be taken at once to get the programme back on course. It remained over the years a hard and unremitting slog for everyone.

I found that if I had to appeal for help to higher authority, Ministers of the new Government personally gave their support wholeheartedly, and even enthusiastically. The Government outwardly, however, remained sensitive to anything to do with POLARIS and were reluctant to encourage much in the way of publicity for the programme and what it was achieving. I ran foul of this years later, when at *Resolution*'s commissioning ceremony at Barrow in October 1967, in answer to a question from the press, I gave my views on the by then dead-end issue of the fifth boat. I was sharply told to keep my mouth shut in future!

During 1966 the next concrete results of the programme began to show. These significantly included the completion of the Royal Naval Polaris School (RNPS), with its formal opening, on schedule, on 30th June, the acceptance into service of *Valiant* at the end of July, the launch of *Resolution* on 15th September, and by the end of the year *Warspite* through her Contractors Sea Trials. The RNPS, with its conspicuous missile launch tower dominating the surrounding apparent chaos of half completed roadways and buildings, amidst seas of mud, threw down the gauntlet to all engaged in the vast construction work yet to be completed in the Faslane/Coulport complex. Vickers at Barrow had achieved wonders, but many problems still remained in the shipyards. Cammell Lairds were lagging badly with their two Polaris submarines, and there was a 'hiccough' in the flow of QT 35/HY 80 steel for the hulls of the hunter-killer submarines, SSN 04 and 05, the contracts for which Vickers had secured as a follow-on to their Polaris work. Orders were about to be placed for two more, SSN 06 and 07, but all was overshadowed by the discovery of hair-line cracks in the welding of *Dreadnought*'s pressure hull. The possible consequences were frightening and a hugely disruptive schedule of ultrasonic testing of all welds in the hulls of all submarines had to be hurriedly ordered. It was accomplished without completely destroying essential orderly progress and was to the enormous credit of all who had to grapple with this devastating problem.

It was time for changes in the Polaris Executive and I had no wish to jeopardize in any way the career prospects of anyone on my staff. I accepted that naval appointments normally lasted for around two years, but that in exceptional circumstances they could possibly be extended to three years. Anything longer might prejudice the individual concerned. A similar custom applied to those in the Civil Service. Bob Lewin was succeeded, as earlier mentioned, as Chief Administrative Officer in 1966 by Peter Nailor, who in turn was succeeded by Michael Power in 1967. Captain Philip Higham relieved Rae McKaig as Deputy CPE in 1966, and, after undertaking the full Polaris training course at Dam Neck – which he did with flying colours – Captain C.H. Hammer took Peter La Niece's place in Washington that summer. Later that year Pat Murphy, the inimitable and trusted SP (Special Projects) Liaison Officer in London, was relieved by Captain J. Love, USN. While Rowley Baker as DPT remained firmly in charge at Bath, further changes at the top included Mr H.J. Tabb, RCNC, (Royal Corps of Naval Constructors) succeeding Mr S.J. Palmer as DPT's Deputy. Lower down the echelon similar changes regularly took place and all were accomplished smoothly and caused not a ripple of disturbance to the programme. The one major exception to this orderly exchange of duties was Charles Shepherd, head of the Polaris Weapon Section at Bath and an absolutely key member of DPT's team. He was quite irreplaceable and I took special measures to retain him in post for the full span of getting Polaris into service, receiving assurances from higher up that in no way would his future career suffer thereby.

On his relief Peter La Niece produced some figures illustrative of the scope of his appointment in Washington, in which he had been responsible not only for close liaison with SPO (Special Projects Office) but was intimately involved in the placing of orders for all U.S. supplied equipment, and in the training of UK personnel in US Naval Establishments or with industry, e.g. Electric Boat Co., Lockheeds. The figures, from April 1963, to June 1966, were

Mileage flown (personally)	–	220,000
Visit Clearances submitted	–	1525
Purchase orders placed	–	over 600
U.K. trainees supervised	–	520
Measurement tons shipped from Charleston (Nov. '64 to June '66)	–	3,300

The Defence Review ordered by the Government in 1966 had little effect on POLARIS, although the 'freeze' on recruitment throughout the Government Service of any additional staff gave rise to minor problems. By the beginning of 1967, I was fairly confident that, if pressure was maintained and barring some frightful accident, an initial major aim would be achieved; perhaps it was the most important of all, the operational deployment of *Resolution* mid-1968, with all necessary supporting facilities available at the base on the Clyde. The remaining targets also seemed not beyond reach.

But there were still omens that were not so good. Cammell Laird, lacking the experience Vickers had gained from building *Dreadnought* and *Valiant*, were dogged by labour troubles and shortages of skilled staff, particularly for the management of their programme. Nevertheless, with things generally shaping up well, I turned my staff's attention increasingly to the problems that would arise when the Polaris force became operational and had to be kept so throughout their lives. This, DPT suggested, should be regarded as twenty years and was the criterion his design team had worked to. Just as special arrangements had had to be made to build the force, so there would have to be special arrangements for its refitting, refuelling and general maintenance, to standards not yet experienced. Rosyth Dockyard was earmarked for the task of major refits and nuclear refuelling, and a start was made on all the work that would be necessary in preparing the yard to undertake this heavy load. A committee under Vice Admiral Sir Raymond Hawkins was charged with recommending how supervision of the task could best be ensured and what, if any, organization would be needed to keep POLARIS up to the mark once the Polaris Executive's task of 'design and build . . .' had been accomplished.

More milestones were successfully passed in 1967. *Renown* and *Repulse* were launched, the base at Faslane was commissioned as HMS *Neptune*, *Resolution*'s Contractor's Sea Trials (CSTs) proved successful and, despite some subsequent teething troubles, she was accepted into service in October, thereupon embarking on a rigorous period of work-up and trials, with the ultimate aim of carrying out her DASO (Demonstration and Shake-down Operation, involving full scale firing of one missile) in February 1968. Training of submarine crews was in full swing and the earlier difficulties of finding enough men of the right calibre, to provide two crews per boat without devastating the manpower of the rest of the Navy, had been satisfactorily overcome.

In 1968 was brought the reward of successful DASOs by both crews of *Resolution* and of her being handed over in June to C-in-C, Home Fleet, her operating authority. She was out of my hands and the Polaris Executive now concentrated on completing the remaining three Polaris submarines and the hunter-killers now under their wing. As the year advanced it became clear that progress on *Repulse* at Barrow (the third SSBN in the programme) was so good that she would be finished before *Renown* at Birkenhead; the programme was adjusted accordingly.

In August 1968, I handed over my task to Rear Admiral A.F. Trewby, who became Assistant Controller (Polaris) (ACP) under the revised

HMS *Resolution* 1968, the first Polaris Submarine.

HMS *Resolution*, 1968.

First firing of a Polaris Missile by H.M.S. *Resolution* 1968. Left to right, Admiral Galantin, USN – Weapons Engineer Officer, RN – Vice Admiral Hugh Mackenzie – Captain C.W.H. Shepherd, RN – Rear Admiral Levering Smith, USN, Port Canaveral, Florida.

Polaris missile, fired by HMS *Resolution*, 1968.

organization now set up, with responsibility for completing the original building programme and for ensuring that resources and facilities, and the organisation behind them, would guarantee the continued operational efficiency of the Polaris force, to the same high standards which had governed the previous five and a half years.

It was sad to leave such a wonderful team which, against all the odds, had accomplished so much; but I felt that, with the first of the submarines operational, it was the right moment to hand over to my successor a 'going' concern, full of confidence and with its tail up.

HMS *Renown* awaiting launch Cammell Lairds, February 1967.

Chapter Nineteen

An active 'retirement'

My naval career ended in August 1968, on the day I finally turned over the whole POLARIS programme to Alan Trewby. Fortunately there had been time to prepare for a smooth transition, both for the programme and for my adapting to a new way of life; about a year earlier the First Sea Lord (Admiral Sir Varyl Begg) had warned me that there would be no further promotion or employment for me once someone had succeeded me in the POLARIS job. He left it largely to me to decide when that should be. At the very beginning it had been made plain that, barring accident or failure, I could expect at least five years in the saddle. Now, faced with this latest declaration, there appeared to me to be two options for bringing to an end my part in the programme, either to be relieved soon after *Resolution*, the first of the submarines, became operational in the summer of 1968, or to prolong the job for a further two years or more until our four submarines were in service. Without hesitation I had decided on the first of these two options and matters were so arranged. I had no wish to prolong the gruelling years, nor find myself in time the senior Vice Admiral in the Navy, sitting for years at the head of the Vice Admiral's list, creating stagnation on it and blocking the promotion of junior officers.

It was a great wrench to say goodbye to all that the Navy had meant to me for over forty years. It was the end of a special way of life, a way that I had never regretted, had mostly greatly enjoyed and had been privileged to experience for so long. Throughout the years the ideal was invariably clear, that of total service to Queen and Country, in the final analysis regardless of self. I had no hard feelings, conditions of service had been, on the whole, fair and reasonable, I had had a very good run with much luck on my side, and there was a great deal for which I could be very thankful. With thoughts of more leisure and of seeing more of my family uppermost in my mind, I was not dismayed by any uncertainties the future might hold; being only just fifty-five I had no intention of doing nothing for the rest of my life.

With domestic issues assuming greater priority, house-hunting for a future family home out of London received early action; job hunting would follow. By the end of June we had found and bought a house in the depths of the Surrey countryside and we moved there from East Sheen within days of my being free to do so. It was school holidays, so the family were all together and not one of us regretted the change from all the noise, rush and fumes of London to the quietness and peace of our new home, even if all

My wife with our granddaughter Anna, 1992.

country smells were not entirely welcome, the more pungent emanating as they did from the nearby pig farm. But we could put up with that, and have done so for over twenty-five years.

Puttenham, sheltering on the south side of the Hog's Back half way between Guildford and Farnham, was the very reverse of the proverbial sleepy village. It thrived on a multitude of societies, institutions and associations which from the moment of our first arrival at Sylvan Lodge, our new home, besieged us with invitations to give them our support and, more importantly, our time. It was beyond our abilities to accept all, but we became quickly aware of the many facets of village life and its varying moods; clearly, we were not going to be allowed to vegetate, even had we wished to. As the years have gone by we have become more and more firmly embedded in the life and ways of the village, with no desire for change.

During my final weeks in the Ministry of Defence I had made a few half-hearted attempts to find in industry or business some gainful form of employment, but I had no great enthusiasm for getting permanently embroiled in the 'rat race'. The recent five years had given me a basinful of the high pressure work involved and I did not relish continuing in the same vein. Not surprisingly, the answers to my inquiries held no promises. In any case jobs could wait until we were fully settled in our new home, a process which included completing some much needed alterations; it was frustrating, and somewhat ironic, that these seemed to be never-ending.

Despite all the expertise gained from managing the POLARIS programme to timely completion, I could not get a simple, or so it seemed to me, building job finished on time. This was a sobering and salutary thought, bringing me down to earth with the problems to be faced in civilian life.

Hard facts – (where was money to come from for our future existence?) – soon forced me to start looking for work, of a congenial kind I hoped. Our private means were minimal and a substantial part of my naval pension had been 'commuted' to provide a capital sum to help pay for our new home – a decision never regretted, for it has been a lasting relief not to have a mortgage hanging over our heads. My retired pay, in consequence, was only £3,000 per annum, exactly half the princely sum, including all allowances, that I had been earning as a Vice-Admiral; mercifully, with inflation about to become rampant, the pension was index-linked. School bills were not yet altogether behind us, and not wishing to see any decline in our standards of living, the search for a job became more imperative. It would not need to be necessarily very lucrative, restoration of income to the previous level was the aim.

Lying in bed in Millbank Military Hospital one evening that autumn, awaiting an operation the next day, my eyes chanced on an advertisement in a back number of 'The Field'. I followed it up and it led a few weeks later to my being offered the post of Director of the recently incorporated Atlantic Salmon Research Trust (ASRT), based on Fishmongers' Hall in the City of London. As an enthusiastic, if not very practised, fisherman since early boyhood, and with pronounced interests in 'conservation', I jumped at the opportunity with delight and anticipation.

Registered as a charity, the Trust was a unique organisation with the designated aim of the conservation of North Atlantic salmon, covering all countries throughout their range. The main threats to salmon were seen to be disease, rife at the time in the form of UDN (Ulcerative Dermal Necrosis), destruction or spoliation of natural habitat, pollution in both fresh water and the sea and, possibly the most serious of all, over-exploitation through uncontrolled and explosively expanding drift-netting at sea in open international waters.

The scope of the job offered a great challenge and held enormous promise, with interests extending internationally into all the salmon-producing countries around the North Atlantic. I was confident that the many new people I would meet would be largely like-minded, fundamentally pro-salmon, though no doubt there would be differences of opinion on how best to achieve the Trust's aims. For money the Trust was entirely dependent on voluntary contributions and initially its funds were very meagre, which meant that any salary could only be very modest. In the early years things were very hard and at times we were scratching the very bottom of the barrel. The work of the Trust since then is a story in itself, on which I can only touch very briefly, but it amply came to take the place of the Navy in furnishing me with a long-lasting sense of purpose. Furthermore, it has provided much happy and friendly companionship over many years with those with whom I have worked.

I took up office in January 1969, in a small room made available by the Fishmongers' Company in their palatial Hall in the City of London, hard by London Bridge. They generously also provided secretarial assistance and though the office was 'below stairs', in actual fact below the kitchens, it was adequate as a beginning. From it I 'surfaced' daily to lunch with the Assistant Clerk. I viewed from his windows the progress of the staggering operation of demolishing London Bridge and its gradual replacement as the new structure rose in its place. The old bridge was transported to some remote spot in the heart of the United States.

My first major task was to organise, in co-operation with our kindred body across the Atlantic, an international conference to be held in Fishmongers' Hall in April 1969. The aim was to put a spotlight on the latest menace to stocks of salmon, manifested by a colossal increase in drift-netting, using miles and miles of invisible nylon monofilament nets, particularly on the high seas to the west of Greenland, which are the feeding grounds of salmon from both Europe and North America.

I was bewildered, as though thrown as a non-swimmer, into very deep water; except for the help of the Fishmongers' Company, whose Clerk was, conveniently, also Secretary to the Salmon and Trout Association, I had no knowledge of people, officials, or organisations, who should be invited to such a conference. Fortunately there was a marvellous tutor at hand, the man at the heart of the original proposal to form the Trust and now one of its first Trustees. Peter Liddell had been granted a Churchill Fellowship in the mid-sixties to study the state of Atlantic salmon throughout their geographical range, during which he had acquired a wealth of facts about people and relevant organizations. He was a giant of a man both physically and mentally and initially he was my lifebelt, the source of all my knowledge. Subsequently, his huge grasp of the problems affecting fisheries and the 'water industry', his immense foresight, initiative and drive guided me and a host of other bodies engaged in the wellbeing of salmon and other fish. His early death was a major tragedy and I lost a great friend.

Adjured to find someone of distinction to give the opening address to this very first international conference on such a little publicised subject as 'North Atlantic Salmon', which was viewed as critical to the success of the Trust and from which it was hoped much would flow, I was persuaded to approach Earl Mountbatten. He accepted the invitation, but on condition that I drafted his speech. Our minds fortunately were on the same lines, and in his address he stated plainly that what was needed to preserve the salmon in the Atlantic was a form of 'Salmon NATO' agreed to by all countries in which the fish was indigenous. The conference ended with a fine-sounding resolution passed by delegates from as far apart as Russia and the United States. As the Cold War was still at its height it was strange, but heartening, to see these two major powers in agreement on one issue. The recommendation said that positive action needed to be taken at Government level to control the Greenland fishery: the only dissenting voices came from our own Ministry of Agriculture, Fisheries and Food. I soon came to realize that any immediate response was a forlorn hope, only the United States was prepared to put pressure on those principally involved in drift-netting. But a seed had been sown. Years later, following another international conference in Edinburgh, there came into existence NASCO, the North Atlantic Salmon Conservation Organization, which gives hope that order and good sense will prevail in controlling the exploitation of salmon in international waters.

From that first conference in London in 1969 there developed a very close bond between the Trust and the transatlantic organisation which had acted as co-sponsor, the International Atlantic Salmon Foundation (IASF). Originally triggered off by Peter Liddell while on his Churchill Fellowship the Foundation had similar aims to the Trust, with full-hearted backing from the United States and Canada. As I had experienced in my days with POLARIS, there was immeasurably more money and resources available on the other side of the Atlantic than we could ever aspire to here, but this did not prevent the two organizations working closely together. Wilf Carter (Dr W.M. Carter), the Director of IASF, saw eye to eye with me on what were the main threats to indigenous stocks of wild salmon and how these threats could best be fought. I have many happy memories of visits to Canada and New York on 'salmon business' and I am proud to have been elected a member of the Board of IASF and to remain, in an honorary capacity, on the Board of the Atlantic Salmon Foundation (ASF) of Canada and the United States, IASF's successor.

Beside many international links I had fingers in a host of pies nearer to home. The Salmon and Trout Association, the Institute of Fisheries Management (another of Peter Liddell's brainchildren), the British Field Sports Society, the Association of Scottish District Salmon Fishery Boards, all had a direct and close interest in salmon, and there were others, too numerous to mention, with a peripheral interest. All had to be cajoled to work together and persuaded to accept a National Policy for Salmon, with which, once agreed, we could, individually or collectively, belabour reluctant or obstructive Ministries and Governments.

The penury of the Trust's early years was finally overcome by a mammoth nation-wide drive in the late seventies, to raise enough capital to ensure that the Trust would have in future sufficient funds available annually to meet its foreseeable needs. Amongst the measures taken to encourage support was the dropping of the word 'Research' from the Trust's title, without in any way altering its underlying aims. The fund-raising campaign was an outstanding success, thanks almost entirely to the determined leadership and efforts of its two ardent organizers, David Clarke and Jean Cormack. Their work as a closely knit team combined to achieve miracles, removing all doubts about the Trust's financial future and its ability to pursue its aims effectively.

In the twenty-five years since I first knew it, the Trust has come a long way and it is now a major voice wherever salmon conservation is concerned, nationally and internationally, particularly in the European Community, whilst it continues to give direct support to research projects.

I was not able to concentrate all my efforts on my chosen subject of 'Salmon', as my naval past raised its head on two occasions soon after I had retired. I was persuaded by its President, Rear Admiral Irving, to join the Society of Underwater Technology and for a short period, until I felt overwhelmed by the speed of its technological advance, I took an active part in its proceedings. The other issue was less easy to avoid and was more sustained. The President of the Navy League (Rear Admiral Earl Cairns, whom I had known of old) was one of the Trustees of ASRT in 1969; desperately searching for someone to fill the too-long vacant post of Chairman of the Navy League, he persuaded me to accept it. For the next five years it fully occupied any spare time I had, with three matters of great concern all requiring resolution. The first issue was its continuing existence in its present form; had it a useful role to play as a 'lobby' fighting for a strong Navy, or should it devote all its efforts and resources to the support of its own youth organziation, the Sea Cadets? The second was, how should it develop its ownership of the little island of Raven's Ait in the Thames at Kingston-on-Thames? And the third, should it build a sea-going training ship for the Sea Cadets? Financial considerations weighed heavily, especially with the two latter subjects, and there were long and involved discussions before the following decisions could be reached. Raven's Ait was to be developed as a comprehensive 'Boating Station' to which Sea Cadets from Units all over the country could come to 'get their feet wet' on a week's training afloat. A square-rigged sail training ship would be designed, built and commissioned to give Sea Cadets the opportunity of a week under sail at sea; and thirdly, complementary to the other two, all effort and resources of the Navy League would be concentrated on the Sea Cadets, the training of youth in the ways of the sea being considered more important than acting as a propaganda machine for the Navy, which now had its own publicity department within the Ministry of Defence. To reflect all this the name 'Navy League' would be changed to 'The Sea Cadet Association'.

These were difficult and far-reaching decisions, not arrived at without much heart-searching and with no guarantee of eventual success, as Raven's Ait subsequently revealed. Splendid buildings and equipment were completed and opened there for the use of Sea Cadet Units and the associated Girls Nautical Training Corps; unfortunately, the project was a failure. The majority of units, spread over all the country, could not afford to make use of the island's facilities and it rapidly became a white elephant, a continuous drain on the Navy League's slender resources. We had over-called our hand and, regrettably, the only solution was to sell the place with all its superb potential for youth training. On the other hand, there was much compensation in the sail training ship, *Royalist*, which has been an outstanding success. I had supported those who had argued long and hard with the Council of the Navy league that they should take the plunge and build her, and I am glad to know that she is still going strong and continues to be well patronised.

Whether it was wise to give up the name of 'The Navy League' remains debatable. I believe it right that effort should be concentrated on youth, but in the changed circumstances of the world and this country's place in it twenty years later, in the nineties, there again seems a need for an authoritative body, independent of the Government, to give voice to all that stems from our dependence on the sea. We may be part of Europe politically, and even connected thereto by the Channel Tunnel, but neither have altered the fundamental fact that seaborne trade still remains vital to our existence.

There was more than enough on my plate to keep me busy throughout the seventies and although the absence of the particular stresses and strains of POLARIS was a relief, the pace of life did not seem to abate very much. Looking back on those years I am sad that I did not make more time to be at home with my family. Such holidays as were possible were confined to a very few weeks in the Highlands of Scotland each summer, joining my brothers when practicable to enjoy salmon fishing on the river Lochy in Inverness-shire and stalking on the wild and rugged hills of nearby Glendessary, as remote and inaccessible a spot as could be wished for – until these hills eventually became too steep for ageing limbs and muscles. The Lochy featured more permanently in my life when I succeeded General Sir William Morgan as Secretary/Manager of the River Lochy Association, the syndicate which owned the salmon fishing rights on the river; though this brought no direct financial gain, it was a delightful job, giving me one or two weeks' fishing each year and keeping me in practical contact with problems endemic to the well-being of the salmon rivers of Scotland.

By 1980 I had been succeeded as Director of the Atlantic Salmon Trust by Gerry Hadoke, an Irish devotee of the salmon with years of wide experience of its habits and of its problems, gained the hard way while Manager of the Foyle Fisheries on the border between Eire and Northern Ireland. My absorption with the Trust's work and progress did not subside for shortly I became its Chairman. But all was nearly brought to a sudden and nasty end, by what might be termed an unexpected re-appearance of the Sword of Damocles, hanging over Maureen's head and mine for a few, brief cataclysmic minutes on, and off, the M1 motorway on a beautiful, calm, sunny evening in mid-July 1982.

Knocked flying by an overtaking car which cannoned off the central barrier into the rear of our car, we somersaulted off the motorway at over sixty-five mph, over the bordering hedge and fence, ending upside down in the adjoining barley field. The petrol tank had been ruptured, all windows

Fishing in Scotland, R Carron, 1994.

were shattered and the inside of the car was immediately ablaze. That we were still alive and conscious was doubtless due to our seat belts, but try as we could, with flames increasing all round, Maureen's could not be released. Mercifully, mine came off so I was able to squeeze out through the broken window, crawl round to her side and drag her flaming body out of the car. First on the scene were a couple from a car fortuitously parked in a nearby lane, two ministering angels who comforted us until police, fire engine and ambulances arrived. There followed months and months in the Burns Unit of Leicester Royal Infirmary; Maureen, with over 40 per cent burns on her body, was desperately ill for a long time; I, with only 15 per cent, got off comparatively lightly. That we both recovered, suffering only relatively minor permanent effects, is thanks to the unceasing care and nursing of the consultants and staff of that Burns Unit of Leciester Royal Infirmary. Supplemented later by those of the Burns Unit of St. Mary's Hospital, Roehampton, to whose care we were transferred when allowed to return home in December; to them all we remain forever enormously grateful.

Inevitably such a traumatic experience changed the pattern of my life, advancing years added their effect and reluctantly I had to accept that the Atlantic Salmon Trust would fare better under a new Chairman. There followed a gradual slide to an easier and more relaxed existence; more time for the garden at Sylvan Lodge and for fishing, now expanded beyond annual excursions to Scottish rivers to embrace that pinnacle of the art of angling, dry-fly fishing for trout on the chalk streams of southern England.

In retirement – a good catch.

In retirement – my dog Dipper witnessing me catch a salmon, 1994.

Maureen had never become addicted as I was, but her contribution behind the scenes in providing for all my wants and needs never ceased, enhancing my enjoyment of this most time-consuming yet relaxing of pastimes. By the end of the eighties life was noticeably less demanding, giving more time for Maureen and me to enjoy to the full the luxury of my being truly retired.

As I pen these final words it is now over twenty-five years since I left the Navy, and though the intervening time has brought new experiences, new pleasures and much fun, despite times of misfortunes and difficulties, it is the Royal Navy that I look back on as having shaped and guided my life after I had left parental care. I cannot help but feel that I have been immensely fortunate in every venture in life, in peace and in war. I value beyond words my more than forty years in what I shall always regard as the finest Service in the world, and with it the companionship I have everywhere found, the latter exemplified especially in the Submarine Service and, when beyond a certain age, the Submarine Old Comrades Association. Brought up in the tradition that the Royal Navy is 'Britain's sure shield' I find the recent drastic cuts in its strength of the gravest concern, raising many doubts as to the country's future security. It appals me that HMS *Dolphin*, the home of the Submarine School and submariners' 'alma mater', should no longer have any operational submarines in commission based there. History teaches us to expect cuts after periods of hostilities or tension, but the present climate of international and national affairs gives no grounds for blithely thinking that the millennium has arrived and that we can have peace forever without paying its costs. The Sword of Damocles is poised over many countries and the world remains a dangerous place; if we neglect our own defences it will be all too easy to lose everything gained from the last war and its immense sacrifices.

To end on a lighter note; a few months ago that proverbial sword appeared to be hanging over the head of our beloved, ageing Labrador and we feared he would not be with us much longer. But a miracle occurred, and as I conclude he is again his former self and has enjoyed, with his master and mistress, a delightful week's spring salmon fishing in Scotland. Perhaps all may yet be well with the world?! Despite the Sword of Damocles.

Appendix I

Passing out examination papers, RNC Dartmouth 1930.

A.E. $\frac{1292}{6}$

PASSING-OUT EXAMINATION OF NAVAL CADETS FROM THE ROYAL NAVAL COLLEGE, DARTMOUTH.

JULY, 1930.

GENERAL HISTORY.

Time allowed, 2 hours.

THREE questions in *Section A should be attempted and any* TWO *in Section B.*

SECTION A.

1. Where are any *four* of the following places and for what are they important : Acre, the Alma, Kandahar, Ladysmith, Lucknow, Pekin, Plevna, Sedan?

2. Describe briefly the importance of any *two* of the following : the rebellion in Greece (1821), the "July Monarchy" (1830), the Polish insurrections of 1831 and 1863, the Treaty of San Stefano (1878), the Franco-Russian alliance (1889).

3. Attempt a character-sketch of any *one* of the following : Gordon, Metternich, Peel, Napoleon III, Lord Salisbury.

4. Why was 1848 called "the year of revolutions"? Sketch briefly the causes of the unrest in Europe in that year.

SECTION B.

5. Show, by means of a sketch-map, the successive stages in the unification of Italy.

6. Sketch and account for the attitude of England towards the unification of Italy.

7. With what objects did Cavour cause Sardinia to intervene in the Crimean War and how far did he achieve his purpose in so doing?

8. Estimate the debt of Italy to Bismarck.

C.672] Wt. 15.2186 6.30 250 H*. (Gp. 11)

P.T.O.

ROYAL NAVAL COLLEGE, DARTMOUTH.

JULY, 1930.

Passing-Out Examination of Naval Cadets.—Seamanship.

Signals—40. *Oral*—60. *Paper*—100.   Total Marks—200.

Time allowed—1 hour.

1. (a) What build are the following : Service boats, and how are (i), (ii) and (iii) rigged?
(i)—Whaler. (ii)—Captain's Galley. (iii)—Pinnace. (iv)—Picket Boat.

   (b) State two occasions when, as Midshipman of a picket boat, you would fly—
(i)—A Captain's pendant, (ii)—an ensign?

   (c) You are Midshipman of—(a) a Service cutter under sail, and (b) a picket boat.
You pass (i) a picket boat with a Captain in the stern sheets
(ii) a barge flying the affirmative, and
(iii) 'sunset' is sounded off.
In each case what would you do?

2. (a) What are the following used for?
(i) Munro shackle, (ii) swifter, (iii) mooring pendant.

   (b) What are the advantages of mooring ship over single anchor.

   (c) How is the cable marked at the 3rd shackle?

3. In Harbour—
   (a) Who constitute the O.O.W.'s staff in a battleship?
   (b) As Midshipman of the morning watch at what time would you call the Officer of the Relieve Decks, and how would you word your call?
   (c) How are the following saluted as they come over the side?
(i) An Admiral. (iii) The Commander of a battle cruiser.
(ii) The Captain of a sloop. (iv) An Air Vice Marshal.

   At Sea—
   (a) What are special sea duty men?
   (b) State two reports which are made to the O.O.W. at sunset.

4. (a) In a fog you hear the following sound signals. What do they mean?
(i) On a siren—two prolonged blasts.
(ii) On a fog horn—three blasts.
(iii) The rapid ringing of a bell for about 5 seconds every minute.

   (b) What lights does 'Nelson' carry (i) at sea, (ii) in harbour?

5. (a) Explain briefly what happens when a fleet alters course—
(i) by compass pendant? (ii) by white pendant?

   (b) What is the signal for 'Divisions in line ahead disposed abeam to starboard'?

6. (a) On what stations are the following ships?
(i) 'Revenge' (ii) 'Frobisher' (iii) 'Hermes'

   (b) What guns has 'Sesame'?

   (c) Why are the Diesel engines not used to propel a submarine while diving?

   (d) What is the Standard Reconnaissance machine of the Fleet Air Arm?

   (e) Explain briefly what is meant by :—
(i) Yard arm group, (ii) Captain of the head, (iii) The D.S.B.
(iv) Half whites. (v) Holiday.

PASSING-OUT EXAMINATION OF NAVAL CADETS FROM THE ROYAL NAVAL COLLEGE, DARTMOUTH.

JULY, 1930.

FRANÇAIS.

2 heures et demie.

PART I.

Traduisez en anglais :—

Le Parisien à la Campagne.

Tout le long de l'année, le Parisien se donne le spectacle du provincial dépaysé dans Paris. En septembre, le provincial prend sa revanche : certes, le Parisien fait une triste figure à l'Opéra avec sa cravate à pois, son gilet à fleurs et ses gants en coton. Mais le Parisien n'a pas une meilleure tournure à la campagne, avec ses bottes vernies, sa veste de velours doublée de satin blanc, ses gants jaunes et ses jambes en pincettes dans un pantalon collant. Les vachères s'arrêtent pour le voir passer, et, n'était la bonne opinion qu'il a de lui-même, le Parisien s'apercevrait bien vite qu'on se moque de lui. Il faut dire aussi que le Parisien, prête énormément à rire dès qu'il a passé la barrière. Ignorant de toutes les choses de la nature, il prend un chêne pour un noyer, un bœuf pour un rhinocéros, des carottes pour des betteraves, et, quand il rencontre une grenouille, qu'il prend naturellement pour un crapaud, il se sauve pour ne pas être empoisonné par la liqueur du batracien.

AUGUSTE VILLEMOT.

PART II.

A.—Complétez les phrases suivantes comme bon vous semblera :—
(1) Dès que . . . , vous vous trouverez en pleine campagne.
(2) Si le Parisien . . . , il s'apercevrait bientôt qu'on se moque de lui.
(3) Il est à souhaiter que . . .
(4) On s'est moqué de lui, sans qu'il . . . .

B.—Indiquez clairement, à l'aide de phrases de votre composition, *que vous traduirez en anglais*, la différence entre :—
1. le col, la colle.
2. le poids, le pois.
3. le noyer, le noyé.
4. ailleurs, d'ailleurs.
5. venir de (faire quelque chose), venir à (faire quelque chose.)
6. par-dessus, au-dessus de.

(C 560) Wt. 55/2198 @30 250 Hw. (Gp.1)

[P.T.O.

---

9. Describe and account for Cavour's policy towards Garibaldi.

10. Comment briefly on any *four* of the following :—
(a) The English politician whom he most admired was Pitt.
(b) In 1846 Cavour was the most unpopular man in Piedmont.
(c) The Church in Piedmont was a political force constantly on the look-out for an opening to retake the position it had lost.
(d) The chief boulder in the path of Italian unity had gone.
(e) The case against the cession of Nice was far stronger.
(f) He, almost alone, rated at its true value the latent military force of Prussia.

PASSING-OUT EXAMINATION OF NAVAL CADETS FROM THE ROYAL NAVAL COLLEGE, DARTMOUTH.

ENGINEERING.

JULY, 1930.

Time allowed, 2½ hours.

[FIVE *questions to be answered. All questions carry equal marks.*]

1. Indicate clearly with the aid of freehand sketches the method of attachment adopted in three of the following cases :—
   (a) Condenser tube in tube plate.
   (b) Boiler tube in tube plate (Yarrow boiler).
   (c) Piston to piston rod of a large reciprocating engine.
   (d) Mushroom valve to spindle of an ordinary screw down valve.
   (e) Whitemetal in a journal bearing brass.
   (f) Yarrow boiler to ship's structure.

2. On the sheet "A" attached are the indicator diagrams obtained from the H.P. cylinder of a double acting reciprocating dynamo engine. Calculate the power developed, neglecting the area of the piston rod. On the "Top" diagram mark the points of "Cut off," "Compression," and "Release."

3. Describe briefly the work involved in the periodical cleaning of a Yarrow boiler.

4. Describe the process of re-metalling the brass of a small bearing.

5. With the ship under running conditions how would you—
   (a) Take the density of a boiler ;
   (b) Test the feed water ;
   (c) Make a smoke screen ?
   How often would you carry out (a) and (b) ?

6. The object of a steam turbine is to convert the potential energy in the steam into work on the rotor.
   Describe as briefly as possible the successive steps in the conversion in—
   (a) An impulse turbine.
   (b) An impulse reaction turbine.
   What is meant by partial admission ?
   What is the corresponding device in a reciprocating steam engine ?

(C.597) Wt.55/2198 6.30 250 H⋆. (Gp. 1)

[P.T.O.

C.—(1) Remplacez les mots en italiques par les pronoms indiqués :—

Pronom *possessif* :—(a) Que pensez-vous de ma maison et de *leur maison* ?

Pronom *interrogatif* :—(b) De *quel accident* parlez-vous ?

Pronom *personnel* :—(c) Je vous présenterai à *ma mère*.

(2) Récrivez les phrases suivantes en mettant au parfait (passé indéfini) les verbes en italiques :—

(a) Ils *courent* bien vite.
(b) *Se coupe-t-elle* le doigt ?
(c) Voilà la peinture qu'ils *descendront*.
(d) Elle *chancela* mais ne *tomba* pas.

(3) Donnez les adverbes qui correspondent aux adjectifs suivants :—

(a) doux.
(b) prudent.
(c) énorme.
(d) pire.

PART III.

Traduisez en français :—

A.—(1) But for your kindness he would have had to wait another two hours.
(2) Come and see us when you like and as soon as you can.
(3) I advise you not to go until it has stopped raining.

B.—Marshal de Villeroi, the governor of Louis XV, wrote a practically illegible hand. One day he sent a letter to Cardinal de Fleury, the young king's tutor, who could not make out a word of what the governor wanted to tell him. He therefore asked him to be so good as to communicate to him his thoughts in a more legible manner. The marshal thereupon wrote another letter, to which Fleury replied: "I regret to say that your second letter is not much more legible than the first one. I beg you not to write to me again, that it may not be said that the king has a governor who cannot write, and a tutor who cannot read!"

PART IV.

Écrivez environ 250 mots sur un des sujets suivants :—

(1) Vous êtes à quelque distance de la côte dans un petit bateau, lorsqu'une tempête s'élève. Décrivez la tempête et racontez ce que vous avez fait.

(2) Il y a des gens qui prétendent que la chasse est cruelle. Êtes-vous de cet avis, et devrait-on y renoncer ?

(3) Comment l'invention de la boussole ("compass") a-t-elle contribué aux progrès de la civilisation ?

A.E. $\frac{1292}{103}$

PASSING OUT EXAMINATION OF NAVAL CADETS FROM THE ROYAL NAVAL COLLEGE, DARTMOUTH.

JULY 1930.
QUESTION 8.
ENGINEERING DIAGRAM.

SHEET B

2

7. Make a line sketch of a typical lay-out of one set of the propelling machinery of a modern geared turbine-driven destroyer. In addition to the main unit, the sketch should show clearly such fittings as—

Turbine adjusting blocks.
Main bearings.
Main thrust block.
Flexible couplings, etc.

8. *Drawing Question.*—Draw to half scale the side elevation of the half coupling shown on attached sheet "B," looking in the direction of the arrow.

5 STUD HOLES 6⅞" P.C.D.

SCREWED ⅝ WHITWORTH.

KEY ½ x ¼ DEEP

5 BOLT HOLES 5¼" P.C.D.

SECTION OF HALF COUPLING

SCALE - HALF SIZE

PASSING-OUT EXAMINATION OF NAVAL CADETS FROM THE ROYAL NAVAL COLLEGE, DARTMOUTH.

JULY, 1930.

MATHEMATICS—I.

Time allowed, 2 hours.

[*All the questions may be attempted.*]

1. The horizontal section of a tank is a circle of 15 ft. diameter. Water flows in at the rate of 10 gallons a minute. By how much is the depth increased in an hour ?

[1 gall. = 277·4 cu. in.].

2. Solve—

(i) $\dfrac{x-2}{x^2-5x+4} - \dfrac{2(x-1)}{x^2-6x+8} + \dfrac{x-4}{x^2-3x+2} = 0$

(ii) $4x - \dfrac{14-x}{x+1} = 14.$

and verify your solution of (i).

3. Prove that the acute angle between a tangent to a circle and a chord drawn through the point of contact is equal to the angle in the greater segment cut off by the chord. A B are points 2 in. apart and the straight line X Y is parallel to A B and 1·5 in. from it. By a geometrical construction find the points P, Q in X Y at which A B subtends an angle of 50°. State the construction.

4. A, B are points on a straight river bank 350 yards apart, and the bearing of B from A is 014°. The bearings of a buoy in the river are 335° from A and 310° from B. Find the distance of the buoy from the bank.

5. What angles less than 360° satisfy the following equations respectively ?—
(1) $\sin\theta = \sin 25°$; (2) $\cos\theta = \cos 35°$; (3) $\tan\theta = \tan 30°$; (4) $\sin^2\theta = \cos^2 49°$.

6. Draw the graph of $(2+x)(4-x)$ and that of $\frac{1}{4}x - 1$ and determine the values of x for which they intersect.

Verify by solving the equation $(2+x)(4-x) = \dfrac{x}{2} - 1.$

7. A rhombus, one of whose angles is 50°, is circumscribed about a circle of 2 in. diameter. Find the length of its sides and those of its diagonals. Find also the length of the shorter arc between points of contact.

8. A plane slopes up at an angle of 10° ; find the angle which a track up it must make with the horizontal edge of the plane to have a slope of 4° only.

PASSING-OUT EXAMINATION OF NAVAL CADETS FROM THE ROYAL NAVAL COLLEGE, DARTMOUTH.

JULY, 1930.

MATHEMATICS—II.

Time allowed, 2½ hours.

[*Not more than SEVEN questions to be answered. Questions marked thus (*) carry more marks.*]

1. A solid consists of a cylinder, of which the height and diameter are both 10 inches, on to one end of which, as base, is fixed a cone, also of height 10 in. Find the volume of the solid. Calculate the radius of a sphere of equal volume. Calculate also the ratio of the total surface of the solid to that of the sphere.

2. The triangle A B C has an obtuse angle at A ; B K, C L are the perpendiculars from B, C to C A and B A produced. Write down two equivalents for B C², using the extension of Pythagoras or the cosine rule, and deduce that certain rectangles are equal. Prove this by an independent method.

3. *State* the meanings assigned to $5°$, $6^{\frac{1}{2}}$ and $7^{-\frac{1}{2}}$. Show by ordinary arithmetic that $10^{·6}$ is approximately 2. What is the corresponding fact as to $\log 2$?

Form the square of $3 - \sqrt{5}$ and show that $3 - \sqrt{5}$ satisfies the equation $x^2 - 6x + 4 = 0$. What is the other solution ?

*4. A ship A is steaming at 20 knots on course 335°. At noon a ship B bears 035° and is distant 8·5 n. ml. At 12.30 p.m. B bears 075° and is distant 3·5 n. ml. Find the actual course and speed relative to A, and the least distance at which A will pass her.

[*To be solved by scale drawing.*]

5. (a) Prove directly from a figure, without assuming a formula for $\sin(A+B)$ that $\sin 2A = 2\sin A \cos A$ and state a formula for $\cos 2A$.

(b) Show that $\cos A \cos B = \frac{1}{2}\{\cos\overline{A-B} + \cos\overline{A+B}\}$ and state the corresponding formula for $\sin A \cos B$.

(c) Find the angles between 0° and 360° which satisfy the equation $\sin\theta + \cos\theta = 1·3$.

*6. A B C D is a square, side 4 in. ; H, K are the mid-points of A B, A D. Taking A B, A D as axes of x and y respectively, form the equations of H C, H D, K C. From the equations show that H D, K C are at right angles, and find the co-ordinates of P their point of intersection. Find also from the equations the angle D H C.

What are the areas of D P K and H P C expressed as fractions of the area of the square ?

[P.T.O.

PASSING-OUT EXAMINATION OF NAVAL CADETS FROM THE ROYAL NAVAL COLLEGE, DARTMOUTH.

JULY, 1930.

NAVIGATION—I.

Time allowed, 2 hours.

D.W. 1m. 25s. slow on G.M.T. ; H.E. 40 ft. ; I.E. 1'—.

1. Zone +1. October 29th, 1929, about 1248, a ship was in D.R. 42° 55′ N., 9° 52′ W., steaming 098° at 15 knots.

1248. Obs. alt. Sun's L.L. 33° 25′·5. D.W.T. 1ʰ 46ᵐ 31ˢ. Sun's T.B. 205°.
1428. C. Finisterre Lt. 020°.
Find the observed position at 1428.

2. Zone +1. October 20th, 1929, at 1122, a ship on her way to Arosa Bay was in D.R. 42° 42′ N., 9° 17′ W., steaming 165° at 15 knots.

1122. Obs. mer. alt. Sun's L.L. 38° 50′.
Soundings showed that the ship was to the Westward of the 50 fathoms line, but other observations were impossible owing to weather conditions.
Explain how the observation of the Sun could enable the navigator to make with safety a point 2 miles 180° of Isla Salvora Light with one alteration of course.
State the exact time when he should alter course, and what the new course should be.

3. At 0850 on a certain day in 1929 a ship was in 42° 7′ N., 9° 0′ W., steaming N. 14° W.
0900. Co. Silietro Lt. S. 37° E.
      Isdas Cies Lt. N. 63° E.
      Lameda Lt. S. 71° E.
Find the observed position at 0900, and from it find the Compass Course to pass Isla Salvora Lt. at a distance of 5′, at a speed of 13 knots, allowing for a 2-knot current setting 090°.
1036. Find the Estimated Position.
1050. Curota Church ʠ Co. Corrubedo Lt. 62° Isla Salvora Lt.
      Fix the ship at 1050.

4. At 2230 a ship was in D.R. 42° 57′ N., 9° 24′ W., steaming 163° at 8 knots. Estimated Current 045°, 1 knot.
2230. C. Finisterre Lt. 120°.
2330. ,,   ,,   ,, 055°.
      Fix the ship at 2330.

2

*7. Evaluate—

(i) $\dfrac{d}{dx}\left\{(x-1)^4 - \dfrac{5}{x^4}\right\}$ when $x = 2$;

(ii) $\displaystyle\int_{-2}^{-3}\left(x^2 - \dfrac{1}{x^2}\right)dx$;

(iii) $\displaystyle\int_{0}^{-3}\sin 2\theta\, d\theta$.

(iv) Using your tables and any method of approximate integration (the simplest is sufficient) show that $\displaystyle\int_{20}^{25}\log_{10} x\, dx$ lies between 6·7 and 6·8.

*8. Sketch the curve $y = x^2 (3 - x)$. Find the equation to the tangent at the point P (1, 2). If this tangent meets the x axis in T, and the curve cuts the x axis in Q, find the area bounded by the x-axis, the straight line T P and the arc P Q.

*9. Find by integration the moment of inertia about its axis of a circular disc of uniform thickness and density (i) in terms of its radius a, thickness t, and density ϱ ; (ii) in terms of its mass and radius.

Find also the M.I. of a uniform sphere about a diameter in terms of its mass and radius.

*10. Five figure tables give these entries :—

sin 14° 54′ = 0·25713.
sin 15°   = 0·25882.
sin 15° 6′ = 0·26050.

What can you deduce from these figures as to the rate at which sin θ is increasing at the point $\theta = 15°$; and how do you harmonise the result with the statement that the differential coefficient of sin θ is cos θ ?

PASSING-OUT EXAMINATION OF NAVAL CADETS FROM THE ROYAL NAVAL COLLEGE, DARTMOUTH.

JULY, 1930.

NAVIGATION.—II.

Time allowed, 2 hours.

[FIVE questions only to be attempted. Questions marked thus (*) carry higher marks than the others.]

1. (a) Give the notation of the Admiralty Chart for the following :—

Wreck (position doubtful) ; ebb tide stream ; 5 fathom line ; eddy ; reported rock whose existence is doubtful.

(b) What is the significance of the following :—Spherical buoy ; pillar buoy carrying a light ; watch buoy ?

(c) Describe the following :—Lt. F. Fl. ; Lt. F. Gp. Fl. (3) ; Lt. Occ. (U).

*2. Define, illustrating with diagrams, the following :—equation of time ; ecliptic ; prime vertical ; rhumb line.

Draw the celestial sphere for an observer in 45° S., showing the positions of two heavenly bodies A and B for which the following are given :—

For A :—T.B. 133° ; Altitude 15°
For B :—Hour Angle 22ʰ ; Declination 10° N.

Estimate from your diagram—

(i) the Hour Angle and Declination of A ;
(ii) the T.B. and Altitude of B ;
(iii) the T.B. and Hour Angle of B at rising.

*3. Zone +7. At 1520 on May 29th, 1929, in Lat. 29° 5′ S., Long. 103° 58′ W., the sun's bearing by Gyro-compass was 308°, the Deck Watch Time being 10ʰ 19ᵐ 5ˢ. Find the error of the compass.

[*D.W.* 1ᵐ 30ˢ *slow on G.M.T.*]

4. Prove the formula for parallel sailing :—

D. Long. = Dep. sec. (Lat.).

At 2310 (Zone + 4) on July 15, 1929, a ship was in Lat. 39° 48′ N., Long. 57° 25′ W. ; course 090° ; speed 9 knots. What was the ship's estimated position at the end of a run of 1,108 miles ?

Find also the zone time (with date) at the end of this run.

[P.T.O.

---

*5. Explain, with diagrams, the corrections to be applied to the observed altitude of the sun's lower limb.

A ship is steaming 290°, 16 knots. The following are the results obtained from altitude observations of two heavenly bodies X and Y :—

X :—At 0520, Intercept 5′·0 " To ", T.B. 350°.
Y :—At 0550, ″   6′·0 " From ", T.B. 100°.

In both instances the observations are worked from the position :—Lat. 37° N., *Long.* 25° 30′ W. By means of a plotting chart, find the position of the ship at 0520 and at 0550.

6. A ship, speed 8 knots, is bound for a port bearing 134° and distant 25′. A current sets N. (Mag.), 2½ knots. Find the course steered and the time to reach the port.

[*Variation* 10° W.]

PASSING-OUT EXAMINATION OF NAVAL CADETS FROM THE ROYAL NAVAL COLLEGE, DARTMOUTH

JULY 1930.

SCIENCE—I.

MECHANICS AND HEAT.

Time allowed, 2 hours.

[*Only* EIGHT *questions are to be attempted, but at least two must be chosen out of each section A, B, and C.*]

> 1 cu. ft. of water weighs 62·5 lbs.
> 1 gallon of water weighs 10 lbs.
> 1 calorie is equivalent to 4·2 joules.
> 1 B.Th.U. is equivalent to 778 ft. lbs.

A.

1. Define the Moment of a Force and state how it is measured ; give one or two units in which it can be expressed. The figure shows a pair of nutcrackers in the act of cracking a nut. Forces of 2 lbs. weight are applied at the end of the arms at right angles to the line bisecting the angle between the arms. A B = 1 in. A C = 5 in. Find the force at right angles to each arm exerted on the nut.

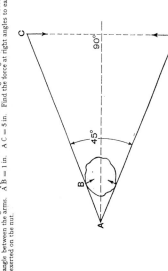

2. Define *velocity ratio* and *mechanical advantage*.

A lifeboat is being hauled up a slip by means of a capstan at the top. Twelve men, each exerting a force of 20 lbs. at right angles to the capstan bars, walk round at 2 m.p.h. while the lifeboat moves up the slip 8 in. a minute.

(a) Calculate the velocity ratio of the system.

(b) If the efficiency is 25 per cent., what is the pull on the lifeboat ?

3. State Archimedes' Principle.

It is desired to construct a raft to carry a 6 in. howitzer, weighing 2 tons. The material available is a number of casks, each having a volume of 10 cu. ft. and weighing 30 lbs. The superstructure of the raft may be taken to weigh 1,000 lbs. and to add nothing to the buoyancy. What is the least number of casks that could be used ?

B.

4. What is meant by a *foot pound, horse-power, a horse-power hour ?*

A waterfall is 100 ft. high. (a) If the whole drop is used for power production, how many foot pounds of energy can be produced from every gallon of water, assuming 15 per cent. loss ? (b) If 1,000 H.P. are required, how many gallons of water must be taken every second through the plant ?

5. Describe an experiment for measuring the coefficient of expansion of iron accurately.

Inch bolts are used for bolting 120 ft. rails to the fish plates of the sleepers. Slots in the fish plates allow freedom of movement. What is the minimum length of slot required for a temperature range of 40° C. ?

[Coefficient of expansion of steel = 0·000012.]

6. Describe fully an experiment for determining the mechanical equivalent of heat with considerable accuracy. What precautions must be taken ?

" The temperature of the water is higher at the bottom of a waterfall than at the top."

(a) Is this statement a possibility ? Give reasons for your answer.

(b) If so, what is the maximum rise in temperature possible for a 400 ft. fall ?

(c) What would the temperature be half-way down the fall ?

7. What do you understand by the term *water equivalent ?*

100 grams of water standing in a thermos flask were at a temperature of 20·2° C., when a further 100 grams at 15·1° C. were run in from a burette. The final temperature was 17·8° C. Calculate the water equivalent of the thermos.

8. What is meant by (a) latent heat of fusion of ice ; and (b) the caloric value of a gas ?

The efficiency of a boiler and furnace plant is 80 per cent. If 600 lbs. of steam at atmospheric pressure are required hourly from water at 15° C., how many pounds of coal, of calorific value 9,000 C.T.U., must be burnt every hour ?

[Latent Heat of Steam is 535 C.T.U. per lb.]

PASSING-OUT EXAMINATION OF NAVAL CADETS FROM THE ROYAL NAVAL COLLEGE, DARTMOUTH.

JULY, 1930.

SCIENCE—II.

Time allowed, 2½ hours.

[*Not more than* FIVE *questions to be attempted. The starred questions carry more marks.*]

[**Take g = 32 ft. ps. ps. : 1 H.P. = 746 Watts.**]

*1. State the laws of friction for solids. What do you understand by the coefficient of friction?

A uniform plank, 20 feet long and weighing 200 lb., in contact with the ground at A, rests upon a rough horizontal cylinder of 6 feet diameter, with axis perpendicular to the plank and fixed to the ground at B, distant 15 feet from A. If the coefficient of friction between the plank and the ground is 0·2, and the ground may be taken as smooth, find the least horizontal force applied to the plank at A that is necessary (i) to move the plank up the cylinder; (ii) to keep the plank from slipping down

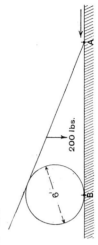

2. A train weighing 300 tons is driven up an incline of 1 in 300, the frictional resistance being 16 lb. per ton. If the tractive force is 9,000 lb., determine (*a*) the velocity at the end of the first mile starting from rest; (*b*) the greatest horse-power at which the engine works.

*3. The mass of a body decreases uniformly from 10 lb. to 5 lb. in 20 seconds. During this time a constant force of 1 lb. weight is acting on the body causing it to move from rest in a horizontal line.

Plot a curve showing the relations between the velocity of the body and the time during which the force acts, and determine the distance covered during the last 10 seconds.

(C 563) Wt.16/180 6/30 250 H.W. (Gp. 1) [P.T.O.

3

C.

9. Explain the terms *magnetic variation* and *magnetic dip*.

Give a neat clear diagram of an electric bell and explain its action.

10. Define *coulomb, ampere* and *volt*.

A battery of E.M.F. 4·2 volts and internal resistance 0·3 ohm is connected through a 2 ohm resistance to a copper voltameter of resistance 0·7 ohm. (*a*) How long will it take to deposit 2 grams of copper? (*b*) How many calories of heat will be liberated in the 2 ohm resistance in one minute?

[Electrochemical equivalent of copper = 0·00033.]

√11. Give a diagrammatic sketch of a shunt motor starter with a no voltage release and show how it is connected to the motor. Explain the action of, and the reason for, the no voltage release.

12. Define a B.O.T. unit.

An electric stove in an hotel is worked by a shilling in the slot meter. It is run off 240 volt mains and has a resistance of 48 ohms. The local price of electrical energy for heating is 1¼ pence a unit. How long will it run, assuming the hotel makes 25 per cent. profit on the takings of the meter?

4. A simple photographic shutter is made of a vertical rectangular sheet of metal with a horizontal slit, and it is let fall freely from a position in which the bottom edge of the slit is 3 inches above the centre of the lens. Find the breadth of the slit in order that it may take 1/60th of a second to pass the centre of the lens.

5. A tram, weighing 12 tons, takes 1 B.O.T. unit of electrical energy while running on the level one mile, starting from rest. The efficiency of the motor and transmission is 70 per cent. and the resistance to motion is 20 lb. per ton.

(a) What will be its speed at the end of the mile ?

(b) If at the end of the mile the speed is then made to remain constant, what current will it be taking from 600-volt mains ?

[Take 1 joule = 3/4 ft. lb.]

*6. Explain the principle of the potentiometer and how it is used to compare E.M.Fs. Describe fully how a large current can be measured by means of the potentiometer. Give a diagram of the connections and state what apparatus would be required.

7. How can a shunt dynamo be controlled conveniently to give a constant P.D. under a varying load ? If a dynamo is required to give constant P.D. without such control, how must it be constructed ? Give a diagrammatic sketch of its electrical windings (only the connections to the armature brushes need be shown).

A shunt dynamo has a P.D. of 100 volts when on open circuit. Armature resistance is 0·5 ohm, and field resistance 100 ohms. Calculate the P.D. when supplying an external circuit with 25 amps.; you may assume that the field magnets are saturated in both cases. What percentage increase of the original speed would be required to bring the P.D. up to 100 volts once more ?

8. Explain what is meant by *mutual induction* and *self-induction*.

Describe and explain the working of the ordinary telephone circuit.

*9. Prove the expression for the equivalent capacity of several condensers arranged in cascade.

The capacities of two condensers connected in cascade are 2 m.f. and 10 m.f. respectively. They are charged through a megohm from 200-volt mains. (a) What are the P.Ds. across each and the charge on each at the instant the current is 80 microamps.? (b) How much energy is stored in the 10 m.f. condenser when fully charged from the 200-volt mains ?

Appendix II

Two Speed Destroyer Sweep.

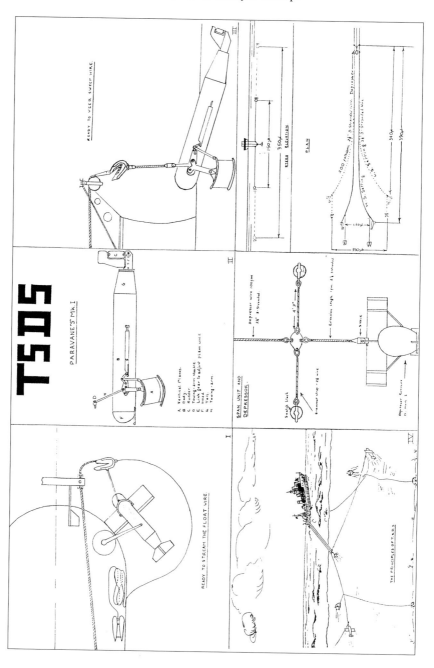

Appendix III

Map of the Mediterranean.

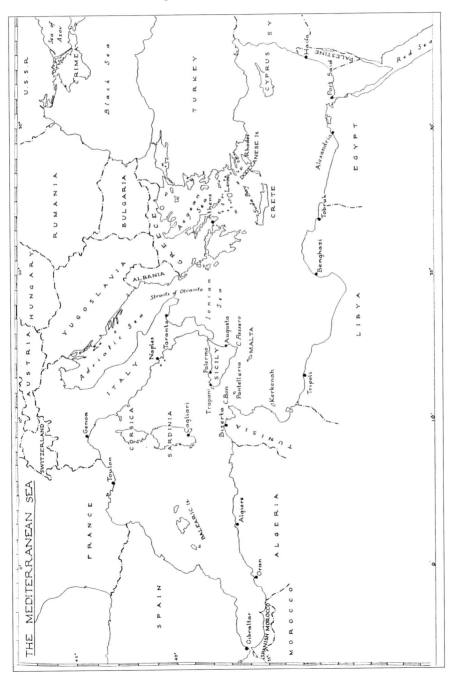

Map of the Indian and SW Pacific Oceans.

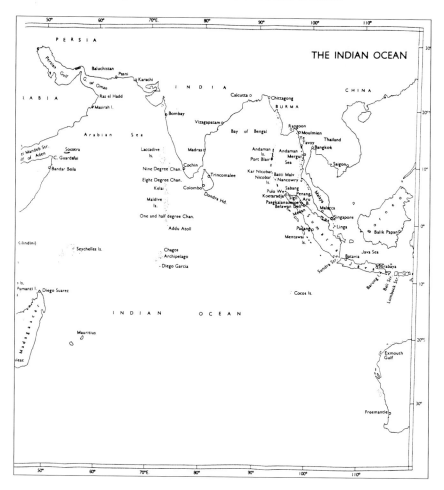

Technical Glossary

'A' gun – the foremost gun, usually on the fo'c'sle.

Algerian Class – Minesweepers.

Abreast – see *abeam*.

Asdic – S./M. detection equipment.

Abeam – A position at right angles to the ship's fore and aft line.

Attack periscope – Monocular, incorporates range finder but with no magnification and very small diameter at top for use in later stages of attack.

'A' class S/M – Completed 1945–48, 1400 tons, 18½ kts. surface.

'B' gun – The second gun from the bow.

Beam – The width of a ship.

Brass-hat – Rank of Commander and above.

Captain (S) – Captain (submarines) - in command of a flotilla/squadron. later (S./M.)

Cutter – A 32ft or 34ft Clinker built ship's boat.

Clockwork mouse – A submarine providing an exercise target for anti-submarine vessels.

Chief Buffer – Chief Boatswain's mate, a Chief Petty Officer. (Co-ordinator of work on the upper deck of a warship)

C.C.R. Pistol – A magnetically induced pistol on a torpedo warhead.

'C' Class – Fleet Destroyers 2500 tons.

CPE – Chief Polaris Executive.

D.A. – Director angle. The angle between the line of sight of the target at the moment of firing and the course of the torpedo.

Dipping Lug Rig – Two masted rig for 34ft cutters. The foresail and mainsail have to be dipped and re-hoisted when tacking.

Dreadnought Submarine – The first British nuclear submarine.

Fo'c'sle – The fore-part of a ship.

F.O. S./M. – Flag Officer, Submarines.

'Hunt' class – Small war-time class of destroyers, 1939–1945.

'H' Class S/M – Completed 1917–1920, 400 tons, 13kts. surface.

I.S.W.A.S. – Earliest type of attack instrument, fitted in submarines until the mid-1930s.

'L' Class – Completed 1917–1922, 900 tons, 17.5 kts. surface.

Make and Mend – half-holiday.

Montagu Rig – The sailing rig of single masted cutters.

M2 Submarine – Original 'M' class (12" gun). Converted to carry a seaplane.

Mark IV Torpedo – Designed 1917, 40 knots maximum.

Mark VIII Torpedo – Designed 1928, 45 knots maximum.

Nautilus – The first nuclear propulsion submarine (US).

'O' Class S./M. – Completed in the 1920s, 1350 tons, 15kts. surface.

'Porpoise' Class S./M. – Minelayers, completed 1934–39, 1800 tons, 25 kts. surface.

'P' Class S./M. – Completed in the 1920s, 1500 tons, 17.5 kts. surface.

Perisher – Submarine Commanding Officers' Qualifying Course.

'Passed over' – Passed over for promotion.

Polaris – Ballistic nuclear missile.

'Q' tank – An internal tank which, when flooded in emergency, gives 10 tons negative buoyancy for quick diving. (T class).

'R' Class S./M. – Completed in the 1920s, 1400 tons, 17.5 kts. surface.

S.S.B.N . – Submarine Submersible Ballistic Nuclear (POLARIS).

S.S.N. – Submarine Submersible Nuclear (attack S/M).

Search Periscope – Binocular and bi-focal with a range finder and high angle search. Magnification 4×.

Snort – Air induction pipe for running diesel engines when dived.

Sea Pressure – Approximately ½ lb. per foot of depth, e.g. 100 ft = 50 lbs.

'Taffrail' – Captain H.T. Dorling, DSO, RN, noted author.

Track Angle – The angle between the course of the target and the torpedo's course. (From 60° to 120° is the ideal track angle for firing torpedoes at a range between 600 yards and 2000 yards.)

Trim – The buoyancy/balance of a submarine when submerged; ideally achieved when in total equilibrium, i.e. neither positively nor negatively buoyant and remaining level, without rising or sinking through the water, known as a 'stopped trim'.

'T' Class S/M – Completed 1938–1945, 1300 tons, 15 kts. surface.

Type XXI U-boat – Entered service 1944 and capable of 16 kts. submerged for one hour. (German)

'U' Class S./M . – Completed 1938–1944, 630 tons, 11 kts. surface.

'V' Class S./M . – Completed 1943–45, 670 tons, 12.5 kts. surface.

Index

Illustrations are noted in *italics* after text references. Continuous text references ignore intervening illustration pages. D = destroyer; HM = Sir Hugh Mackenzie; S/M = submarine.